Communications
in Computer and Information Science 124

Tai-hoon Kim   Jianhua Ma   Wai-chi Fang
Byungjoo Park   Byeong-Ho Kang
Dominik Ślęzak (Eds.)

U- and E-Service, Science and Technology

International Conference, UNESST 2010
Held as Part of the Future Generation
Information Technology Conference, FGIT 2010
Jeju Island, Korea, December 13-15, 2010
Proceedings

 Springer

Volume Editors

Tai-hoon Kim
Hannam University, Daejeon, South Korea
E-mail: taihoonn@hnu.kr

Jianhua Ma
Hosei University, Tokyo, Japan
E-mail: jianhua@hosei.ac.jp

Wai-chi Fang
National Chiao Tung University, Hsinchu, Taiwan
E-mail: wfang@mail.nctu.edu.tw

Byungjoo Park
Hannam University, Daejeon, South Korea
E-mail: bjpark@hnu.kr

Byeong-Ho Kang
University of Tasmania, Hobart, Australia
E-mail: byeong.kang@utas.edu.au

Dominik Ślęzak
University of Warsaw & Infobright, Warsaw, Poland
E-mail: dominik.slezak@infobright.com

Library of Congress Control Number: 2010940208

CR Subject Classification (1998): H.4, I.2, C.2.4, I.2.11, H.3, C.2

ISSN   1865-0929
ISBN-10   3-642-17643-7 Springer Berlin Heidelberg New York
ISBN-13   978-3-642-17643-2 Springer Berlin Heidelberg New York

springer.com

© Springer-Verlag Berlin Heidelberg 2010
Printed in Germany

Typesetting: Camera-ready by author, data conversion by Scientific Publishing Services, Chennai, India
Printed on acid-free paper   06/3180

Preface

Welcome to the proceedings of the 2010 International Conference on u- and e-Service, Science and Technology (UNESST 2010) – one of the partnering events of the Second International Mega-Conference on Future Generation Information Technology (FGIT 2010).

UNESST brings together researchers from academia and industry as well as practitioners to share ideas, problems and solutions relating to the multifaceted aspects of u- and e-services and their applications, with links to computational sciences, mathematics and information technology.

In total, 1,630 papers were submitted to FGIT 2010 from 30 countries, which includes 223 papers submitted to UNESST 2010. The submitted papers went through a rigorous reviewing process: 395 of the 1,630 papers were accepted for FGIT 2010, while 50 papers were accepted for UNESST 2010. Of the 50 papers 8 were selected for the special FGIT 2010 volume published by Springer in the LNCS series. 27 papers are published in this volume and 15 papers were withdrawn due to technical reasons.

We would like to acknowledge the great effort of the UNESST 2010 International Advisory Board and members of the International Program Committee, as well as all the organizations and individuals who supported the idea of publishing this volume of proceedings, including SERSC and Springer. Also, the success of the conference would not have been possible without the huge support from our sponsors and the work of the Chairs and Organizing Committee.

We are grateful to the following keynote speakers who kindly accepted our invitation: Hojjat Adeli (Ohio State University), Ruay-Shiung Chang (National Dong Hwa University), and Andrzej Skowron (University of Warsaw). We would also like to thank all plenary and tutorial speakers for their valuable contributions.

We would like to express our greatest gratitude to the authors and reviewers of all paper submissions, as well as to all attendees, for their input and participation.

Last but not least, we give special thanks to Rosslin John Robles and Maricel Balitanas. These graduate school students of Hannam University contributed to the editing process of this volume with great passion.

December 2010

Tai-hoon Kim
Jianhua Ma
Wai-chi Fang
Byungjoo Park
Byeong-Ho Kang
Dominik Ślęzak

Organization

Organizing Committee

General Co-chairs	Jianhua Ma (Hosei University, Japan) Wai-chi Fang (National Chiao Tung University, Taiwan)
Program Co-chairs	Byungjoo Park (Hannam University, Korea) Frode Eika Sandnes (Oslo University College, Norway) Byeong-Ho Kang (University of Tasmania, Australia)
Publicity Co-chairs	Tai-hoon Kim (Hannam University, Korea) Aboul Ella Hassanien (Cairo University, Egypt)
Publication Chair	Bongen Gu (Chungju National University, Korea)

Program Committee

Alexander Loui
Antonio Coronato
Biplab Kumer
Birgit Hofreiter
Bok-Min Goi
Ch. Chantrapornchai
Chao-Tung Yang
Costas Lambrinoudakis
David Taniar
Dorin Bocu
George Kambourakis
Hai Jin

Hakan Duman
Hans Weigand
H.-D. Zimmermann
Helmar Burkhart
Hiroshi Yoshiura
Hongli Luo
Hongxiu Li
Hsiang-Cheh Huang
Igor Kotenko
Irene Krebs
Isao Echizen
J.H. Abawajy

Jianhua He
Kuo-Ming Chao
Ling-Jyh Chen
Mei-Ling Shyu
Nguyen Manh Tho
Rami Yared
Raymond Choo
Regis Cabral
Sajid Hussain
Seng W. Loke
Seong Han Shin
Sheng Zhong

Table of Contents

Design and Implementation of a Threaded Search Engine for Tour Recommendation Systems*

Junghoon Lee[1], Gyung-Leen Park[2], Jin-hee Ko[1],
In-Hye Shin[1], and Mikyung Kang[2],**

[1] Dept. of Computer Science and Statistics,
Jeju National University, 690-756, Jeju Do, Republic of Korea
{jhlee,jhko,ihshin76}@jejunu.ac.kr
[2] University of Southern California - Information Sciences Institute, VA22203, USA
glpark@jejunu.ac.kr, mkkang@isi.edu

Abstract. This paper implements a threaded scan engine for the $O(n!)$ search space and measures its performance, aiming at providing a responsive tour recommendation and scheduling service. As a preliminary step of integrating POI ontology, mobile object database, and personalization profile for the development of new vehicular telematics services, this implementation can give a useful guideline to design a challenging and computation-intensive vehicular telematics service. The implemented engine allocates the subtree to the respective threads and makes them run concurrently exploiting the primitives provided by the operating system and the underlying multiprocessor architecture. It also makes it easy to add a variety of constraints, for example, the search tree is pruned if the cost of partial allocation already exceeds the current best. The performance measurement result shows that the service can run even in the low-power telematics device when the number of destinations does not exceed 15, with an appropriate constraint processing.

1 Introduction

With the development of vehicular telematics networks, many new services can be provided to drivers according to their vehicle types. For example, a rent-a-car driver can retrieve a bunch of real-time information on the current traffic condition as well as the tourist attraction he wants to visit. In addition, a taxi driver can pick up a passenger according to the dispatch system [1]. Such telematics services will evolve along with the development of new vehicular communication technologies and the performance upgrade of telematics devices. With the ever-growing communication speed and the sufficient computing power, more

---

* This research was supported by the MKE(The Ministry of Knowledge Economy), Korea, under the ITRC(Information Technology Research Center) support program supervised by the NIPA(National IT Industry Promotion Agency). (NIPA-2010-(C1090-1011-0009)).
** Corresponding author.

T.-h. Kim et al. (Eds.): UNESST 2010, CCIS 124, pp. 1–7, 2010.

sophisticated services can be developed and provided to the users, even though they need to process a great volume of data and run a complex algorithm.

Tour planning is considered to be one of the most promising telematics services, especially for rent-a-car drivers on the tourist place [2]. Its main function is to decide the tour schedule based on personal preference, current traffic condition, tourist attraction information, and so on, as shown in Figure 1. In most tourist places, the information on each tourist attraction is usually organized already in the database, or sometimes in ontology [3]. Such information covers the details on each tour point including how to reach, how much time it takes on average, activity to do, and so on. Hence, the amount of data and their processing grows significantly. Meanwhile, Jeju province in the Republic of Korea has diverse kinds of unique tourist attractions, such as beaches, volcanoes, cliffs, mountains, subsidiary islands and so on, while hosting a lot of tour activities including ocean sport, golf, hiking, and the like within a relatively small area. Since so many diverse tour plans are possible, the tourist needs the assistance from an intelligent tour planning system [4].

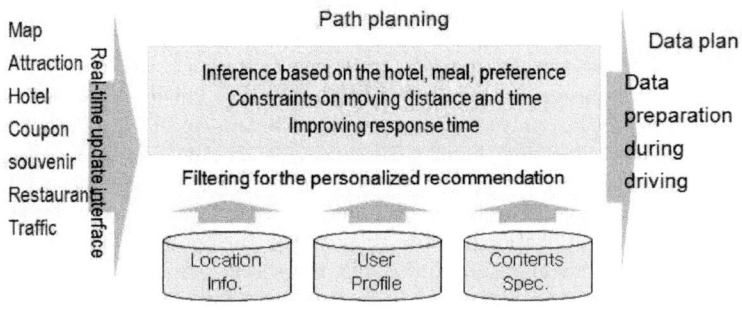

Fig. 1. Tour planning system

Generally, the tour recommender system consists of two steps [5]. First, the system selects the candidate POIs sorted by their ranks or scores determined by the system-specific criteria and algorithms. The second step filters candidate POIs to generate a corresponding tour schedule, considering calculated ranks, given time constraint, user location, and current traffic condition as shown in Figure 2. Particularly, for a tourist who accesses and retrieves information via a telematics device inside rent-a-car, it is necessary to minimize the response time to say nothing of the number of user-system interactions. Computing an optimal route for multiple POIs is an instance of TSP (Traveling Salesman Problem) which is known to be NP-hard, and the number of candidate POIs is extremely critical to the response time.

Obviously, the efficient heuristic and the multithreaded program are two best strategies to speed up the computation time for a complex problem. TSP is one of the most classical computation-intensive problems for which a lot of famous heuristic methods have been developed [1]. Most of them, including

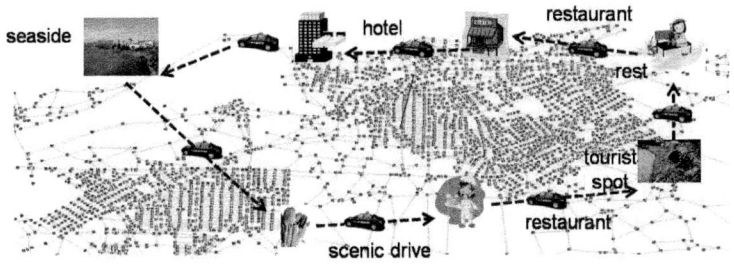

Fig. 2. Example of a tour schedule

Lin-Kernighan algorithm, achieved great improvement in computation speed and accuracy [6]. However, existing schemes mainly consider just the distance between the destinations, so it is quite difficult to integrate additional constraints a driver may specify and submit in tour planning. For example, lunch time must be put between 12:00 and 13:00 on a specific restaurant type, or the museum must be visited prior to beach area. Without an efficient heuristic, the time complexity of $O(n!)$ is very sensitive to the number of POIs that are to be scheduled. Moreover, those services need to process a great amount of data including personal preference, detailed POI attributes, and the navigation-scale road network [7].

Even though the execution time grows too much to be used for larger n, a strong constraint can prune the unnecessary branch in the search space tree. Moreover, along with a well-defined constraint, the multithreaded execution can further improve the computation time without sacrificing the accuracy of the final solution. For the sake of verifying how fast the multithreaded program can response to the user request, actual implementation and application to the real data is important. In this regard, this paper is to build a multithreaded computing framework for the tour planning service and measure its performance, aiming at providing convenient tour schedule to vehicular telematics users. The framework includes threaded search engine and constraint processing primitives.

This paper is organized as follows: After issuing the problem in Section 1, Section 2 designs and implements the threaded search engine for the tour schedule Performance measurement results are demonstrated to reveal the practicality of our implementation in Section 3. Finally, Section 4 summarizes and concludes this paper with a brief introduction of future work.

2   System Design and Implementation

The overview of our framework is described in Figure 2. The first step is to process the road network represented by the ESRI shape file format. Based on this, a route between every pair of POIs can be calculated. In integrating the up-to-date traffic condition, a commercial or civilian service is available in most cities including Jeju. This information is mapped to the road network. Second,

POI details have been organized in travel ontology by another member of our research team [3]. Third, POIs are classified by their characteristics first and necessary fields are defined, while each field is associated with the appropriate attribute [8]. Additionally, how to specify the user preference and constraint was researched in [9]. Here, user preference is defined by geographical terrain preference, time preference, and activity preference, based on general attributes such as demographic information, tour history, and tour motivation.

As a preliminary step to integrate all these components, this paper implements the multithreaded search space scan engine which assigns subtrees in the search space to each thread. The multiprocessor architecture is now commonly available in PCs, notebook computers, and even in vehicular telematics devices. In this architecture and the Windows-based operating system, each thread is allocated to each processor and executed. The tour schedule service can run either on the in-vehicle telematics device or on the remote high capacity server and then transmitted to the driver via the appropriate wireless communication channel. Our implementation runs on the machine equipped with Intel Core2 Duo CPU working at 2.4 GHz clock, 3.0 GB memory, and Windows Vista operating system, while the measurement of actual execution time can give us a useful guideline, for example, where the service is placed, how much constraint can be combined, up to how many destinations the service can provide the reasonable service level, and the like.

To begin with, this paper makes a program which calculates the distance between each of n nodes using the A* algorithm [10]. Classical Dijkstra's algorithm consumes too much time, as the number of pairs gets larger for larger n. Even if A* algorithm cannot always find the optimal solution, its execution time is much short [8]. Moreover, one-to-many version of A* is also available [11]. In the subsequent version, we will implement a thread that works in background to update the cost between the major POIs according to the traffic condition change. For n POIs, it is necessary to visit $n!$ leaf nodes, each of which corresponds to a complete schedule, if we don't have another constraints. Furthermore, each of n top-level subtrees has $(n-1)!$ leaf nodes. In the dual CPU platform, the tour planner creates two equal-priority threads, each of which processes $\frac{n}{2}$ subtrees. If no other constraint is given, the execution time of each thread is the same. Otherwise, it is advantageous to create n threads and allocate them one by one each time a thread completes scanning one subtree.

Next, constraint processing can prune unnecessary branch traversal in the search space tree. Basically, after the search procedure reaches a leaf node, that is, when a complete schedule is built, the cost for the schedule is calculated. If the cost is less than the current best, namely the smallest cost, the current best will be replaced by the new one. However, if the cost for an incomplete schedule already exceeds the current best, it is useless to execute the remaining allocation, as adding a new entry will make the cost increase monotonously. Accordingly, our implementation checks the cost of partial allocation before proceeding to the next entry allocation. Moreover, for the real-life tour schedule, such constraints listed in Section 1 can further narrow the search space, reducing the execution time. It has the same effect as the reduction in the number of destinations, which is critical in $O(n!)$ search space processing.

3   Performance Measurement

This section measures the performance of our system implementation. Figure 3 plots the measurement result for the actual execution time of our implementation. The experiment makes the number of POIs change from 7 to 12. For simplicity and without losing generality, the cost between each node is selected randomly. As shown in this figure, the execution time is insignificant until n reaches 8, where single-threaded version takes $0.01sec$ and the dual-threaded version $0.007\ sec$, respectively. For the number of POIs less than or equal to 10, it takes less than a second. When the number of nodes is 11, it takes 8.8 seconds to make a tour schedule in threaded version, cutting the computation time almost by half. The thread context switch and management overhead prevents further improvement. From here, the program can clearly take advantage of the threaded execution. However, if the number exceeds 12, even the dual-threaded version cannot provide a reasonable execution time without a well-defined constraint processing.

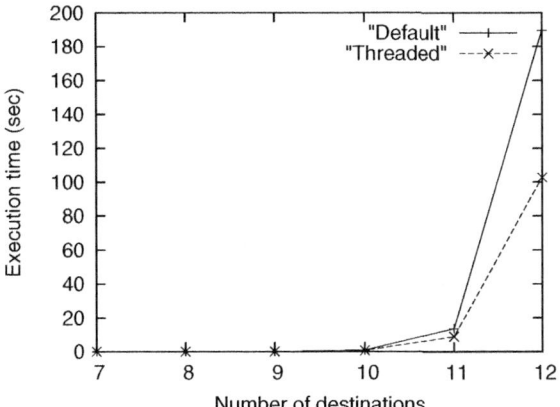

Fig. 3. Execution time measurement

Anyway, this result indicates that the tour planner can work also on the telematics device when n is less than 10. For a single day trip, the number of POIs generally lies in this range. In addition, threaded version can achieve the computation speed-up almost proportional to the number of CPUs when n is larger than or equal to 10, significantly reducing the response time.

Figure 4 plots the effect of constraint processing. For two threads, each thread routine stores its own current best to alleviate the interference between the threads in accessing the shared variable. Even if the single common current best can further reduce the search space, mutual exclusion on the shared variable takes indisregardable overhead. The execution time is just 0.39 *sec*, while the non-constrained version takes 102.7 *sec* as shown in Figure 3 and Figure 4. In our experiment, the execution time is less than 30 *sec* until the number of POIs is 17, but it goes to 700 *sec* when the number of POIs is 18. After all, this experiment reveals that an efficient heuristic or strong constraint can significantly improve the execution time. The tour schedule is highly likely to have strong constraints, as the tourist has different requirements according to his tour length, preference, and the like. So, our framework can work efficiently in the real-life environment.

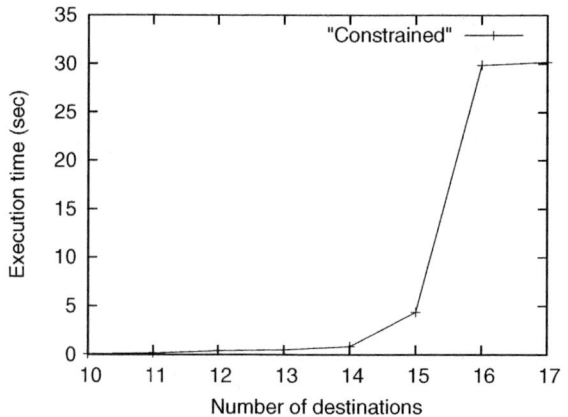

Fig. 4. Effect of constraint processing

4 Concluding Remarks

This paper has designed and implemented a threaded scan engine for the $O(n!)$ search space for the tour recommendation system and measured its performance. The implemented system allocates the subtree to the respective threads and makes them to run concurrently on a multiprocessor architecture. In addition, the constraint processing primitive is added to prune the subtree when the partial allocation in progress has no hope to make a solution better than the current best. The measurement result shows that the service can run even in the telematics device for the single day trip, even without any constraint processing. In our experiment, the execution time is less than 30 *sec* until the number of POIs is 17 on an average performance personal computer. Based on this implementation, an efficient service framework can be built for the development of prospective vehicular telematics services by integrating existing POI ontology, mobile object database, personalization profile.

At the next step, we are to classify the constraints that may be given to our search engine and measure their effect, namely, how much each constraint group can reduce the search space. The constraint may be time-based, sequence-based, similarity-based, group-based, and so on.

References

1. Lee, J., Park, G., Kim, H., Yang, Y., Kim, P.: A Telematics Service System Based on the Linux Cluster. In: Shi, Y., van Albada, G.D., Dongarra, J., Sloot, P.M.A. (eds.) ICCS 2007. LNCS, vol. 4490, pp. 660–667. Springer, Heidelberg (2007)
2. Ricci, F., Werthner, H.: Case Base Querying for Travel Planning Recommendation. Information Technology & Tourism 4, 215–226 (2002)
3. Choi, C., Cho, M., Choi, J., Hwang, M., Park, J., Kim, P.: Travel Ontology for Intelligent Recommendation System. In: Asia International Conference on Modelling and Simulation, pp. 637–642 (2009)
4. Lee, J., Kang, E., Park, G.: Design and Implementation of a Tour Planning System for Telematics Users. In: Gervasi, O., Gavrilova, M.L. (eds.) ICCSA 2007, Part III. LNCS, vol. 4707, pp. 179–189. Springer, Heidelberg (2007)
5. Nasraoui, O., Petenes, C.: An Intelligent Web Recommendation Engine Based on Fuzzy Approximate Reasoning. In: Proceeding of the IEEE International Conference on Fuzzy System, vol. 2, pp. 1116–1121 (2003)
6. Lin, S., Kernighan, B.W.: An Effective Heuristic Algorithm for the Traveling-Salesman Problem. Operations Research 21, 498–516 (1973)
7. Letchner, J., Krumm, J., Horvitz, E.: Trip Router with Individualized Preferences (TRIP): Incorporating Personalization into Route Planning. In: Eighteenth Conference on Innovative Applications of Artificial Intelligence (2006)
8. Lee, S., Kim, S., Lee, J.: Yoo. J.: Approximate Indexing in Road Network Databases. In: ACM Symposium on Applied Computing, pp. 1568–1572 (2009)
9. Kang, E., Kim, H., Cho, J.: Personalization Method for Tourist Point of Interest (POI) Recommendation. In: Gabrys, B., Howlett, R.J., Jain, L.C. (eds.) KES 2006. LNCS (LNAI), vol. 4251, pp. 392–400. Springer, Heidelberg (2006)
10. Goldberg, A., Kaplan, H., Werneck, R.: Reach for A*: Efficient Point-to-point Shortest Path Algorithms. MSR-TR-2005-132. Microsoft (2005)
11. Shin, S., Lee, S., Kim, S., Lee, J., Im, E.: Efficient Shortest Path Finding of K-nearest Neighbor Objects in Road Network Databases. In: ACM Symposium on Applied Computing, pp. 1661–1665 (2010)

Analysis of the Position Effect to the Vehicle Speed and Stop Probability*

Junghoon Lee[1], Gyung-Leen Park[1,**], Hye-Jin Kim[1],
Min-Jae Kang[2], Cheol Min Kim[3], and Jinhwan Kim[4]

[1] Dept. of Computer Science and Statistics
[2] Dept. of Electronic Engineering
[3] Dept. of Computer Education
Jeju National University, 690-756, Jeju Do, Republic of Korea
{jhlee,glpark,hjkim82,minjk,cmkim}@jejunu.ac.kr
[4] Dept. of Multimedia Engineering, Hansung University
kimjh@hansung.ac.kr

Abstract. This paper addresses how to manage the location history data collected from the Jeju taxi telematics system and analyzes the effect of the report position in a link to the average speed and stop probability. The analysis cannot only quantify how much the speed value, included in each location report, will be accurate in calculating the actual link speed but also locate bottle-neck links. Using the road network represented by an ESRI shape format, a map match scheme is designed to calculate the position from one of the two end points. Then, the statistical analysis runs database queries on the vehicle speed and stop probability for all records, for the records having the passenger-on status, and for the records belonging to the hot links. The investigation finds that the speed difference between the middle and end points of a road segment can reach 13 kmh on average and locates intersections that blocks vehicle traffic.

1 Introduction

Nowadays, it has become possible to use cell phones and GPS devices to collect the movement patterns of people and transportation systems as well as their spatial and social use of streets and neighborhoods [1]. This data collection can make it possible to efficiently run urban actuators such as traffic lights, street signs, and even inhabitants. In addition, we can get a lot of information on traffic pattern, vehicle speed, and passenger's waiting time provided that we are targeting at moving objects in a transportation system [2]. Generally, such an analysis requires large-scale data manipulation, raw data processing, and

---

* This research was supported by the MKE(The Ministry of Knowledge Economy), Korea, under the ITRC(Information Technology Research Center) support program supervised by the NIPA(National IT Industry Promotion Agency). (NIPA-2010-(C1090-1011-0009)).
** Corresponding author.

T.-h. Kim et al. (Eds.): UNESST 2010, CCIS 124, pp. 8–16, 2010.

intelligence in dealing with the unique features of the respective moving objects. As for the vehicle object, it moves at very high speeds over the wide area, its trajectory must follow the road network, and its movement varies according to the vehicle type such as taxi, bus, truck, and the like [3].

For location tracking, a vehicle should be able to determine its location, typically represented by latitude and longitude, by means of a GPS (Global Positioning System) receiver. Then, vehicles report to the central server via an appropriate wireless interface, regardless of whether it infrastructure-based or ad-hoc style. The cellular network, such as 3G or CDMA (Code Division Multiple Access) in Korea, belongs to the infrastructure network and provides ubiquitous connection to all moving objects, even though it's not cost-free and its bandwidth is quite limited. A shorter report period, or frequent reports, necessarily creates more accurate and refined tracking data. However, due to the communication cost, the resolution of the tracking data must be compromised, even though the communication rate is usually negotiable with the telecommunication company. As the report keeps accumulating, the large-scale spatial database is needed for efficient data storage and processing.

Nominated as the telematics model city by the national government of the Republic of Korea, Jeju area has launched many research projects, product developments, and pilot system verification for the last few years. Among these, the Taxi telematics system keeps track of the location of each taxi for an efficient taxi dispatch, creating movement history data for tens of member taxis [4]. The collected location data can also yield value-added information such as pick-up and drop-off patterns, passenger travel time and distance, and dispatch delays [5]. To say nothing of such vehicle-related information, we can also get the road-specific information after associating the coordinate to the road segment, for example, the vehicle speed distribution on the road, whether an intersection needs to install a traffic signal, or whether its traffic signal blocks traffic. For such analysis, it is important to know where the report occurs on the road segment. In this regard, this paper is to design a method to match the location to a road segment and analyze the effect of such report position to the actual vehicle speed and stop probability.

This paper is organized as follows: After issuing the problem in Section 1, Section 2 describes the main features of location history data. Section 3 describes the details on how hot analyze the position effect and shows the analysis result. Finally, Section 4 summarizes and concludes this paper with a brief introduction of future work.

2   Location History Data

In the Jeju taxi telematics system, each taxi reports the location record consisting of time-stamp, taxi ID, latitude, longitude, heading, speed, and status, either every 1 or 3 minutes according to whether the taxi is carrying a passenger or not. Its values are mainly achieved from the GPS receiver and the telematics device in each taxi. Just the taxi ID and status comes from the telematics device which has a dedicated ID and represents the current taxi status. The status field can have 4 values, namely, *empty*, *passenger-on*, *dispatched*, and *in-rest*. Our information processing framework adds two fields, namely, link and position fields to this basic record. The map match module searches the link closest to the received coordinate from the digital map, calculates the position ratio in the link, and stores in position field as shown in Figure 1. The position ratio can have the value of 0 through 1. If it is 0.5, the report is created in the middle of a road segment. Not just for the traditional navigation system, map matching is becoming more important since vehicles are used as traffic probes in estimating the current road speed and building a statistical traffic delay model [6].

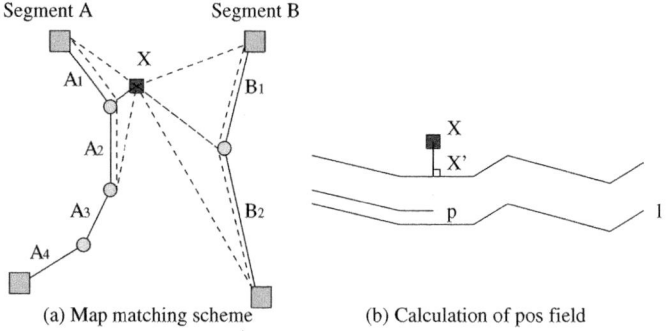

(a) Map matching scheme   (b) Calculation of pos field

Fig. 1. Additional fields processing

We have the road network of Jeju area in an ESRI shape file format which sequentially stores each line segment, or link. Each link, basically connecting two intersections, is further divided into a series of subsegments. A link also specifies a boundary box that embraces the whole segment. For a given record having point, X, the map match module first finds the segments to which X is included using the bounding box information. Here, considering the GPS and map plotting error, we add 10 m error margin. For candidate segments, the area is calculated for each triangle made up of X and two consecutive points along the segment as shown in Figure 1(a). The segment having the smallest area is the link for the point X. After selecting the matched segment, we can draw a perpendicular line and find the meet point as shown in Figure 1(b). In the figure, l denotes the total length of a line segment and it is calculated by the sum of the lengths of all subsegments. p is the length from the start point to the meet point, X'. The ratio of p to l is set to the value of the position field. As such, the whole record is completed and stored in the relational and spatial databases as shown in Table 1.

Using this location history database, our previous work has conducted several analyses. First, after building the information processing framework, the dispatch

Table 1. Location record organization

field	type	description
tstamp	datetime	time
tid	char(6)	taxi ID
x	double(11,10)	latitude
y	double(11,10)	longitude
dir	double(3,2)	direction
speed	double(3,2)	speed of vehicle
status	int(2)	current taxi status
link	int(6)	matched link
pos	double(3,2)	position ratio

delay and distance are estimated by tracing the status change [7]. Second, to get the passengers' travel pattern, the hourly travel distance and the travel time are estimated for each passenger transaction [8]. Third, for the sake of reducing the empty taxi ratio, the taxi-side waiting time is analyzed by measuring the time interval between two adjacent travels [9]. Fourth, we filter the hot pick-up points and their temporal and spatial distribution to recommend empty taxis to the area in which they can pick up a passenger [10]. Fifth, based on the GUI implementation to select the path of interest [11], the speed field of each record is investigated to check whether the location history data can be used for link speed estimation [12].

3 History Data Analysis

3.1 Preliminaries

In our previous effort to get diverse information from the Jeju taxi telematics system, we have discovered that the speed field is significantly affected by the position in the line segment. In addition, many passenger pick-ups are done near an intersection, possibly making the road more dangerous and interfering right-turn vehicles. The position field indicates how close the coordinate is to the intersection, making the record more descriptive. For example, if this field gets closer to either 0.0 or 1.0, the point is located near an intersection. It implies that the certainty of map matching result diminishes. In addition, if a vehicle is not moving at such a spot, it must be waiting for the traffic signal to change, so the corresponding record must be excluded in estimating the link speed. After all, the location record is stored in the database and a sophisticated analysis will extend the information range we can get.

Road networks for the path recommendation and the traffic information service are different in their granularity. In Jeju area, the official road network for the traffic information service consists of about 1,100 nodes and 3,200 links as shown in Figure 2. It is much coarser compared with the road network for path finding, and can't be used for map matching. As contrast, the road network for

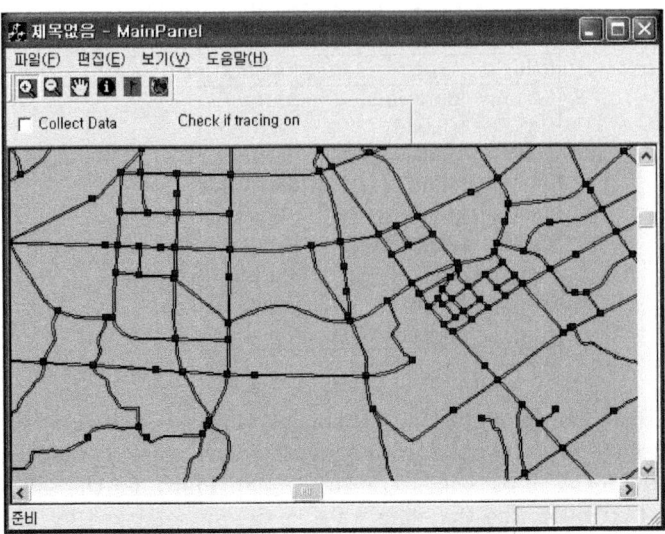

Fig. 2. Road network for the traffic information service

path finding is made up of about 17,000 nodes and 25,000 links, as will be shown in Subsection 3.3. For a link which contains just two endpoints in memory, many points are included in a disk file or database to represent the shape of actual road segments. It takes a long time to match a location point to a specific road segment. If the road network gets more complex, the map matching procedure must be built on an efficient indexing scheme and spatial database. Up to now, we just store the road network in a sequential file and the relational database.

3.2   Validity of Link Speed

This subsection estimates the average speed according to the position in the road segment. Two experiments will plot 3 curves. First, the speed fields of the whole records are averaged after being grouped by the position ratio. Second, only the records having the passenger-on status are averaged to eliminate the case an empty taxi is waiting for a passenger without moving. Third, just the hottest 10 links having the largest number of reports are selected in calculating the average. For such a case, the average is highly likely to be accurate. The experiment converts the position ratio into discrete values from 0.1 to 1.0 by rounding to the nearest tenth. For a road segment, if the position field is 0, it is the westmost point, namely, the start point at the west. On the contrary, if it is 1, it is the eastmost point. Our shape file stores in this way, and other files can be converted like this. It is easily expected that the speed in the middle of the road segment is higher than that in the end points, where a traffic light may be installed or the car slows down to check other traffic.

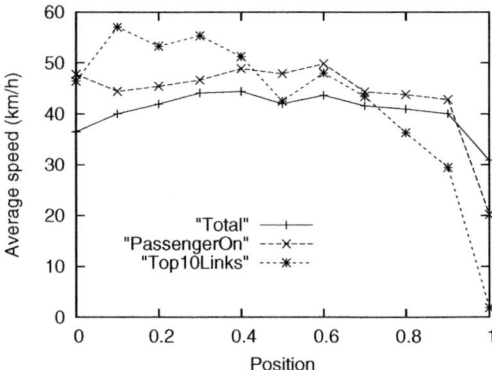

Fig. 3. Average speed vs. position

For the case of whole records, the difference between the middle point and the end point is about 13 kmh on average. The top 10 link case includes the road segment where an empty taxi waits for a passenger. As the taxi is not moving, such a link has many reports. Interestingly, they wait around the east end point more than around the west end point, so the average speed is almost 0 when the position is 1.0. The speed difference is almost 53 kmh. For the case of carrying a passenger, we can assume that the taxi is moving at the speed the road network permits. Even in this case, the eastmost point has the lowest speed, indicating that the traffic signal system is quite unfair. The difference reaches 27 kmh.

Next, Figure 4 plots the stop probability according to the position field. It is also expected that the two end points have the higher stop probability. The result conforms to the case of Figure 3. We can see the differences of 4.2 %, 26.8 %, and 65.8 %, respectively. Even for the curve of passenger-on case, the east end shows a higher stop probability, indicating longer waiting time in front of the traffic signal.

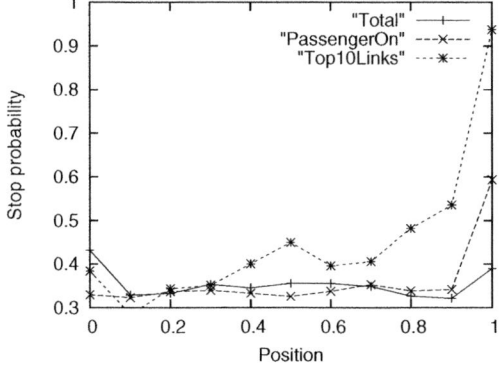

Fig. 4. Stop probability vs. position

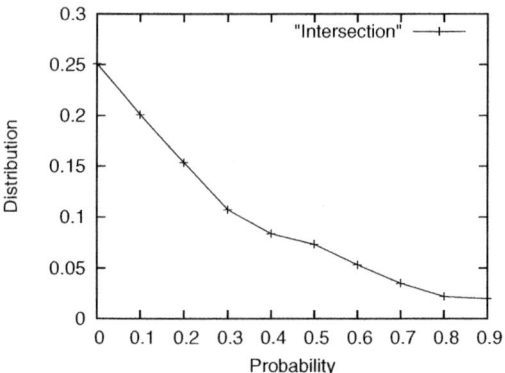

Fig. 5. Link distribution

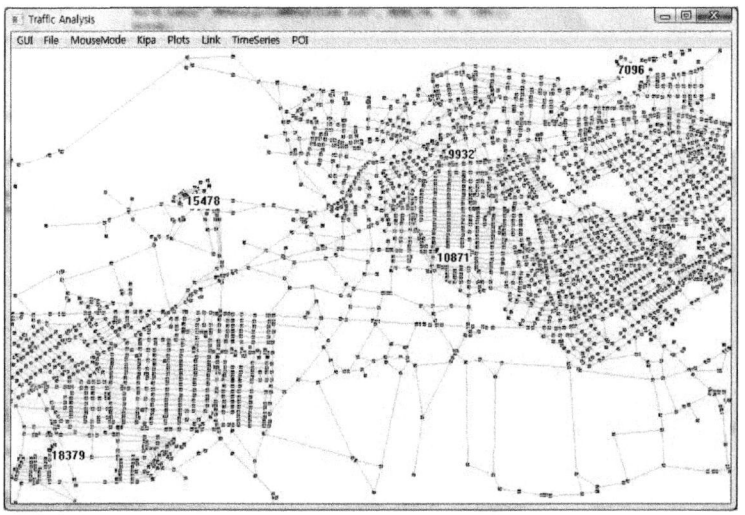

Fig. 6. Bottleneck link plotting

3.3 Locating the Bottleneck Intersection

This subsection attempts to identify the intersection which is likely to block traffic. To this end, the estimation procedure finds the number of records having speed of 0 and groups by the link ID. Then, the records having the position value of less than 0.1 or greater than 0.9 is selected to calculate the ratio between them. Next, the probability distribution is generated as shown in Figure 5. This figure indicates that 25 % of links do not have the record having speed of 0 at two end points. For about 0.25 % of links, more than 90 % of records have the speed of 0 near the two end points. Namely, on such a road segment, the vehicles stop at the intersection 9 out of 10 times, indicating that it has some problem in the traffic management.

Figure 6 depicts the architecture of our information processing framework. The road network is converted to the graph data structure to provide basic map functions such as zoon-in, zoom-out, and pan. Moreover, this framework provides the graphic user interface capable of mapping between WGS (World Geodetic System) and device coordinates, searching and marking specific nodes or links. Here, the figure shows the link ID on which many vehicles stop at both end points. If several links are located in the dense area, some links IDs are overwritten. The locations of digits correspond to the heavy traffic area such as the airport, the city hall, the market, and newly-built residential area. Like this way, we can find the problem of the traffic system using the location history data.

4   Concluding Remarks

This paper has described how to manage the location history data collected from the Jeju taxi telematics system and how to organize the location record. An analysis has been conducted to quantify the effect of the report position in a link to the average speed and stop probability. The analysis estimates how much the speed value, included in each location report, will be accurate in calculating the actual link speed and locates bottle-neck links. Using the road network represented by an ESRI shape format, a map match scheme has been implemented to calculate the position from the west end point. The position filed makes it possible to investigate the road network condition at a specific time instance The analysis finds that the speed difference. between the middle and two end points of a road segment can reach 13 kmh and locates the 20 intersections that blocks vehicle traffic.

The location history data and digital road maps are complementary each other. The road map is created by companies using the specialized vehicles equipped with GPS to drive the road and record data. An emerging alternative is to use GPS data from ordinary vehicles driving their regular route [13]. Even though our system is built on top of an existing road map, it can help to correct the map error by detecting the change in the road network as well as locating intersections. Particularly, we have implemented the user interface that filters the location history records belong to a specific path [11]. Regardless of the path length, the refined investigation can be conducted to the area of interest. As future work, we will keep researching what we can get from the location history data and how to do, for example, appropriately distributing the taxis over the city area to reduce the empty taxi ratio and waiting time. In our approach, the taxis will play a role of urban actuators.

References

1. Clabrese, F., et al.: Urban Computing and Mobile Devices. In: Pervasive Computing, vol. 6, pp. 52–57 (2007)
2. Ahmadi, H., Abdelzaher, T., Gupta, I.: Congestion Control for Spatio-Temporal Data in Cyber-Physical Systems. In: Proc. ACM/IEEE International Conference on Cyber-Physical Systems, pp. 89–98 (2010)

3. Hariharan, R., Toyama, K.: Project Lachesis: Parsing and Modeling Location Histories. In: Egenhofer, M.J., Freksa, C., Miller, H.J. (eds.) GIScience 2004. LNCS, vol. 3234, pp. 106–124. Springer, Heidelberg (2004)

4. Lee, J., Park, G., Kim, H., Yang, Y., Kim, P., Kim, S.: Telematics Service System Based on the Linux Cluster. In: Shi, Y., van Albada, G.D., Dongarra, J., Sloot, P.M.A. (eds.) ICCS 2007. LNCS, vol. 4490, pp. 660–667. Springer, Heidelberg (2007)

5. Green, P.: Driver Distraction, Telematics Design, and Workload Managers-Safety Issues and Solutions. In: Proceedings of the 2004 International Congress on Transportation Electronics, pp. 165–180 (2004)

6. Newson, P., Krumm, J.: Hidden Markov Map Matching Through Noise and Sparseness. In: 17th ACM SIGSPATIAL International Conference on Advances in Geographic Information Systems, pp. 336–343 (2009)

7. Lee, J., Park, G.: Design and Implementation of a Movement History Analysis Framework for the Taxi Telematics System. In: 14th Asia-Pacific Conference on Communications (2008)

8. Lee, J.: Traveling Pattern Analysis for the Design of Location-Dependent Contents Based on the Taxi Telematics System. In: International Conference on Multimedia, Information Technology and its Applications, pp. 148–151 (2008)

9. Lee, J.: Analysis on the Waiting Time of Empty Taxis for the Taxi Telematics System. In: International Conference on Convergence and Hybrid Information Technology, pp. 66–69 (2008)

10. Lee, J., Shin, I., Park, G.: Analysis of the Passenger Pick-up Pattern for Taxi Location Recommendation. In: International Conference on Networked Computing and Advanced Information Management, pp. 199–204 (2008)

11. Lee, J., Hong, J.: Design and Implementation of a Spatial Data Processing Engine for the Telematics Network. In: Applied Computing and Computational Science, pp. 39–43 (2008)

12. Lee, J.: Traffic Information Processing Using the Location History Data on the Vehicular Telematics System. In: ECTI-CON, pp. 756–759 (2009)

13. Fathi, A., Krumm, J.: Detecting Road Intersections from GPS Traces. In: Sixth International Conference on Geographic Information Systems (2010)

Approach to Privacy-Preserve
Data in Two-Tiered Wireless Sensor Network
Based on Linear System and Histogram

Van H. Dang[1], Sven Wohlgemuth[2], Hiroshi Yoshiura[3],
Thuc D. Nguyen[1], and Isao Echizen[2]

[1] University of Science, VNU-HCM, 227 Nguyen Van Cu, Dist 5, HCMC, Vietnam
dhvan@fit.hcmus.edu.vn, ndthuc@fit.hcmus.edu.vn
[2] National Institute of Informatics. 2-1-2 Hitotsubashi, Chiyoda-ku, Tokyo 101-8430, Japan
wohlgemuth@nii.ac.jp, iechizen@nii.ac.jp
[3] The University of Electro-Communications. 1-5-1 Chofugaoka, Chofu-shi,
Tokyo 182-8585, Japan
yoshiura@hc.uec.ac.jp

Abstract. Wireless sensor network (WSN) has been one of key technologies for the future with broad applications from the military to everyday life [1,2,3,4,5]. There are two kinds of WSN model models with sensors for sensing data and a sink for receiving and processing queries from users; and models with special additional nodes capable of storing large amounts of data from sensors and processing queries from the sink. Among the latter type, a two-tiered model [6,7] has been widely adopted because of its storage and energy saving benefits for weak sensors, as proved by the advent of commercial storage node products such as Stargate [8] and RISE. However, by concentrating storage in certain nodes, this model becomes more vulnerable to attack. Our novel technique, called zip-histogram, contributes to solving the problems of previous studies [6,7] by protecting the stored data's confidentiality and integrity (including data from the sensor and queries from the sink) against attackers who might target storage nodes in two-tiered WSNs.

Keywords: two-tiered wireless sensor network, histogram, linear system.

1 Introduction

We shall consider two-tiered WSNs with three main actors. Sensors are in charge of sensing data. The sink receives queries from users, contacts the inner network to get answers, and returns them to users. Storage nodes stores data from sensors and seek answers for queries from the sink. This makes query processing more efficient because the sink needs to contact a few storage nodes instead of all the sensors. Because storage nodes may contain vital data, we should recognize that they are vulnerable to attack. Therefore, we shall assume that storage nodes are not trustworthy but the sink is completely trustworthy. In this paper, we solve the problem in a two-tiered WSN of un-trustworthy storage nodes; that is, we devise a way to protect confidentiality and integrity of data from sensors and queries (modeled as range queries) from the sink.

T.-h. Kim et al. (Eds.): UNESST 2010, CCIS 124, pp. 17–30, 2010.

Challenges of the problem are limited memory, communication bandwidth, storage space, and energy supply of regular sensors. A typical sensor, MicaZ from CrossBow, has 128KB of program memory, 4KB of data memory, a 250-kbps bandwidth, and a 2.4 GHz frequency [9,10]. Because price of sensors becomes the predominant problem, we shall assume that the hardware constraints of WSNs will remain constant for some time [11].

The privacy problem in two-tiered WSNs has not been covered much. There are only three studies concerning it. One is Sheng & Li's state-of-the-art scheme [6]; the others are Chen & Liu's [7] and Rui Zhang, Jing Shi & Yanchao Zhang's [17]. The state-of-the-art method has two main drawbacks. Firstly, it uses bucketization. As mentioned in [13], the entire bucketization scheme and the exact probability distribution of values may be estimated. Secondly, if the data are concentrated in a few buckets, this method incurs a cost to empty the buckets in order to ensure integrity. This increases the transmission cost. Finally, as mentioned in [7], this method is not suitable for multi-dimensional data; sensors may be equipped with multiple sensing modules measuring temperature, humidity, pressure, etc. However, Sheng & Li's scheme is just for one-dimensional data. Note that we also consider only one-dimensional data. The method of Chen & Liu [7] also has two drawbacks. Firstly, the encrypted parts of the data must be in ascending order. If there is a problem of transmitting packets in the wrong order, this will cause errors and possibly false negatives about attacks. Secondly, communication is costly without Bloom Filters. The solution of the authors is of course to use Bloom Filters. However, this technique brings with it false positive errors. In addition, although it referred to the problem of replicated values in data, the paper did not present a clear solution. The method reduces the cost in comparison with the state-of-the-art method [6] in the case of multi-dimensional data. However, our concern is one-dimensional data, so we will not look any further into this advantage. Finally, reference [17] aims to ensure integrity for multi-dimensional data by using methods called, probabilistic spatial crosscheck, probabilistic temporal crosscheck, random probing, and hybrid scheme composed of these three methods.

We propose a novel method called zip-histogram to provide privacy for data in the system. The ideas behind this method are to build a histogram, i.e., a set of values, and to compress the histogram to decrease the communication cost. The compression is based on systems of linear equations and a shared key technique. For range queries from users, the sink converts them into random forms and sends them to the storage nodes. Storage nodes always return the whole converted histogram to the sink. Therefore, the secrecy of the queries is sure to be protected. The storage nodes also perform queries without knowing the content of the original histogram. The efficiency of the method depends on zip-histogram. It must compress the histogram into an acceptable size and recover the histogram. Compared with the previous studies, our method has advantages and disadvantages: It discloses nothing about queries, while the others disclose some information, and it has benefits for high-frequency data. However, it must send the whole histogram, although the communication cost is lowered.

2   System Model and Threat Model

2.1   System Model

Although the model of a two-tiered WSN was described in previous studies [6,7], it will be useful to describe it here briefly. We shall concentrate more on the flow of data in the model. To have a full view of data flow, we include other actors connected to the system. The first is the environment that the sensors sense the data from. The second is the users that request the sink to send queries to the storage node.

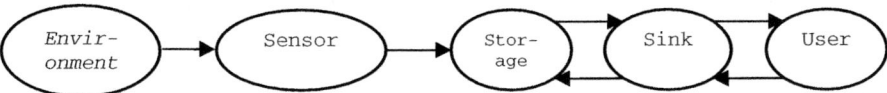

Fig. 1. System model

(1) Phase 1 – Sensing and sending data
A regular sensor consists of three main components: processing, transferring, and sensing units [14]. The sensing unit collects (senses) data from the environment (the natural environment, the human body, etc.), and the processing unit preprocesses the data. The transferring unit sends data to the nearby storage. To ensure privacy, the data must be converted into a meaningless form (by the processing unit) before it is sent. In addition, to save energy during the transfer, the data is not sent per item. Instead, the sensor senses the data during a time period (called a time slot). Then, for each time slot, the sensor sends a set of data items in converted form to the storage node: i,t, $convert(d1,...,dm)$, where i is the identification of the sensor, t is the time slot, and $\{d1,...,dm\}$ is the set of original data.

(2) Phase 2 – Storing data
The data stored in the storage node has a meaningless form: i,t, $convert(d1,...,dm)$

(3) Phase 3 – Requesting query
The user sends a query to the sink. We shall concentrate on range queries, i.e., queries for data belonging to a range $[a,b]$. We assume that the connection between the user and the sink is secure. Form of query: t, $[a,b]$

(4) Phase 4 – Sending query
After receiving a request from the user, the sink preprocesses the query so that the storage node will not recognize what the query means. Then the sink sends the converted query to storage. Form of query: t, $convert([a,b])$

(5) Phase 5 – Processing query and replying
The storage node searches for data which satisfies the query after it receives the query from the sink. However, all data are meaningless to the storage, and so is the query. The problem we want to solve is how can we process query with encrypted data? The storage node returns the result in converted form to the sink: $convert(result)$.

(6) Phase 6 – Verifying the reply
The sink must have way to check if the reply is correct and complete. If the reply is correct and complete, the sink returns the results to the user. Form of results: $result$

2.2 Threat Model

We shall consider one type of privacy attack called camouflage adversaries. One can insert a node or compromise nodes in order to hide in the sensor network. These nodes can conduct privacy analyses [15].

There are two kinds of sensor in the system: normal sensor nodes and storage nodes. If a sensor node is compromised, the data in it will be stolen. However, data in other nodes will still be secure. Because the number of sensors in a network is very large compared to only one or few compromised sensors, this kind of attack does not cause much damage. If the storage node is compromised, however, it may cause a lot of damage because the node stores all data from all sensors. The storage node then can reveal the original data or send a wrong result back to the sink as a query result.

Therefore, we want to ensure the confidentiality and integrity of data sent from the sensors to the storage, the data in storage, the queries from the sink, and the results from the storage to sink.

- Data confidentiality: Data sent from the sensor to the storage and the data in storage should be kept secure.
- Query confidentiality: A query from the sink to the storage should be kept secret in storage.
- Data integrity: The sink must be able to identify if replies from storage have been interfered with in some way. For example, the storage node does not reply with all results or changes the results before sending.

Fig. 2. Data in threat model

3   Related Work

The main contribution of Chen&Liu [7] is to use prefix membership verification and a Bloom Filter (optional) to improve the power usage and data storage in case of multi-dimensional data. They also proposed a new structure called neighbourhood chain to provide integrity.

The basic idea is to convert a set of sensors data into a set of consecutive ranges (in ascending order), then convert those into a minimum set of prefixes. After that, they convert the bound values of the range query into sets of prefixes. They use prefix membership verification to find the ranges included in the range query. The second idea is structure neighborhood chaining that links separate data items into concatenations of pairs of consecutive items. The concatenations not only include information about the current data items but also about the previous item; therefore, they can be used to check the integrity of data.

Chen&Liu's scheme has two main drawbacks: Firstly, the encrypted parts must be in ascending order. If packets are not transferred in the right order, this will cause errors and may lead to false negatives about attacks. Secondly, the costs of communication are too high without Bloom Filters. The solution of the authors is to use Bloom Filters. However, this technique is subject to false positive errors. In addition, although it refers to the problem of replicated values in the data, the paper did not clarify the solution. This method reduces costs compared to the state-of-the-art method [6] for multi-dimensional data. However, we are only concerned with one-dimensional data Our approach fixes the cost for different numbers of items and does not require the order of data items to be kept.

The main idea of the S&L Scheme [6] is to partition a domain of data into buckets, each assigned a label. Each data item is identified by which bucket it belongs to. All data values in the same bucket are encrypted in the same block. the whole input and assigned a corresponding label. For each empty bucket, the sensor creates an encoding number which is used for the sink to verify that the bucket is empty. The sensor sends all data to nearby storage. When the sink wants to query a range, it converts the range into a minimal set of bucket labels and sends these labels to the storage nodes. The storage nodes search for data with the labels and returns the data to the sink. The sink then decrypts all data from storage and verifies it using encoding numbers.

There are two main drawbacks with this scheme. Firstly, it uses bucketization method. As mentioned in [13], using this technique, the entire bucketization scheme and the exact probability distribution of the values may be estimated. Secondly, if the data is concentrated in a few buckets, the scheme costs extra size for empty buckets to ensure integrity. This increases the transmission cost. Furthermore, as mentioned in [7], this scheme is not suitable for multi-dimensional data in case sensors are equipped with multiple sensing modules capable of measuring temperature, humidity, pressure, etc. The authors' method and ours are for one-dimensional data. Our approach prevents the data probability from being approximately estimated.

For multi-dimensional data, reference [16] proposed query-result completeness verifications called probabilistic spatial crosscheck, probabilistic temporal crosscheck, random probing, and hybrid crosscheck. The key idea of probabilistic spatial crosscheck is to embed relationships among data generated by different sensor nodes. If the storage node omits part of the data in the response, the network owner can decide with certain probability that the query result is incomplete by inspecting the relationships among other returned data. The temporal crosscheck relies on queries for consecutive epochs. In the random probing scheme, the network owner probes random nodes from which no data were returned in the query result. The hybrid scheme is a combination of spatial crosscheck, temporal crosscheck, and random probing [16]. This scheme is more effective than the one of using an encoding number in [6]. However, it still has a chance of failing of verification.

4 Our Approach

4.1 Theory

(1) Histogram technique
Instead of sending raw data, we propose to send a histogram of data. For the sake of easy reading, we shall formalize the situation as follows:

The sensor node needs to send m data items: $d = \{d_i\}_{i=1}^m$. These may or may not contain duplicate values. Each data item belongs to a data range: $D = [1, n]; d_i \in D, \forall i$.

Therefore, the histogram of data spans the whole range: $H = \{h_i\}_{i=1}^n$, where h_i means the counts of value i in d.

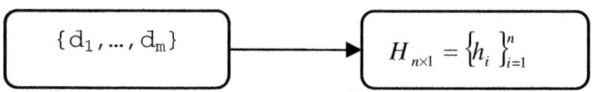

Fig. 3. Histogram technique

With this approach, the communication cost goes up if the data range is large (n is large). This is not what we want. We want as small a communication cost as possible. Furthermore, if possible, we want to keep the communication cost fixed.

(2) Algebraic approach

Our approach uses a linear rectangular system of n variables with just k $(k<n)$ equations to keep the communication cost fixed.

Let the coefficience matrix be: $A_{k \times n}$ $(k<n)$ $A_{k \times n}(k < n) = \{a_{ij}\}$. Let the histogram of data be: $H_{n \times 1} = \{h_i\}_{i=1}^n$. The histogram is preprocessed before sending, as follows:

$$T(H) = A_{k \times n} \times H_{n \times 1}^T \quad \text{(We call } T(H) \text{ the zip-histogram.)}$$

The dimension of $T(H)$ is therefore $k \times 1$. n (i.e., the size of H) reduces to k (the size of $T(H)$). Moreover, for any value of n, the reduced size is always fixed at valueto k. These are what we want.

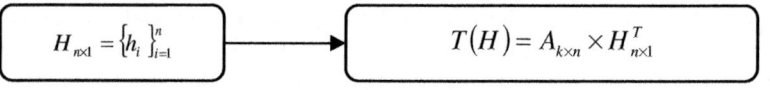

Fig. 4. Zip-histogram

(3) Noise technique and Encryption scheme

After converting the histogram into a zip-histogram, we apply a noise technique N or encryption scheme E to the zip-histogram to make it meaningless:

$$D' = N(T(H)) \quad \text{or} \quad D' = E(T(H)) = AES(T(H)).$$

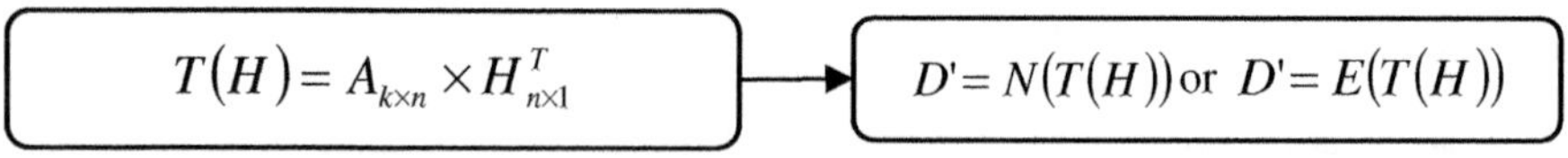

$$T(H) = A_{k \times n} \times H_{n \times 1}^T \longrightarrow D' = N(T(H)) \text{ or } D' = E(T(H))$$

Fig. 5. Noise technique and Encryption scheme

The noise technique creates noisy information by using a hash function with a shared key between the sensor and the sink, as well as the time slot t and value of bin i as parameters.

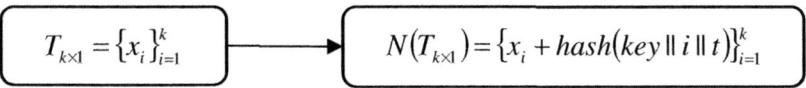

$$T_{k\times 1} = \{x_i\}_{i=1}^k \qquad\qquad N(T_{k\times 1}) = \{x_i + hash(key \parallel i \parallel t)\}_{i=1}^k$$

Fig. 6. Noise histogram

Regarding the encryption scheme, there are some researches about suitable ciphers for WSNs. Up to now, symmetric ciphers such as Skipjack, MISTY1, and Rijndael [11] have been more suitable. We shall assume that the security and memory costs of these ciphers will be acceptable for sensors for some time to come. Note that the commercial sensor node MicaZ from CrossBow supports AES [9].

4.2 Our Approach

Phase 1 – Sensing and sending data
A sensor senses a set of data from the environment during a time slot. The sensor creates the corresponding histogram from the set of data and uses a linear system with a rectangular coefficience matrix to zip the histogram. After that, it may use a noise technique or an encryption scheme to convert the zip-histogram into a meaningless form. The result is sent to storage.

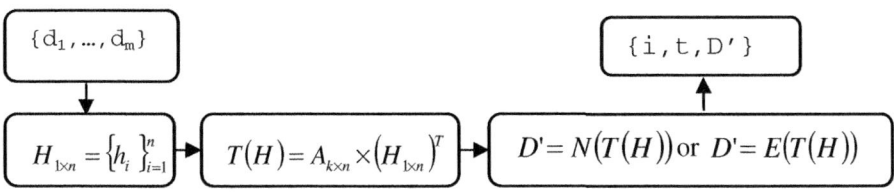

$$\{d_1, \dots, d_m\} \qquad\qquad \{i,t,D'\}$$

$$H_{1\times n} = \{h_i\}_{i=1}^n \quad T(H) = A_{k\times n} \times (H_{1\times n})^T \quad D' = N(T(H)) \text{ or } D' = E(T(H))$$

Fig. 7. Phase 1

Phase 2 – Storing data
The data in the storage node are meaningless: $\{\{i,t,D'\}\}$

Phase 3 – Requesting query
We assume that all the queries are range queries. Note that the queries in most sensor network applications can be easily modeled as range queries [7].
    The user sends a query request to the sink: $t,[a,b]$

Phase 4 – Sending query
The sink then converts the range query into a time slot and sends it to storage.

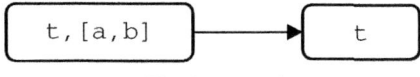

$$t,[a,b] \qquad\qquad t$$

Fig. 8. Phase 4

Phase 5 – Processing query and replying
After the storage receives a set of tags from the sink, it chooses data with the right
time slot and sends back it to the sink: { i,t,D'}chosen

Phase 6 – Verifying, filtering and answering to users
After receiving a reply from the storage, the sink does the reverse process of phase 1
to get the original data. The sink then filters the data to get the right query results and
returns them to the user.

$$D' = N\big(T(H)\big) \text{ chosen or } D' = E\big(T(H)\big)\text{chosen}$$ Result

$$T(H) = A_{k\times n} \times \big(H_{1\times n}\big)^T$$ → $$H_{1\times n}$$ →   {d_i}   →   {d_i}chosen

Fig. 9. Phase 6

4.3 Challenge of Our Approach

The challenge of our approach is in this step.

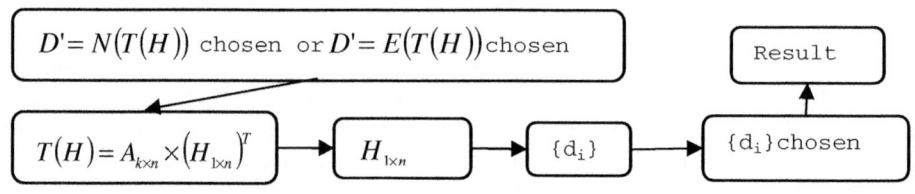

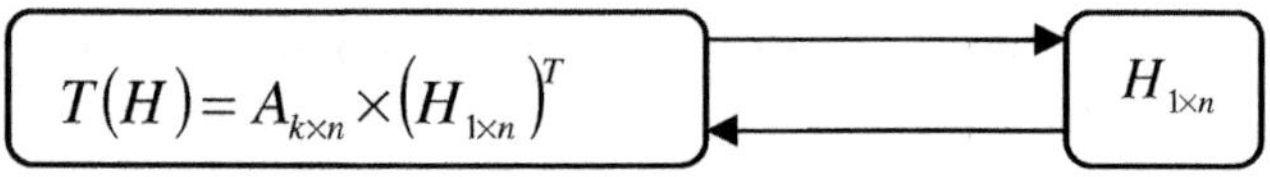

$$T(H) = A_{k\times n} \times \big(H_{1\times n}\big)^T$$ $$H_{1\times n}$$

Fig. 10. Challenge

There is no problem to convert $H_{1\times n}$ into $T(H)$. But there is a big problem in trying to find $H_{1\times n}$ from $T(H)$.

Let $\big(H_{1\times n}\big)^T$ be the solution of the nonhomogeneous system: $A_{k\times n} \times X_{n\times 1} = T_{k\times 1}$.

This nonhomogeneous system has more variables than the number of equations.
Therefore, if this system is consistent (i.e., it has solutions), it will have countless
solutions. Moreover, it is hard to decide which solution is a real result of $H_{1\times n}^T$. The
only constraints on $H_{1\times n}^T$ are that all items of the histogram must be zero or positive

integers and $\sum_{i=1}^{n} h_i = m$.

4.4 Solution

Our approach is to build a coefficient matrix $A_{k\times n}$ satisfying these conditions:

$A_{k \times n} \times X_{n \times 1} = C_{k \times 1}$ has multiple solutions, and $A_{k \times n} \times X_{n \times 1} = C_{k \times 1}$ has only one solution satisfying the above two constraints ($x_i \geq 0, \forall i$ and $\sum_{i=1}^{n} x_i = m$).

The principle of our approach is as follows:

Let two of the solutions of the system be X^1, X^2

$$X^1 = \left\{ x_i^1 \right\}_{i=1}^{n} \; ; \; X^2 = \left\{ x_i^2 \right\}_{i=1}^{n}$$

$$A_{k \times n} X^1 = C_{k \times 1} = \begin{bmatrix} a_{11} & .. & a_{1n} \\ .. & & \\ a_{k1} & .. & a_{kn} \end{bmatrix} \begin{bmatrix} x_1^1 \\ .. \\ x_n^1 \end{bmatrix} = \begin{bmatrix} \sum_{i=1}^{n} a_{1i} x_i^1 \\ \sum_{i=1}^{n} a_{ki} x_i^1 \end{bmatrix} = \begin{bmatrix} c_1 \\ .. \\ c_k \end{bmatrix}$$

$$A_{k \times n} X^2 = C_{k \times 1} = \begin{bmatrix} \sum_{i=1}^{n} a_{1i} x_i^2 \\ \sum_{i=1}^{n} a_{ki} x_i^2 \end{bmatrix} = \begin{bmatrix} c_1 \\ .. \\ c_k \end{bmatrix}$$

We deduce: $\begin{bmatrix} \sum_{i=1}^{n} a_{1i} x_i^1 \\ \sum_{i=1}^{n} a_{ki} x_i^1 \end{bmatrix} = \begin{bmatrix} \sum_{i=1}^{n} a_{1i} x_i^2 \\ \sum_{i=1}^{n} a_{ki} x_i^2 \end{bmatrix} = \begin{bmatrix} c_1 \\ .. \\ c_k \end{bmatrix}$

From this we have:

If $\begin{bmatrix} \sum_{i=1}^{n} a_{1i} x_i^1 \\ \sum_{i=1}^{n} a_{ki} x_i^1 \end{bmatrix} = \begin{bmatrix} \sum_{i=1}^{n} a_{1i} x_i^2 \\ \sum_{i=1}^{n} a_{ki} x_i^2 \end{bmatrix} = \begin{bmatrix} c_1 \\ .. \\ c_k \end{bmatrix}$ then X^1, X^2 cannot be solutions at the same time.

* Generate all possible solutions from constraints

We generate all possible solutions from the following constraints:

$$X = (x_i)_{i=1}^{n} \; ; \; 0 \leq x_i \leq m \; ; \; \sum x_i = m$$

Let $\left\{ X^j \right\}, j \in J$ be all possible solutions.

* Necessary conditions for the system to have only one solution

$$\forall j_1, j_2 \in J, AX^{j_1} \neq AX^{j_2} \Leftrightarrow \begin{bmatrix} \sum a_{1i} x_i^{j_1} \\ .. \\ \sum a_{ki} x_i^{j_1} \end{bmatrix} \neq \begin{bmatrix} \sum a_{1i} x_i^{j_2} \\ .. \\ \sum a_{ki} x_i^{j_2} \end{bmatrix}$$

Instead, we can limit the conditions as follows:

$$\forall j_1, j_2 \in J, \sum a_{1i} x_i^{j_1} = \sum a_{1i} x_i^{j_2}; ..; \sum a_{(k-1)i} x_i^{j_1} = \sum a_{(k-1)i} x_i^{j_2}; \sum a_{ki} x_i^{j_1} \neq \sum a_{ki} x_i^{j_2}$$

Along that way, the following is the way to generate matrix $A_{k \times n}$:

The first *(k-1)* rows of $A_{k \times n}$ can be generated randomly.

The last row of $A_{k \times n}$ must be generated so that it satisfies:

If $\sum_i a_{ri} x_i^{j_{f1}} = \sum_i a_{ri} x_i^{j_{f2}}, \forall r \in \{1,.., k-1\}, j_{f1}, j_{f2} \in J$ then

$$\sum_i a_{ki} x_i^{j_{f1}} \neq \sum_i a_{ki} x_i^{j_{f2}} \text{ or } \sum_i a_{ki} x_i^{j_{f1}} - \sum_i a_{ki} x_i^{j_{f2}} \neq 0$$

Accordingly, we get a system of inequalities

$$\left\{ \sum_i a_{ki} x_i^{j_{f1}} - \sum_i a_{ki} x_i^{j_{f2}} \neq 0 \right\}, \forall j_{f1}, j_{f2} \in J \Leftrightarrow \left\{ \sum_i a_{ki} \left(x_i^{j_{f1}} - x_i^{j_{f2}} \right) \neq 0 \right\}, \forall j_{f1}, j_{f2} \in J$$

Therefore, we can express this system as products of matrices $A_{k*} B \neq 0$

where $B = \left\{ x^{j_{f1}} - x^{j_{f2}} \right\} = \begin{pmatrix} x_1^{j1} & x_1^{j2} & .. \\ x_2^{j1} & x_2^{j2} & .. \\ .. & & \\ x_n^{j1} & x_n^{j2} & .. \end{pmatrix}$, $A_{k*} = \begin{pmatrix} a_{k1} & a_{k2} & .. & a_{kn} \end{pmatrix}$ is the

last row (kth row) of the coefficient matrix A.

$$A_{k*} B = \begin{pmatrix} a_{k1} & a_{k2} & .. & a_{kn} \end{pmatrix} \begin{pmatrix} x_1^{j1} & x_1^{j2} & .. \\ x_2^{j1} & x_2^{j2} & .. \\ .. & & \\ x_n^{j1} & x_n^{j2} & .. \end{pmatrix} \neq 0$$

(*) Solutions of the system of inequalities
Our system is simpler than ordinary systems of inequalities, because we just need to find one arbitrary solution (not all solutions) of a system in the form "$\neq$" (not <, $\leq, >, \geq$).

The system is as follows: $\begin{pmatrix} a_{k1} & a_{k2} & .. & a_{kn} \end{pmatrix} \begin{pmatrix} x_1^{j1} & x_1^{j2} & .. \\ x_2^{j1} & x_2^{j2} & .. \\ .. & & \\ x_n^{j1} & x_n^{j2} & .. \end{pmatrix} \neq 0$

Each inequality's geometry is plain (the volume is zero). All possible values not in those geometries are solutions of the system. The only way for the system of inequalities to have no solutions is if the intersection of those geometries is spread over the whole space. This is impossible; therefore, the system always has solutions.

(*) **Heuristics for solving the system of inequalities**

Table 1. Heuristics

```
Input: Matrix B

Output: (a_{k1}, a_{k2},..., a_{kn})

Program:
Let
     α_i be the number of rows of B which have a value at column i
     different from 0 and a product of that row and (a_{k1}, a_{k2},..., a_{kn})^T
     different from 0.
     β_i be the number of rows of B which have a value at column i
     different from 0 and product of that row and (a_{k1}, a_{k2},..., a_{kn})^T equal
     to 0.
     γ be the number of rows of B having a product of row and
     (a_{k1}, a_{k2},..., a_{kn})^T equal to 0
For j = 1 to n
        Initialize a_{ki} = 1
End for

val1 = 2
For j = 1 to n
        Choose a_{kj} with the maximum β_j. If there are many values    a_{kj}
with the same maximum β_j, choose a_{kj} with the minimum α_j
        While (true) do
                if (a_{kj} = val2) makes γ smaller
                        Assign x_j = val 1
                        val1 = val + 1
                        Break;
                end if
        End while
    End for
End for
```

4.5 Analysis

Firstly, for any range queries from users, the sink converts them into random forms. Therefore, the secrecy of the queries is sure to be protected.

Secondly, because the idea behind our method is using histogram, it has benefits for high-frequency data case.

Thirdly, the histogram is converted into a zip-histogram. This prevents the data probability from being approximately estimated.

Finally, the computational security of our method depends on the difficulty of solving a rectangular linear system and a hash function (if we use noise technique referred to in section 4.1).

However, our method still has a number of un-resolved problems, as follows.

4.6 Other Un-resolved Challenges

The first problem is building the matrix: $B = \left\{ x^{j_{f1}} - x^{j_{f2}} \right\} = \begin{pmatrix} x_1^{j1} & x_1^{j2} & .. \\ x_2^{j1} & x_2^{j2} & .. \\ .. \\ x_n^{j1} & x_n^{j2} & .. \end{pmatrix}$

from the *(k-1)* rows of the coefficient matrix: $A_{(k-1) \times n} = \begin{bmatrix} a_{11} & .. & a_{1n} \\ & .. & \\ a_{(k-1)1} & .. & a_{(k-1)n} \end{bmatrix}$

Since $\sum x^{j_{f1}} = \sum x^{j_{f2}} = m \Rightarrow \sum \left(x^{j_{f1}} - x^{j_{f2}} \right) = 0 \Rightarrow \sum x_*^{j1} = \sum x_*^{j2} = ... = 0$, we solve

the following equations to find B: $\begin{bmatrix} a_{11} & .. & a_{1n} \\ .. & & \\ a_{(k-1)1} & & a_{(k-1)n} \\ 1 & ... & 1 \end{bmatrix} \begin{bmatrix} x_1^{j1} \\ \\ .. \\ \\ x_n^{j1} \end{bmatrix} = 0$

with the constraints: $\left| x_1^{j1} \right|, .., \left| x_1^{j1} \right| \leq m$,

and the following system is consistent:

$$\begin{bmatrix} x_1^{j_{f1}} \\ .. \\ x_n^{j_{f1}} \end{bmatrix} - \begin{bmatrix} x_1^{j_{f2}} \\ .. \\ x_n^{j_{f2}} \end{bmatrix} = \begin{bmatrix} x_1^{j1} \\ .. \\ x_n^{j1} \end{bmatrix} ; \sum x_i^{j_{f1}} = \sum x_i^{j_{f2}} = m; 0 \leq x_i^{j_{f1}}, x_i^{j_{f2}} \leq m$$

The second problem is solving $T(H) = A_{k \times n} \times (H_{1 \times n})^T$ to find $H_{1 \times n}$.

Similarly, we solve the following equations to find H:

$$\begin{bmatrix} T(H) \\ m \end{bmatrix} = \begin{bmatrix} A_{k \times n} \\ (1 \quad .. \quad 1) \end{bmatrix} \times (H_{1 \times n})^T \text{ with constraints } (0 \leq h_i \leq m)$$

The current solution is an exhaustive search (trial and error). Although this computation can be performed by a sink with a powerful computational ability, we should find a more effective method to solve these equations.

5 Conclusion

We proposed a novel method called zip-histogram to convert data before sensors send it to storage. We also specified the challenges, advantages, and disadvantages of this method. The method keeps the communication cost fixed for any type of data. However, the cost of computations at the sink has not been resolved yet and should be studied in subsequent research. The method does not reveal any information about data, unlike the other two state-of-the-art methods [6,7]. Although we believe that the computation cost of the sensor is reasonably small because of the simplicity of the matrix multiplication operations, experimental evaluations also need to be performed to verify this supposition. Finally, we should mention that this method may be extended in order to make it work for multi-dimensional queries. In so doing, the cost will increase linearly with the number of dimensions.

References

1. 21 ideas for the 21st century. Business Week, 78–167 (1999)
2. 10 emerging technologies that will change the world. Technology Review 106 (2003)
3. Burrell, J., Brooke, T., Beckwith, R.: Vineyard Computing: Sensor Networks in Agricultural Production. IEEE Pervasive Computing 3(1), 38–45 (2004)
4. Chong, C.-y., Kumar, S.P.: Sensor networks: evolution, opportunities, and challenges. Proceedings of the IEEE 91(8), 1247–1256 (2003)
5. Xu, N., et al.: A Wireless Sensor Network for Structural Monitoring. ACM SenSys (2004)
6. Sheng, B., Li, Q.: Verifiable privacy-preserving range query in two-tiered sensor networks. In: The 27th Conference on Computer Communications (INFOCOM), Phoenix, AZ (2008)
7. Chen, F., Liu, A.X.: SafeQ: Secure and Efficient Query Processing in Sensor Networks. In: Proceedings of the 29th Annual IEEE Conference on Computer Communications (INFOCOM), San Diego, California (March 2010)
8. Stargate, http://platformx.sourceforge.net/home.html
9. MicaZ datasheet,
   http://www.xbow.com/products/Product_pdf_files/Wireless_pdf/
   MICA2_Datasheet.pdf
10. Stankovic, J.: How Things Work: Wireless Sensor Networks. IEEE Computer (October 2008) (invited paper)
11. Law, Y.W., Doumen, J., Hartel, P.: Survey and benchmark of block ciphers for wireless sensor networks. ACM Trans. Sen. Netw. 2(1), 65–93 (2006)
12. Gaubatz, G., Kaps, J.-P., Ozturk, E., Sunar, B.: State of the Art in Ultra-Low Power Public Key Cryptography for Wireless Sensor Networks. In: PERCOMW Proceedings of the Third IEEE International Conference on Pervasive Computing and Communications Workshops, pp. 146–150 (2005)
13. Hore, B., Mehrotra, S., Tsudik, G.: A privacy-preserving index for range queries. In: Proceedings of the thirtieth international conference on very large data bases, Toronto, Canada, vol. 30, pp. 720–731 (2004)
14. Khemapech, I., Duncan, I., Miller, A.: A Survey of Wireless Sensor Networks Technology. In: Merabti, M., Pereira, R. (eds.) PGNET, Proceedings of the 6th Annual PostGraduate Symposium on the Convergence of Telecommunications, Networking & Broadcasting, pp. xx–xx. EPSRC, Liverpool (June 2005)

15. Padmavathi, G., Shanmugapriya, D.: A Survey of Attacks, Security Mechanisms and Challenges in Wireless Sensor Networks. International Journal of Computer Science and Information Security (IJCSIS) 2(1&2) (2009)
16. Shi, J., Zhang, R., Zhang, Y.: Secure Range Queries in Tiered Sensor Networks. In: Proc. IEEE INFOCOM (2009)
17. Zhang, R., Shi, J., Zhang, Y.: Secure multidimensional range queries in sensor networks. In: Proceedings of the tenth ACM international symposium on Mobile ad hoc networking and computing, New Orleans, LA, USA, pp. 197–206 (2009)

Fine-Grained Access Control for Electronic Health Record Systems

Pham Thi Bach Hue[1], Sven Wohlgemuth[2], Isao Echizen[2],
Dong Thi Bich Thuy[1], and Nguyen Dinh Thuc[1]

[1] Faculty of Information Technology, University of Science, VNU – HCMC
227 Nguyen Van Cu street, District 5, Ho Chi Minh City, Vietnam
{ptbhue,dtbthuy,ndthuc}@fit.hcmus.edu.vn
[2] National Institute of Informatics, 2-1-2 Hitotsubashi, Chiyoda-ku, Tokyo, Japan
{wohlgemuth,iechizen}@nii.ac.jp

Abstract. There needs to be a strategy for securing the privacy of patients when exchanging health records between various entities over the Internet. Despite the fact that health care providers such as Google Health and Microsoft Corp.'s Health Vault comply with the U.S Health Insurance Portability and Accountability Act (HIPAA), the privacy of patients is still at risk. Several encryption schemes and access control mechanisms have been suggested to protect the disclosure of a patient's health record especially from unauthorized entities. However, by implementing these approaches, data owners are not capable of controlling and protecting the disclosure of the individual sensitive attributes of their health records. This raises the need to adopt a secure mechanism to protect personal information against unauthorized disclosure. Therefore, we propose a new Fine-grained Access Control (FGAC) mechanism that is based on subkeys, which would allow a data owner to further control the access to his data at the column-level. We also propose a new mechanism to efficiently reduce the number of keys maintained by a data owner in cases when the users have different access privileges to different columns of the data being shared.

Keywords: Access control, fine-grained access control, database encryption.

1 Introduction

Health information today, which is mainly stored on paper, is scattered and disconnected. An EHR system is a concept defined as a sysmtematic collection of electronic health information about individuals that can be shared via the Internet across various health care settings such as: hospitals, clinics, and pharmacies etc. EHR systems provide online services where patient's health records are created, used, exchanged, stored, and retrieved. There are three main entities in the EHR scenario: the *data owner* - i.e. patient who is the subject of the health records made available for controlled external use; the *user* – individual or organization that requests data from the EHR system; and the *server* - an organization that receives the data sent from the data owners and makes it available for distribution to clients.

T.-h. Kim et al. (Eds.): UNESST 2010, CCIS 124, pp. 31–38, 2010.
© Springer-Verlag Berlin Heidelberg 2010

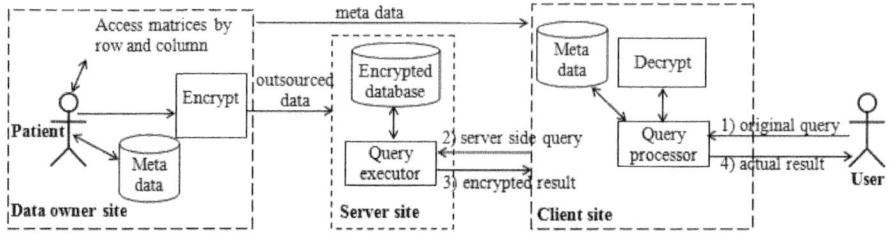

Fig. 1. Block diagram of an EHR system

In EHR systems, however, the patients' data is stored on an external server, which is typically not under their control, and it is assumed that this server cannot be trusted with the confidentiality of the database's content. It is important to protect the health data of patients from unauthorized access by intruders and even the server's operators.

In existing EHR systems such as Google Health or Microsoft HealthVault, patients cannot control the providers' usage of their personal data. Database encryption was regarded as a solution for protecting data from unauthorized disclosure. Existing encryption schemes assume that the client has complete access to the query results [8]. Such encryption schemes do not fit applications such as the EHR system, where the data owner often requires the enforcement of access restriction to different users. Some access control mechanisms have recently been proposed, but by using them, the data owners can only control access at the tuple-level and they are not able to restrict access to some of the more sensitive attributes of the data being shared ([1], [3], [4], [16]).

The contributions of this study are: (a) a new access control mechanism called FGAC, which would allow a data owner to further control the access to his data at the column-level, (b) a new mechanism to efficiently reduce the number of keys maintained by the data owner when users have different access privileges to different columns of the data being shared.

2   Privacy Requirement by Legislation

Privacy is described as *"[...] the claim of individuals, groups, or institutions to deter-mine for themselves when, how, and to what extent of information about them is communicated to others"* [15]. This description of privacy as informational self-determination has been a basis for health data protection regulations such as HIPAA [9], European Data Protection Direction 95/46/EC [5], and Data Protection Act of Japan [11]. From them, and based on [7], we derive the following privacy requirements for an EHR system:

Requirement 1: Every patient should be able to control the flow of information related to himself/herself. This requirement is very important for information systems to preserve patients' privacy as defined above. Since patient's records are stored on a service provider's site and the patient is not given enough information about the provider to decide if they are trustworthy, this leads to

Requirement 2: Patients should not be forced to trust any party except ones direct-ly involved with their treatment. Accessing entire medical records is not always essen-tial. Any intended purpose of use, disclosure, or request of protected health informa-tion should be at a necessary minimum. This is stated by

Requirement 3: Patients can limit usage and disclosure of their personal records to the necessary minimum. Linking information from several data requests could possibly generate unintended information about patients. This results in

Requirement 4: Access requests to the patients' data cannot be used to establish the profiles or additional knowledge about patients. Although the privacy mechan-isms are implemented, they have no value if the user cannot verify that they work correctly. To counter this problem we state

Requirement 5: User should be able to verify that the result returned from the un-trustworthy server is trustworthy. Security solutions used in an EHR system must fulfill the above-mentioned five requirements.

3 Attack Model and Privacy Problems

Patients are required to trust the provider when using Microsoft HealthVault [13] or Google Health [6]. They cannot control whether the providers really adhere to their promises to protect their data and disclose personal data only to parties the patients have agreed to. So, Microsoft HealthVault and Google Health fail to guarantee re-quirements 1 and 2, and thus, any of the remaining requirements. The encryption scheme proposed by Hacigümüs et al. [8] can protect data from unauthorized access and fulfills requirements 1 and 2. However, this scheme assumes that a user has full access to the outsourced databases, so it does not fulfill requirement 3 and cannot be used in EHR systems in which the users should have different access privileges to the patients' health records and in which sensitive information needs to be limited in use and disclosure. Using the proposed access control mechanisms ([4], [16], [3]), patients are unable to restrict access to some sensitive columns, so requirement 3 is not guaranteed. Requirements 4 and 5 must be fulfilled by solutions for ensuring user privacy and query assurance, respectively, and they are out of the scope of this paper. In this paper, we address the first three privacy requirements. It raises the questions: *"What encryption scheme is suitable for fine-grained access control by the data own-er?"* and *"How to manage the access control policies in an EHR system?"*

4 Related Work

Recent access control approaches combine cryptographic protection and authorization access control and enforce access control via selective encryption, which means users can decrypt only the data they are authorized to access [1]. They exploit a struc-ture called the user tree hierarchy to represent the relationship between users and information items. The key for accessing lower-level nodes is based on the keys of their predecessors by using a family of one-way functions [14]. However, the complexity of the algorithm for building the tree hierarchy is exponential and it needs reconstruction after most of the modifications of the access control policies have been accomplished. Zych et al. [16] presented a key management scheme that was based on a partial order between the user groups and used the Diffie-Hellman key generation algorithm for the key derivation. The algorithm for constructing the hierarchy and the generation scheme are very complex and costly. El-khoury et al. [4] suggested a key management scheme using a structure called binary trie. A binary trie was constructed based on the access control policies which are modeled via an access matrix. Keys ring for each group of user are generated based on this binary trie structure. The key management complexity is reduced and most of the data access policy updates do not require significant changes to the structure, which reduces the number of key generations and data re-keyings. De Capitani di Vimercati et al. [3] proposed a two-layer access control mechanism that is based on the application of selective encryption. This solution has the benefits of being faster and less costly when the authorization policy is updated. However, all of the above-mentioned encryption schemes and access control mechanisms can only support tuple-level access control and fail to guarantee requirement 3. By using them, the data owners cannot restrict access to some of the more sensitive attributes of the shared data or have to partition the relation containing the shared data into fragments with the full share. This creates a lot of relations, and thus creates difficulties in effectively managing the database and query processing.

5 Approach for Fine-Grained Access Control in EHR System

The database encryption with subkeys first proposed by Davida et al. [2] had the advantages of record orientation, security, and each field can be accessed under a different key. Using it, a user can read only some given fields depending on the readable subkeys he has without revealing all the attributes' values. We suggest using the encryption scheme proposed by Hacigümüs et al. [8] for EHR systems, but with a modification of the encryption function. The encryption scheme with subkeys is used instead of the block cipher techniques, such as AES, RSA, or DES as in original scheme. For each relation $R(A_1, A_2, ..., A_n)$, the data owner stores encrypted relation $R^S(etuple, A_1^S, A_2^S, ..., A_n^S)$ on the server, where the attribute *etuple* is the encryption form of a record using the encryption scheme with subkeys. The data owners follow these steps to protect their data:

Step 1: The data owners encrypt their data by tuples and thereby they grant access to their data by tuples. They first partition their data into disjoined row categories. Each row category consists of one or more rows. Users who have the same privileges to a row category are gathered into a single group. The data owners describe the access policies to their data by using an access matrix, called an access matrix by row (Table 1).

Step 2: The data owner constructs the binary trie for the access matrix by row [4] to decide the number of keys that will be used to encrypt the data (Fig. 2). The data owner restricts the access to the sensitive columns by giving out only the subkeys corresponding to the columns that the user has access permission to. The key derivation method which is described in section 6, is used to derive the necessary keys (Table 2).

Step 3: If the users in a group have different access privileges to different columns of a row category, the data owner describes the access policies using other access matrices, and each is called an access matrix by column, and manages the keys by using the binary trie. Users hold only some of the subkeys and derive the necessary ones to read the data with the granted permission. Appropriate keys are communicated to users by the data owner via a secure channel. Using our approach, the patient's data is protected from unauthorized disclosure and the patient can restrict access to sensitive columns of the data being shared. Our approach fulfills requirements 1, 2, and 3.

Table 1. Access matrix by row

	r_1	r_2	r_3	r_4	r_5
g_1	0	1	1	0	0
g_2	1	1	0	1	1
g_3	1	1	1	0	0
g_4	1	1	1	1	0

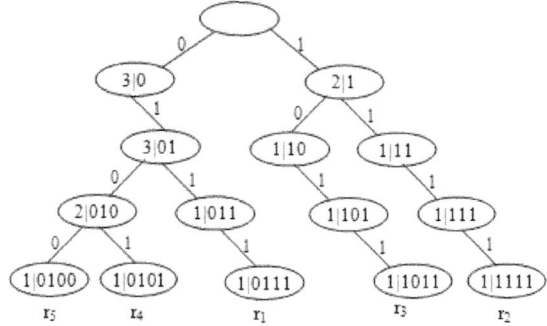

Fig. 2. Binary trie structure for access matrix by row

Table 2. Keys held by each group of users and keys must be derivable

	Keys held	Keys derived
g_1	k_1	k_{1111}, k_{1011}
g_2	k_{01}, k_{11}	k_{0111}, k_{1111}, k_{0101}, k_{0100}
g_3	k_{011}, k_{101}, k_{111}	k_{0111}, k_{1111}, k_{1011}
g_4	k_{0111}, k_{1111}, k_{1011}, k_{0101}	

6 Key Management for Fine-Grained Access Control in EHR System

Database Encryption with Subkeys: There are variations when using the Chinese Remainder Theorem (CRT) for encrypting a database ([2], [12], [10]). In EHR systems, the convenience for a user to access data at a service provider is important, therefore an encryption scheme requiring less keys held by each valid user was chosen. We use an encryption with subkeys developed by Davida et al. [2] in EHR systems.

Let C_i be the ciphertext of an encrypted record, and let d_j be the reading subkey for field j. There are m records in a relation and n fields in each record. The encryption procedure is done by forming $C_i = \sum_{j=1}^{n} e_j \left(r_{ij} || x_{ij} \right) mod\ D, for\ i = 1, 2, ..., m;$

where $D = \prod_{j=1}^{n} d_j$, x_{ij} is the value of field j of record i, || is the concatenation, r_{ij} is the random value for field j used for preventing attacks originated from using CRT, r_{ij} $||x_{ij} < d_j$, e_j is the encryption key for field j, and b_j is the multiplicative inverse of D/d_j with moduli d_j. In addition, the decryption procedure is: $r_{ij} || x_{ij} = C_i \bmod d_j$, j = 1, ..., n. By discarding the random bit r_{ij}, one can obtain the jth field data x_{ij} of record i.

Key Derivation Method: When using an encryption scheme with subkeys, the key of a security class SC_i consists of multiple different subkeys (d_{i1}, d_{i2}, ..., d_{in}), d_{ij} is a prime and also the decryption key used for decrypting the jth attribute. The key of security class SC_j, which is an immediate child of SC_i, is computed by ($f_1(d_{i1})$, $f_2(d_{i2})$, ..., $f_n(d_{in})$), and each f_i is a one-way function [14]. The key of the security class SC_j also consists of multiple subkeys, each subkey must be a prime too (for properly using the CRT). So, each function f_i must be a one-way function that receives a prime number as the input and outputs a prime number, appendix.

Column-level Access Control: If a user group has full access authorization to all the columns of a row category, each user in this group holds all the subkeys of each key assigned to each group. By derivation, they obtain the actual keys to access all the columns of the row category with authorization. If a user group has access authorization to only some attributes of a row category, and the access authorizations are the same to all the members of the group, they are given appropriate subkeys to access the corresponding columns. In the cases when different users in a user group G have different access privileges to different columns of a row category, the data owner describes these privileges by using other access matrices, called access matrix by column. The number of rows of this matrix is equal to the number of subgroups of users in the group G and the number of columns it has equals to the number of groups of columns with different access authorizations. We construct the binary trie structure corresponding to this column access matrix. Each subgroup of users holds just some subkeys. These subkeys can then be used to derive other subkeys in order to access the other columns with granted permission.

Key Management: In our proposed access control mechanism, each user owns some subkeys (which are used to derive other subkeys) to access the fields he has access authorization for. Management of the number of subkeys is difficult for users. We propose using the key management method in [10] to handle this problem.

(1) Assigns each field a public prime number p_j, j =1, 2, ..., n.
(2) Computes the secret master key MK_i by CRT for user i:
    $MK_i = d_j \bmod p_j$ for some j $1 \le j \le (n+1)$ where d_{n+1} and p_{n+1} are random secret key and the prime number of a dummy field used to prevent users from colluding to disclose the secret master key of user i.
    User i keeps only the secret master key MK_i.
(3) To read the field j, user i computes $d_j = MK_i \bmod p_j$ to get subkey d_j.

7   Conclusion and Future Work

We have proposed a new fine-grained access control mechanism based on subkeys. Our proposal has the following characteristics:

(1) It allows a data owner to further control the access of their data at the column-level.
(2) It efficiently reduces the number of keys maintained by a data owner when users have different access privileges to different columns of the data being shared. These subkeys are encrypted one time more (using CRT) so that each user holds only one secret master key, but they can derive the necessary subkeys to access data with authorization.

For future work, we will investigate the dynamic cases of access control in which the users and the privileges changed frequently. We will also analyze the system's performance when we implement our proposals.

Acknowledgement

We would like to thank Niraj Shah for his helpful comments.

References

1. Damiani, E., De Capitani di Vimercati, S., Foresti, S., Jajodia, S., Paraboschi, S., Samarati, P.: Key Management for Multi-User Encrypted Databases. In: Proc. of the 2005 ACM Workshop on Storage Security and Survivability, pp.74–83 (2005)
2. Davida, G.I., Wells, D.L., Kam, J.B.: A Database Encryption System with Subkeys. ACM Transactions on Database Systems 6(2), 312–328 (1981)
3. De Capitani di Vimercati, S., Foresti, S, Jajodia, S., Paraboschi, S., Samarati, P.: Over-encryption: Management of Access Control Evolution on Outsourced Data. In: VLDB, pp. 123–134 (2007)
4. El-khoury, V., Bennani, N., Ouksel, A.M.: Distributed Key Management in Dynamic Outsourced Databases: a Trie-based Approach. In: First Int. Conf. on Advances in Databases, Knowledge, and Data Applications, pp. 56–61 (2009)
5. European Commission, Directive 95/46/EC of the European Parliament and of the Council of 24 Oct. 1995 on the protection of individuals with regard to the processing of personal data and on the free movement of such data. Official Journal of the European Communities, L 281, 395L0046, 31–50 (1995)
6. Google, Health Privacy Policy,
   http://www.google.com/intl/en-US/health/privacy.html
7. Haas, S., Wohlgemuth, S., Echizen, I., Sonehara, N.,Müller, G.: On Privacy in Medical Services with Electronic Health Records. In: IMIA SiHIS, CoMHI (2009)
8. Hacigümüs, H., Iyer, B.R., Li, C., Mehrotra, S.: Executing SQL over encrypted data in the database-service-provider model. In: SIGMOD, pp. 216–227 (2002)
9. Health Insurance Portability and Accountability Act of 1996 (HIPAA) Privacy Rule
10. Hwang, M.S., Yang, W.P.: A Two-Phase Encryption Scheme for Enhancing Database Security. J. Systems Software, Elsevier Science, 257–265 (1995)
11. Japanese Government: Act on the Protection of Personal Information (2005),
    http://www5.cao.go.jp/seikatsu/kojin/foreign/act.pdf
12. Lin, C.H., Chang, C.C., Lee, C.T.: A record-oriented cryptosystem for database sharing. In: Int. Computer Symposium, pp. 328–329 (1990)

13. Microsoft, HealthVault Privacy Policy (2009),
    `https://account.healthvault.com/help.aspx?`
    `topicid=PrivacyPolicy`
14. Sandhu, R.S.: Cryptographic implementation of a Tree Hierarchy for access control, pp.
    95–98. Elsevier, Amsterdam (1988)
15. Westin, A.F.: Privacy and Freedom. Atheneum, New York (1967)
16. Zych, A., Petkovic, M., Jonker, W.: Efficient key management for cryptographically en-
    forced access control, pp. 410–417. Elsevier Science, Amsterdam (2008)

Appendix

We present a method for constructing a one-way function that receives a prime as an input and gives a prime as an output. Using this algorithm, the users with the same privileges will generate the same keys at different times for deriving keys to access the specific data.

Theorem

Assume that $n - 1 = F \times R = (\prod_{i=1,...,s} p_i^{a_i}) \times R$, where $R < \sqrt{n}$, and an integer b such that $b^{n-1} \equiv 1 \pmod{n}$ exists and $\gcd(b^{(n-1)/p_i} - 1, n) = 1$, $i=1,..., s$. Then n is a prime.

Algorithm G: Generating a prime of d digits with a given seed a.
(1) Generate a Q that has d-2 digits using the consecutive hash values of seed a:
    $Q = h(a)\|...\|h(a)$, where $\|$ is the concatenation operator.
(2) Find the greatest R such that $(R < Q)$ and $(1 + RQ \equiv 1 \pmod 6)$.
(3) If $p = RQ + 1$ is a pseudo-prime with base 2 and 3 then return p.
(4) $R = R+6$.
(5) Goto (2).

Generating key function

Let h be a one-way hash function h: $Z_n \rightarrow H$, i.e. given $y \in H$, it is hard to find $x \in Z_n$ such that $h(x)=y$, where H is the hash value space. For example, MD5 and SHA are two popular one-way hash functions. Let g be a generating prime function g: $H \rightarrow P$, where P is a prime space. Let f: $Z_n \rightarrow P$ be defined by $f = g \circ h$, then f is a one-way function. Indeed, given $y=f(x)=g(h(x))$, because h is a one-way hash function, it is hard to find $x \in Z_n$ such that $y=f(x)=g(h(x))$. To generate a prime, we use the combination of the above generating prime function and the hash function SHA.

Algorithm F: Generating key based on a given prime p.
(1) Compute $a = SHA(p)$.
(2) Generate a prime q using the algorithm G with seed a.

On Indiscernibility in Assessments

Sylvia Encheva

Stord/Haugesund University College,
Faculty of Technology, Business, and Maritime Sciences,
Bjørnsonsg. 45, 5528 Haugesund, Norway
sbe@hsh.no

Abstract. In this work we focus on the issue of providing individual help to students in terms of hints. Once a student is suggested to solve a problem via an intelligence tutoring system an immediate question arises on how to provide automated assistance if the student experiences some difficulties in solving that problem. While hints turn out to be quite useful in that matter, the discussion on how to deliver them is still open.

Keywords: Learning, assessment, intelligent systems.

1 Introduction

Learning management systems (LMS) facilitate sequencing of content and creation of a practical structure for teachers and students. While being very useful with respect to content delivery they appeared to be insufficient for developing higher level thinking skills. Learning management systems are educational software that among other things should track students' progress and provide tailored feedback. They however cannot make reasonable inferences and provide personalized assistance. A serious step forward satisfying such requirements is the involvement of intelligent software agents. Generally speaking they are supposed to achieve particular goals in an autonomous fashion, taking responsibility for its own actions, the creation of its own plans, and the establishment of its own sub-goals.

Intelligence tutoring systems have been discussed by many authors. In [22] such a system is defined as "educational software containing an artificial intelligence component. The software tracks students' work, tailoring feedback and hints along the way. By collecting information on a particular student's performance, the software can make inferences about strengths and weaknesses, and can suggest additional work." An intelligent tutoring system is defined in [23] as a "computer system" based on "artificial intelligence" designed to deliver content and provide feedback to its user. The topic received a lot of attention from the research community since the 1980's. However it seems that the process of providing adequate help to users based on their individual responses is still open.

In this work we assume that several hints are associated with a problem presented to a student via an intelligent tutoring system. In order to find the most optimal sequence for presenting these hints to the student we arrange them

T.-h. Kim et al. (Eds.): UNESST 2010, CCIS 124, pp. 39–47, 2010.

in different levels based on previous responses, learning stiles and orientations, and the theory of weak orderings.

The rest of the paper is organised as follows. Section 2 contains definitions of terms used later on. Section 3 explains how to rank hints according to personal responses. Section 4 contains the conclusion of this work.

2   Background

Developing a cognitive tutor involves creating a cognitive model of student problem solving by writing production rules that characterize the variety of strategies and misconceptions students may acquire. Cognitive tutors have been successful in raising students' mathematical test scores in high school and middle-school classrooms, but their development has traditionally required considerable time and expertise, [7]. The Cognitive Tutor, [6] is able to understand student knowledge and problem-solving strategies through the use of a cognitive model. A cognitive model represents the knowledge that an ideal student would possess about a particular subject.

Learning styles describe the influence of cognitive factors where learning orientations describe the influence of emotions and intentions, [10] and[18]. Learning orientations describe an individual's disposition to approach, manage, and achieve learning intentionally and differently from others, [25].

Student navigation in an automated tutoring system should prevent students from becoming overwhelmed with information and losing track of where they are going, while permitting them to make the most of the facilities the system offers, [9]. A personalized intelligent computer assisted training system is presented in [16]. An intelligent tutoring system that uses decision theory to select the next tutorial action is described in [13]. A taxonomy for automated hinting is developed in [19]. The role of hints in a Web based learning systems is considered in [5].

Two very interesting problems are considered in [3], namely the problem of determining a consensus from a group of orderings and the problem of making statistically significant statements about ordering. An ordered set (or partially ordered set or poset) is an ordered pair $(P, \leq)$ of a set P and a binary relation $\leq$ contained in $P \times P$ called the order (or the partial order) on P such that the relation is $\leq$ reflexive, antisymmetric, and transitive.

Two elements a and b where $a \neq b$ and $a, b \in P$ are comparable if $a \leq b$ or $b \leq a$, and incomparable otherwise. A relation I is an *indifference* relation when given AIB neither $A > B$ nor $A < B$ has place in the componentwise ordering. A partial ordering whose indifference relation is transitive is called a *weak ordering*.

If given two alternatives, a person is finally choosing only one. The natural extension to more than two elements is known as the 'majority rule' or the 'Condorcet Principle'. A relation $R(L_1, L_2, ..., L_k)$ is constructed by saying that the pair $(a, b) \in R$ if (a, b) belong to the majority of relations L_i. The linear orderings a b c, b c a and c a b leading to $R = \{(a, b), (b, c), (c, a)\}$ (three-way tie), illustrate the 'paradox of voting'. The probability of the voting paradox for weak orderings is calculated analytically for the three-voter-three-alternative case. It appears that the probability obtained this way is considerably smaller than in the corresponding case for linear orderings, [21].

A 'social welfare function' maps k-tuples of the set of linear orderings of any $b \subset A$ to single linear orderings of B, where A is a set of at least three alternatives, [1]. An existing social welfare function is provided in [3].

3 Hints

Hints are designed to provide a description of how to sove a current problem. A complete solution should be provided only as a last resort.

Our approach is based on the well know principle that stating that a successful problem solving can be achieved by a decomposition of the original problem into sub problems that can be easily solved. In addition we consider the design issues pointed in [26], i.e.

- When should the tutor give a hint about the next step? Should it wait for the student to ask? Should it give unsolicited hints when it detects guessing or floundering?
- What step should the tutor suggest? For instance, if there are multiple paths to a solution, and the student appears to be following a long complex one, should the tutor suggest starting over?
- How can the tutor give hints that maximize learning, keep frustration under control, and allow the student to finish the problem?

In this particular case a problem that has to be solved by a student is followed by three hints called a, b, and c. According to the history in a database these hints can be placed in two or three levels:

- two levels
  - one of the elements a, b, c is ranked higher than the other two while those two are of equal importance
  - one of the elements a, b, c is ranked lower than the other two while those two are of equal importance
- three levels
  - consecutive ordering

The expressions an 'element a' and a 'hint a' are used interchangeably in this content.

Cases where two of the elements are placed on the same level can be seen in Fig. 1, Fig. 2, Fig. 3, and Fig. 4.

Cases where all elements have different levels are presented in Fig. 5, Fig. 6, and Fig. 7.

Summaries of possible structures for three and four elements where all elements are presented can be seen in Fig. 8 and Fig. 9 respectively.

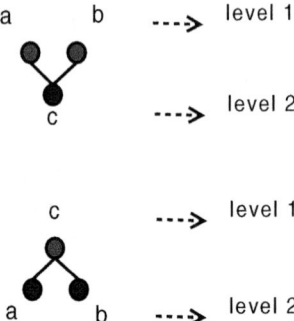

Fig. 1. Elements a, b, c are changing levels of belonging

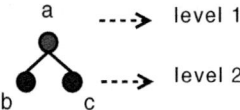

Fig. 2. Two levels case where one of the elements a, b, c is ranked higher than the other two while those two are of equal importance

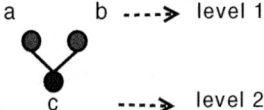

Fig. 3. Two levels case where two of the elements a, b, c are of equal importance and are ranked higher than the third

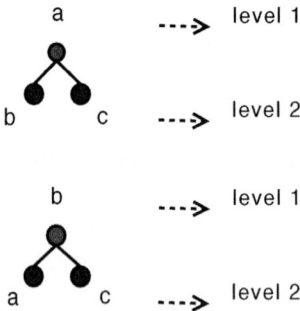

Fig. 4. Elements a, b, c have the same structure in both orderings

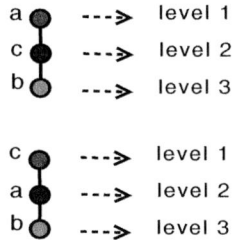

Fig. 5. Two of the elements a, b, c are changing levels of belonging within the same structure of three different levels of helpfulness

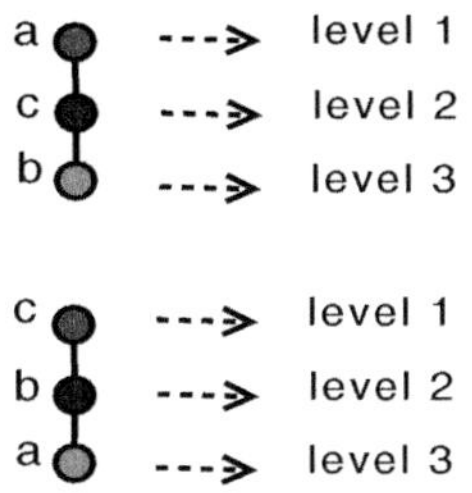

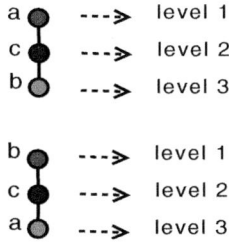

Fig. 6. All elements a, b, c are changing their levels of belonging within the same structure of three different levels of helpfulness

a ●   ---> level 1
c ●   ---> level 2
b ○   ---> level 3

b ●   ---> level 1
c ●   ---> level 2
a ○   ---> level 3

Fig. 7. Two of the elements a, b, c are changing levels of belonging within the same structure of three different levels of helpfulness

Hints placed on the same level can be further classified using rough sets theory. This can help to avoid 'a danger in going off the rails' when developers of the technologies don't keep in mind what psychologists and other experts have discovered about how people learn [22].

From a classical stand point of view a concept is well defined by a pair of intention and extension. Existence of well defined boundaries is assumed and an extension is uniquely identified by a crisp set of objects. In real life situations one has to operate with concepts having grey/gradual boundaries, like for example partially known concepts, [20], undefinable concepts, and approximate concepts,[11].

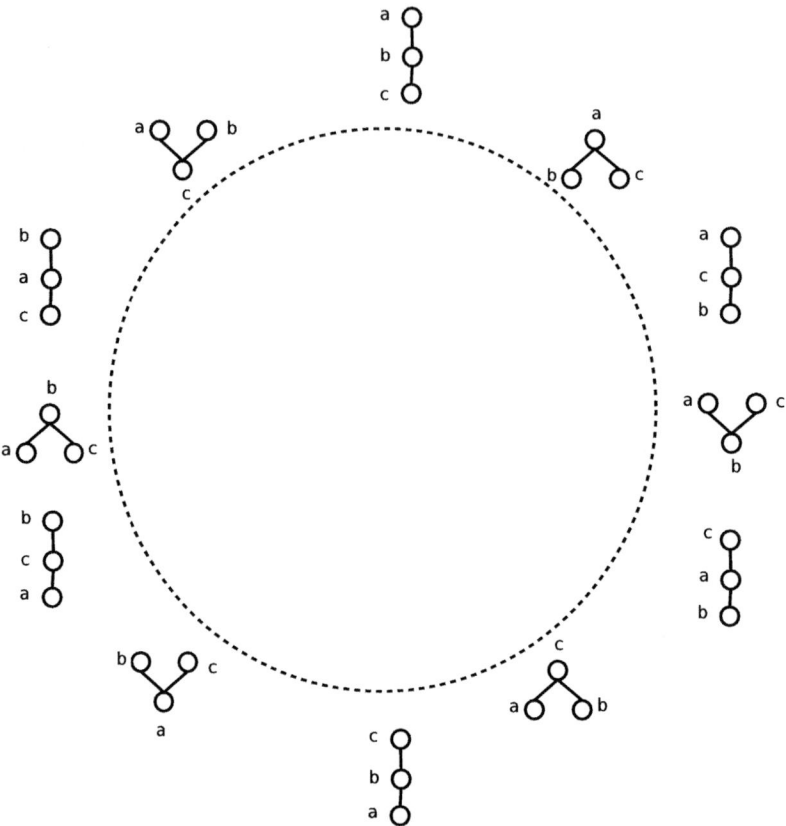

Fig. 8. Structures for three elements

Rough Sets were originally introduced in [14]. The presented approach provides exact mathematical formulation of the concept of approximative (rough) equality of sets in a given approximation space, [15]. An *approximation space* is a pair $A = (U, R)$, where U is a set called universe, and $R \subset U \times U$ is an indiscernibility relation.

Equivalence classes of R are called *elementary sets* (atoms) in A. The equivalence class of R determined by an element $x \in U$ is denoted by $R(x)$. Equivalence classes of R are called *granules* generated by R.

Definitions often used for describing a rough set $X, X \subset U$ are:

– the *R-upper approximation* of X,

$$R^\star(x) := \bigcup_{x \in U} \{R(x) : R(x) \cap X \neq \varnothing\}$$

– the *R-lower approximation* of X,

$$R_\star(x) := \bigcup_{x \in U} \{R(x) : R(x) \subseteq X\}$$

level 4

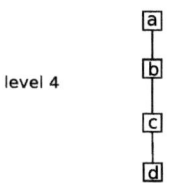

level 3

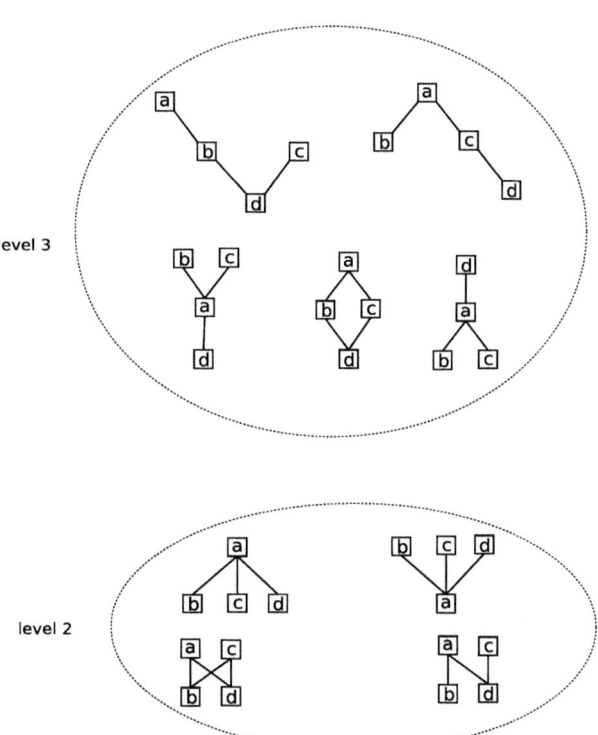

level 2

Fig. 9. Structures for four elements

– the *R-boundary region* of X,

$$RN_R(X) := R^\star(X) - R_\star(X)$$

It is important to mentioned the need of a large pool of problems related to an intelligent tutoring system. according to [26], a 13 week semester requires 130 problems at minimum, and the number of problems can go up to 500 if course designers want freedom to choose their own problems.

Another important issue is related to response clustering. Clusters' of respondents sharing the same preferences enable the viewer of such information to understand the propensity of a given 'cluster' to behave, react, respond, and perform, [27]. Cluster analysis considers the problems of measuring similarities between samples as well as the problem of the partitioning sets of samples into clusters.

4   Conclusion

Ranking of hints based on students' responses presents a better picture of the learning progress compare to interviews with individual students or group representatives.

References

1. Arrow, K.J.: Social Choice and Individual Values, 2nd edn. Wiley, New York (1951)
2. Berg, S.: Condorcet's Jury Theorem and the Reliability of Majority Voting. Group Decision and Negotiation 5(3), 229–238 (1996)
3. Bogart, K.P.: Some social sciences applications of ordered sets. In: Rival, I. (ed.) Ordered Sets, Reidel, Dordrecht, pp. 759–787 (1982)
4. Breuker, J.: Components of Problem Solving and Types of Problems. In: Dong, Z., Van de Velde, W., Schreiber, G. (eds.) EKAW 1994. LNCS, vol. 867, pp. 118–136. Springer, Heidelberg (1994)
5. Brunstein, A., Krems, J.: Helps and Hints for Learning with Web Based Learning Systems: The Role of Instructions. In: Lester, J.C., Vicari, R.M., Paraguaçu, F. (eds.) ITS 2004. LNCS, vol. 3220, pp. 794–796. Springer, Heidelberg (2004)
6. http://www.carnegielearning.com/web_docs/Whitepaper_Edweek.pdf
7. http://ctat.pact.cs.cmu.edu/
8. http://www.learning-styles-online.com/overview/
9. Encheva, S., Tumin, S.: Automated Discovering of What is Hindering the Learning Performance of a Student. In: Zhou, X., Li, J., Shen, H.T., Kitsuregawa, M., Zhang, Y. (eds.) APWeb 2006. LNCS, vol. 3841, pp. 521–531. Springer, Heidelberg (2006)
10. Keefe, J.W.: Learning style: An overview. In: NASSP's Student learning styles: Diagnosing and proscribing programs, pp. 1–17 (1979), Reston, VA. National Association of Secondary School Principles
11. Marek, V.W., Truszczynski, M.: Contributions to the theory of rough sets. Fundamenta Informaticae 39(4), 389–409 (1999)
12. Martinez, M.: Building interactive Web learning environments to match and support individual learning differences. Journal of Interactive Learning Research 11(2) (2001)
13. Mayo, M., Mitrovic, A.: Optimising ITS behaviour with Bayesian networks and decision theory. International Journal of Artificial Intelligence in Education 12, 124–153 (2001)
14. Pawlak, Z.: Rough Sets. International Journal of Computer and Information Sciences 11, 341–356 (1982)
15. Pawlak, Z.: Rough Sets: Theoretical Aspects of Reasoning About Data. Kluwer Academic Publishing, Dordrecht (1991)
16. Pecheanu, E., Segal, C., Stefanescu, D.: CDVE 2004. LNCS (LNAI), vol. 3190, pp. 1229–1234. Springer, Heidelberg (2003)

17. Schworm, S., Renkl, A.: Learning by solved example problems: Instructional explanations reduce self-explanation activity. In: Gray, W.D., Schunn, C.D. (eds.) Proceeding of the 24th Annual Conference of the Cognitive Science Society, pp. 816–821. Erlbaum, Mahwah (2002)
18. Stewart, K.L., Felicetti, L.A.: Learning styles of marketing majors. Educational Research Quarterly 15(2), 15–23 (1992)
19. Tsovaltzi, D., Fiedler, A., Horacek, H.: A Multi-dimensional Taxonomy for Automating Hinting. In: Lester, J.C., Vicari, R.M., Paraguaçu, F. (eds.) ITS 2004. LNCS, vol. 3220, pp. 772–781. Springer, Heidelberg (2004)
20. Yao, Y.Y.: Interval-set algebra for qualitative knowledge representation. In: Proceedings of the Fifth International Conference on Computing and information, pp. 370–374 (1993)
21. Van Deemen, A.: The Probability of the Paradox of Voting for Weak Preference Orderings. Social Choice and Welfare 16(2) (1999)
22. http://www.aaai.org/AITopics/pmwiki/pmwiki.php/AITopics/IntelligentTutoringSystems
23. http://design.test.olt.ubc.ca/Intelligent_Tutoring_System
24. http://www.engsc.ac.uk/journal/index.php/ee/article/view/62/97
25. http://www.trainingplace.com/source/research/learningorientations.htm
26. http://www.learnlab.org/opportunities/summer/readings/06IJAIED.pdf
27. http://www.wipo.int/pctdb/en/wo.jsp?wo=2007035412

Flexible Ubiquitous Learning Management System Adapted to Learning Context

Ji-Seong Jeong[1], Mihye Kim[2], Chan Park[1], Jae-Soo Yoo[1], and Kwan-Hee Yoo[1,*]

[1] Department of Information Industrial Engineering, Department of Information
Communication Engineering, Department of Computer Education and IIE,
Chungbuk National University,
410 Seongbongro Heungdukgu Cheongju Chungbuk, South Korea
{farland83,szell,yjs,khyoo}@chnu.ac.kr
[2] Department of Computer Science Education, Catholic University of Daegu,
330 Hayangeup Gyeonsansi Gyeongbuk, South Korea
mihyekim@cu.ac.kr

Abstract. This paper proposes a u-learning management system (ULMS) appropriate to the ubiquitous learning environment, with emphasis on the significance of context awareness and adaptation in learning. The proposed system supports the basic functions of an e-learning management system and incorporates a number of tools and additional features to provide a more customized learning service. The proposed system automatically corresponds to various forms of user terminal without modifying the existing system. The functions, formats, and course learning activities of the system are dynamically and adaptively constructed at runtime according to user terminals, course types, pedagogical goals as well as student characteristics and learning context. A prototype for university use has been implemented to demonstrate and evaluate the proposed approach. We regard the proposed ULMS as an ideal u-learning system because it can not only lead students into continuous and mobile 'anytime, anywhere' learning using any kind of terminal, but can also foster enhanced self-directed learning through the establishment of an adaptive learning environment.

Keywords: Learning management system, ubiquitous learning management system, u-learning system.

1 Introduction

The e-learning environment that began with the advent of the personal computer, modern communications, broadcasting, and digital technology in education has moved from m-learning, which emphasizes mobility, to t-learning, which utilizes television, both analog and digital, as a medium for learning. Today, it continues to evolve into the u-learning environment, which enables users to learn at any time and any place, using wired or wireless networks, regardless of the type of device. That is,

---

* Corresponding author.

T.-h. Kim et al. (Eds.): UNESST 2010, CCIS 124, pp. 48–59, 2010.

the current learning environment is becoming a ubiquitous environment where all communication media are interconnected through wired or wireless networks with sensors and radio frequency identification (RFID) embedded objects in our surroundings [1].

E-learning can be defined as a form of learning that utilizes computers, networking, and broadcasting technologies, through which people acquire and develop new knowledge and skills, individually or collaboratively [2]. M-learning enhances the transportability of e-learning and promotes mobile learning using wireless communications technology with portable devices such as personal digital assistants (PDAs) and pocket-size terminals [3]. T-learning makes use of analog or digital television, using one-way or two-way audio/video and data broadcasting [4].

Ubiquitous learning (u-learning) is a new form of mobile technology with sensors and wireless communications [2]. It has provided new directions for learning, while initiating a ubiquitous learning environment in which students can learn continuously and overcome limitations of time and place. It can be said that u-learning is a comprehensive learning system built on the core features of ubiquitous computing, such as pervasiveness, portability, embeddedness, connectivity, and context awareness. Hence, by inferring a student's learning context and level of knowledge, u-learning can create a more creative and individualized self-directed learning environment, leading to an optimized learning environment for students [5].

In e-learning, learning management systems (LMSs) cater to overall educational, administrative, and deployment requirements [6]. There are many different kinds of LMSs and representatives, including Moodle (Modular Object-Oriented Dynamic Learning Environment) [7], [8], LAMS (Learning Activity Management System) [9], [10], Blackboard [11], [12], and Sakai [13], [14]. However, the existing LMSs cannot easily accommodate various types of terminal in the ubiquitous environment, such as personal media players (PMPs), smart phones, and other portable devices, because the systems were designed to operate in a limited, PC-based environment. In other words, the current LMSs need to be updated to support new devices. They usually operate on PC-based web browsers and Microsoft Windows. Thus, the systems are not ideal for supporting mobile learning [15]. Moreover, in existing LMSs, the learning activities provided for courses are fixed and are not capable of flexibly adapting to a student's level of knowledge, learning style, or course type.

We propose a u-learning management system (ULMS) that automatically accommodates various terminals without modifying the existing system appropriate to the ubiquitous learning environment. The functions, formats, and learning activities of the system for courses and students are dynamically and adaptively constructed at runtime based on the situational learning context, such as user terminal, course type, pedagogical goals, student profile, and environment. Context is an essential feature in designing a more adaptive mobile learning system [16], and "learning must occur embedded in the context in which it occurs" [17]. That is, a stronger view of learning theory puts more emphasis on the significance of learning context [17], context awareness, and adaptation in mobile learning [18]. Based on this view of learning theory, we seek to develop a context-aware u-learning system by taking into account the knowledge of the surrounding conditions. We aim to establish an optimally adaptive learning environment that allows students to learn and receive education 'anytime, anywhere,' and using any kind of terminal by seamlessly adapting the functions and formats of the system to the user terminal and learning context. Note that the contents of this paper have been partially reported in earlier work [15], [19].

This paper is organized as follows. Section 2 reviews the existing literature on LMSs and adaptive e-learning systems. Section 3 describes the main components, additional functions, and supporting tools of the proposed u-learning management system. Section 4 gives examples of implementing features. In Section 5, we offer conclusions and future research ideas.

2 Related Work

A learning management system (LMS) is a software application for administrating, tracking, delivery, and reporting of educational programs [20]. There are many different types of LMSs based on development platforms, purposes and features; however, they generally share many common characteristics such as managing users (including user registrations and profiles), creating and managing courses, learning content and activities, administrating assessments, tests and educational records, generating reports, supporting course calendars and bulletin boards, among others. The well-known LMSs are Moodle [7], [8], LAMS [9], [10], Blackboard [11], [12] and Sakai [13], [14], among many others.

Moodle [7], [8] is a course management system (CMS) similar to a learning management system. It is a free web application that allows educators to create online courses that focus on interaction and collaborative learning. Moodle has many features typical of an e-learning platform and can be used for education, training, and business settings [7]. It also supports the use of web 2.0 technologies such as blogs, wikis, and web applications [11]. LAMS [9], [10] is a learning activity management system "for designing, managing, and delivering online collaborative learning activities" [9]. It provides a visual authoring environment for creating learning activities and their sequences. LAMS can be used for individual tasks, small group work, or whole class activities. Blackboard [11], [12] is a course and content management system that supports the management of e-learning, transaction processing, and online communities for synchronous learning and collaboration. Sakai [13], [14] is a community of academic institutions that develop a common collaboration and learning environment. It is also known as CMSs, LMSs, or Virtual Learning Environments (VLE). The Sakai software supports many of the common features of CMSs, including generic collaboration tools such as a wiki, announcements, mailing list distribution and archiving, forums, and an RSS (Really Simple Syndication) reader. However, these are all limited in the aspect of supporting not only personalization, but also user terminals. They were designed to operate in a limited, PC-based environment, thus it is difficult to accommodate various types of user terminals in the ubiquitous environment. And they also provide only static fixed courses so that they do not allow users to have a highly customized and self-directed learning experience based on their learning characteristics and circumstances.

In response to these problems of the existing LMSs, some projects were performed to make LMSs adaptive and personalized. The e-learning platform iLearn [21], [22] attempted to provide personalization for learners based on learners' pedagogical needs and learning styles within common LMSs. To determine the customized e-learning package for a specific learner, it uses the semantic processing engine based on semantic web technologies. The GRAPPLE [23], [24] project has been launched to integrate an adaptive learning environment with existing LMSs to provide learning contents and activities tailored to students' needs. It includes five LMSs, three open-source LMSs (Claroline, Moodle, and Sakai), and two commercial LMSs (IMC CLIX and learn eXact). The GRAPPLE adaptive learning environment supports an authoring tool to allow course creation, a user model framework for providing a proper user data, and an adaptive learning engine to deploy adaptive courses and guidance. It provides personalization based on individual goals, level of knowledge, learning styles, context of use, as well as group characteristics and goals with collaborative work [24]. However, these are also limited in terms of support adapted to various forms of user terminals in the ubiquitous environment, even though they have proceeded to support personalization based on user profiles and pedagogical goals. Furthermore, they only focus on adaptive features to address the limited personalization within existing LMSs, rather than develop an overall u-learning management system adequate for the ubiquitous learning environment.

3 Ubiquitous Learning Management System

The proposed u-learning management system undertakes the overall administration of educational tasks related to teaching and learning in a u-learning environment, including teaching and learning support, and learning-content management. The system also offers tools such as a learning-content creator, learning-content viewer, and multimedia editor, as well as additional functions, such as student profile analysis, inference engine, e-portfolio, and search functions. These functions allow the user to manage system users, administer courses, track and record learning activities, and generate diverse e-portfolios for these activities. In addition, the system manages online education and facilitates collaborative learning. Above all, the system enables continuous education regardless of time and place by supporting different forms of system interfaces adapted to various user terminals.

Communication between the system and user terminals is accomplished by a simple object access protocol (SOAP), which guarantees system security and enables interoperability between programs running in different operating systems. Furthermore, each function in the system is developed as a module based on object-oriented architecture and component-based development, and the realized learning system is automatically built by selecting and combining these components in an arrangement tailored to a specific user terminal. That is, the realized functions, formats and interfaces of the system appropriate to the user terminal are dynamically assembled from the components at runtime.

3.1 System Architecture

Fig. 1 shows the architecture of the proposed u-learning management system. The architecture consists of five main components: user connection, teacher support, student support, administration support, and course management.

User Connection. Users can connect to the system using a variety of terminals. First, the system identifies the connected user terminal and automatically reformulates the functions and formats of the system to suit the user terminal. Then, the learning

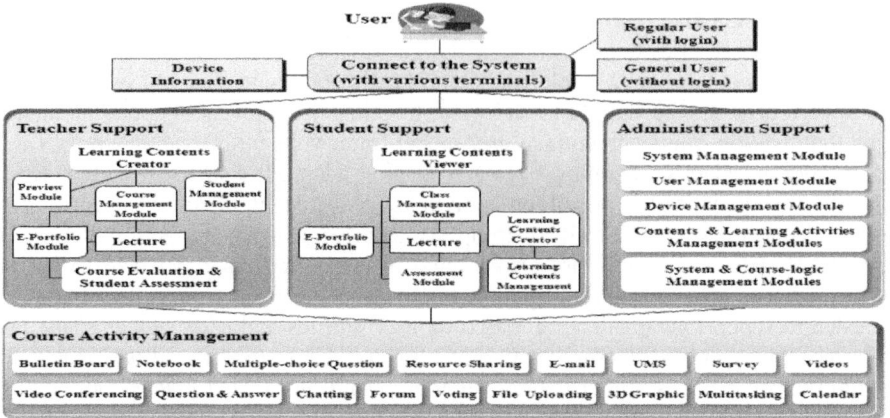

Fig. 1. Architecture of the proposed u-learning management system

system provides this derived user interface to the user. The system also dynamically chooses a display resolution according to the user's network bandwidth and terminal type. For example, when a user connects to the system with a PMP over a network link with low bandwidth, the system displays the learning content at low resolution and with low-level text rather than at high resolution with colored graphics or videos.

Teacher Support. This feature provides an environment in which teachers can open and operate regular courses by building up teaching and learning modules and creating content. This feature supports instructor-led activities that allow instructors to open and run courses, create content, conduct quizzes, surveys and reports, and manage students. Course materials can be previewed and modified. Teachers can also monitor the students' progress and learning activities while running the courses. In addition, teachers can evaluate the overall status of their students' understanding and achievement and provide comprehensive evaluation results to the students at the end of the course. Teachers can also check all activity information using e-portfolios.

Student Support. This feature assists students in their general learning activities. Students can search through courses and check their progress in the courses in which they are registered. They can also use the system to check their records and class assignments, take quizzes or examinations, and review their improvement using e-portfolios provided in various forms. Furthermore, students can create their own informal lectures and share them with other students.

Administrator Support. This feature allows administrators to direct the learning system by managing users, content, activities, and the flow of courses. This function interface also allows administrators to control information on all devices connected to the system. Administrators may need to arrange the development of some modules for newly released terminals.

Course Management. This feature allows users to create and use learning activities such as bulletin boards, notebooks, e-mails, unified messaging services (UMS), single-choice/multiple-choice questions, surveys, videos, resource sharing, video conferencing, chatting, voting, file uploading, multitasking, forums, Q&As, 3D graphics, and calendar. These learning activities are all implemented as modules (components). Then, the learning activities for a specific course are dynamically constructed at runtime based on course type and student learning context. Providing the course content in this flexible configuration is more helpful to teachers and students, resulting in seamless context adaptation in mobile learning. In addition, all interactions between users and the system are logged in databases that are systemically managed through e-portfolios. Users can view the log information in real-time. This way, teachers and students can monitor their teaching and learning processes. Users can easily create learning content without installing additional software and freely customize the web page layout of the learning system. Furthermore, they can add other web-based functions.

3.2 Support Tools

The tools provided by the system include a learning content creator, multimedia editor, and content viewer. We set up a rich internet application (RIA) environment with Flex2 to enhance the usability of these tools through a more interactive interface.

3.2.1 Learning Content Creator

Fig. 2 shows in detail the internal structure of the learning content creator. The content creator consists of three main modules: dynamic interface, user-created content (UCC) multimedia edit, and content management [19]. The sequence of a learning process is designed with learning activity units.

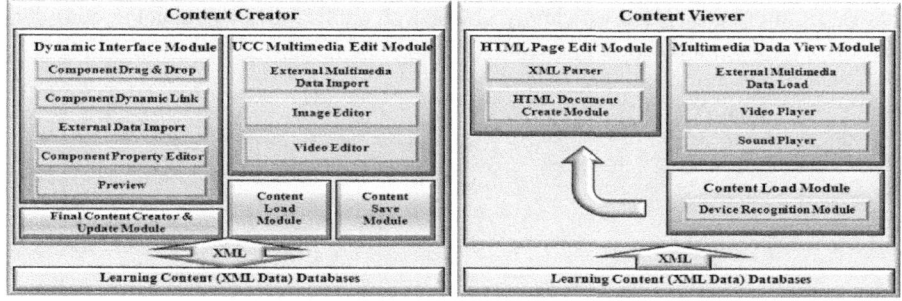

Fig. 2. Internal structure of the learning content creator (left) and content viewer (right)

The dynamic interface module provides the design environment for learning activities. It arranges each learning activity using drag-and-drop, and allows users to design the sequence of learning activities, add details, and import external content. The UCC multimedia edit module loads the multimedia editor. It allows users to import external multimedia data and edit images and videos. The content management module manages created learning activities, converts them into extensible markup language (XML) format, and saves the XML data to the u-learning content database. Each designed learning activity is created and saved to a data file in the XML structures, along with an index of its contents and learning sequence. Then, the XML data files are integrated into one XML document file based on the sequences of each learning activity, and the XML document file is saved to the database. This module also manages XML metadata to support the conversion of XML files to Sharable Content Object Relation Model (SCORM) format.

3.2.2 Learning Content Viewer

The learning content viewer consists of the three modules shown at the right in Fig. 2. First, there is an HTML authoring module, which builds web pages presented to users. This module converts XML data into HTML documents using an XML parser and optimizes the HTML documents to suit the user's device. The second module is the multimedia data viewer, which displays videos and images in a web browser. The third module is the content loader, through which users can access the learning content from the learning content databases [19].

3.2.3 Multimedia Editor

The proposed system provides an authoring/editing tool that allows users to edit multimedia such as images and videos and import them as data to the learning content. Various other multimedia editing tools are widely used; these tools are generally based on ActiveX. This means that users must download and install these tools before they can be used. However, Asynchronous JavaScript and XML (Ajax) techniques allow the immediate use of the multimedia editor, which is provided by the proposed system, without installing anything first. Fig. 3 illustrates how Ajax techniques work in the system. Ajax-based web applications run in web browsers. Here, a web browser is used as a client. A client requests data from a database server using XMLHttpRequest and function codes with JavaScript. The XMLHttpRequest object provides a method for asynchronous data exchange between browser and server [25]. Therefore, users can more easily and efficiently utilize web applications by reducing consideration of their computing environment.

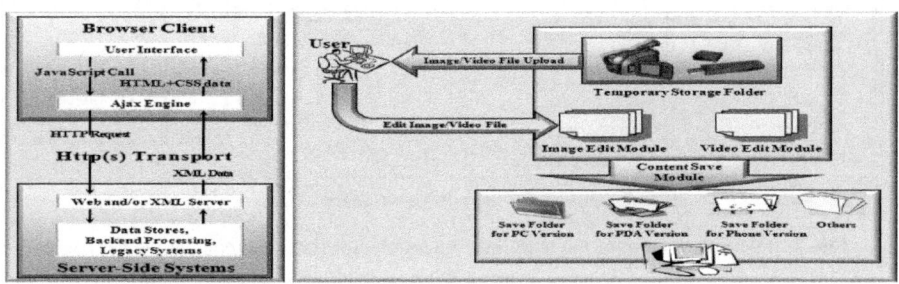

Fig. 3. Ajax web application model (left) and internal structure of the multimedia editor (right)

The multimedia editing tool was designed to edit images and videos, but it also includes a simple tool that allows users to edit educational cartoons. Fig. 3 shows the working structure of the multimedia editor. Users can load image/video files into the multimedia editing server. The uploaded files are stored in a temporary folder on the server, and the users can edit the files using a variety of editing functions, such as filtering, resizing, reversing, cropping, revolving, rotating, inserting frames, adjusting, merging, encoding inserting captions, and others. Edited files are saved in a number of different versions corresponding to each terminal and are separately managed [19].

3.3 Additional Functions

The u-learning management system provides a number of additional functions, such as analysis of student characteristics, an inference engine, e-portfolios, and learning content search. To facilitate a more effective self-directed learning environment, the system supports some functions for the analysis of a student's background knowledge, level of understanding, learning style and preferences, learning history, and learning context [26]. The proposed u-learning system provides the student analysis functions which consist of a number of component units, such as academic achievement and individual information (transcript, résumé, self-introduction, internships, learning styles and preferences, learning coaching, and learning history), learning results, learning assessments, learning goals, and other associated activities (volunteer activities and recommendation letters). And we also provide the inference functions for diagnosing and analyzing each student's characteristics and content needs through the overall learning process. To analyze the appropriateness of learning content for each student, we employ three data mining methods: proportional reporting ratio (PRR) [27], reporting odds ratio (ROR) [28], and the information component (IC) of the Bayesian confidence propagation neural network [29].

The e-portfolio system included in the proposed u-learning system manages and presents the learning processes in various forms with text and multimedia, including audio, video, images, and graphics. The system consists of two main modules: the teacher-support module and student-support module. The teacher-support e-portfolio includes course information for ongoing classes. Teachers can design and suggest the syllabus to students based on the students' learning status, which involves their attendance, bulletin board participation, learning participation, questions, debates, quizzes, assignment scores, grades, and previously taken courses. This e-portfolio also includes teaching history, research history, and educational background. The student-support e-portfolio includes course information for the classes in which the student is enrolled. It aims to improve student learning abilities by facilitating an enhanced, self-directed learning environment through the analysis and accommodation of various student learning orientations, based on individual learning activities. The e-portfolio also includes student name, identification (ID) and social security number (SSN), résumé, self-introduction, and study plan.

The search function in our proposed system helps teachers and students easily locate the learning content they want through text-based retrieval and/or XML-based retrieval mechanisms.

4 Examples

A prototype has been implemented to demonstrate and evaluate the proposed approach. The system was developed using ASP.NET 2.0, Microsoft SQL 2.5, and Visual Studio .NET 2003 on Windows 2008 and Microsoft Internet Information Services (IIS) 6.0 as a web server. We adapted the RIA-based Microsoft Silverlight 2.0 to maximize the user experience of creating learning content and activities.

Fig. 4 shows the main screen of the system, which consists of five main menus: 'my lecture,' 'my study,' 'portfolio,' 'community,' and 'user service,' on a desktop computer. Under the 'my lecture' menu, teachers can manage courses they have opened and check the registered student information. After opening lectures, teachers can add related lecture notes. Each lecture note is composed of several activities in various forms with text and multimedia objects; that is, the contents of a lecture note consist of a number of activities. Fig. 5 shows the process of creating a lecture note by adding an image activity. Students also can open their own informal lectures and share them with others.

Fig. 4. Main screen of the u-learning management system

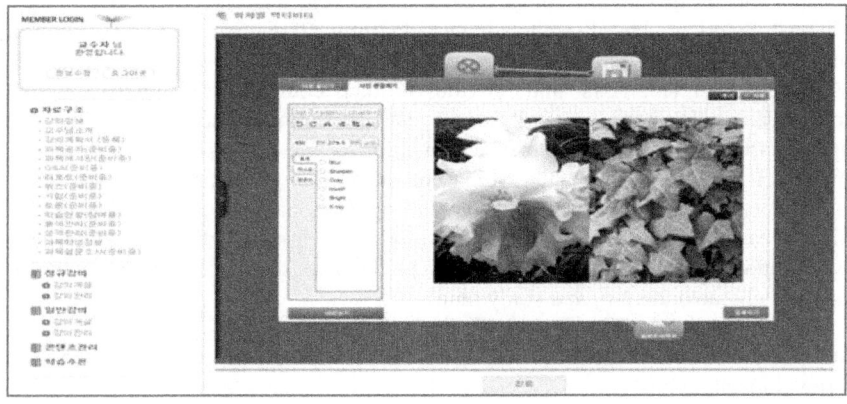

Fig. 5. Example of the creating of a lecture note by adding an image

Under 'my study,' students can register, take lectures, manage courses they have taken, and check their records and required materials. Under the 'portfolio' menu, a user can freely create various forms of e-portfolio by combining supported learning elements. Users can also view information on all teaching and learning activities, as well as the activity log of system events. All interactions between the system and users are logged to identify factors that could later help in enhancing learning activities. Fig. 6 shows examples of screens connected using a smart phone.

Fig. 6. Examples of screens connected using a smart phone (a) initial screen (b) login screen (c) course inqurey screen

5 Conclusion

Through this study, we proposed a ubiquitous learning management system (ULMS) that automatically adapts to various types of terminal. The functions and formats of the learning system are dynamically configured according to the user terminal. There-fore, the system allows students to learn using wired or wireless networks, with any kind of terminal, without being limited by time or place. Furthermore, to support an enhanced, self-directed learning environment, the system dynamically constructs course learning activities at runtime based on course types, pedagogical goals, and student learning circumstances and characteristics (student background knowledge, learning styles, preferences, and learning context), with an emphasis on the signifi-cance of adaptation to context in learning.

The basic architecture of the system is composed of five main functions: user con-nection, teacher support, student support, administration support, and course man-agement. The system also provides several tools, including a learning-content creator and viewer, which allow users to create and view a variety of educational content. The tools also include an Ajax-based multimedia editor, which allows users to edit multimedia data such as images and audiovisuals and insert the multimedia data into learning content. Furthermore, the system provides a number of additional functions that can analyze student characteristics and infer similarities between students and learning content to provide a highly personalized, independent, and self-directed learning environment. The system also allows users to create various types of e-portfolio. The ultimate purpose of these additional functions is to provide a more customized learning service. Finally, the system offers two search mechanisms to help users more readily locate the learning content they need.

In addition, the proposed u-learning system develops each function as a component unit based on an object-oriented approach. It automatically and dynamically builds the learning system interface by compiling in real time functions corresponding to each terminal environment. Using the fixed interface approach makes it necessary to develop a new system version to support new terminal types; but with this dynamic interface approach, the system needs only to add certain modules to process the new terminal type. Thus, we regard the proposed ULMS as an ideal ubiquitous learning system optimized for a ubiquitous environment that supports uninterrupted learning activities using various terminals regardless of time and location.

We have not yet completed development of the proposed approach, and a number of issues still remain. Practical trials must be conducted to further evaluate the proposed system. Also, investigations into improvements suggested by students in a wide range of case studies should be continued. Nonetheless, our system is valuable for ubiquitous learning because it provides students not only an 'anytime, anywhere' continuous and mobile learning experience with any device but also an enhanced, customized learning environment created by analyzing student learning circumstances and characteristics.

Acknowledgement

This research was financially supported by the Ministry of Education, Science Technology (MEST) and National Research Foundation of Korea(NRF) through the Human Resource Training Project for Regional Innovation.

References

1. Curtin, J., Kauffman, R.J., Riggins, F.J.: Making the 'Most' Out of RFID Technology: A Research Agenda for the Study of the Adoption, Usage, and Impact of RFID. Information Technology and Management 8(2), 87–110 (2007)
2. Liu, G.-Z., Hwang, G.-J.: A key step to understanding paradigm shifts in e-learning: Towards context-aware ubiquitous learning. British Journal of Educational Technology 40(6) (2009)
3. Rushby, N.: Editorial. British Journal of Educational Technology 36(5), 709–710 (2005)
4. Dosi, A., Prario, B.: New Frontiers of T-Learning: the Emergence of Interactive Digital Broadcasting Learning Services in Europe. In: ED-Media 2004, 4831–4836 (2004)
5. Jung, S.M., Ko, B.S., Shin, S.W., Seo, J.H.: Understanding of u-learning. Korean Education & Research Information Service (KERIS), Issue Report RM 2005-54, Republic of Korea (2005)
6. Learning management system, http://en.wikipedia.org/wiki/Learning_management_system
7. Moodle, http://moodle.org/
8. Moodle-Wikipedia, http://en.wikipedia.org/wiki/Moodle
9. LAMS, http://www.lamsinternational.com/
10. LAMS-Wikipedia, http://en.wikipedia.org/wiki/LAMS
11. Blackboard, http://www.blackboard.com/
12. Blackboard Inc., http://en.wikipedia.org/wiki/Blackboard_Learning_System
13. Sakai, http://www.efrontlearning.net/
14. Sakai Project, http://en.wikipedia.org/wiki/Sakai_Project

15. Park, C., Sung, D.-O., Han, C.D., Jang, Y., Lee, H.J., Yoo, J.-S., Yoo, K.-H.: COLMS: Components Oriented u-Learning Management Systems in Ubiquitous Environments. International Journal of Contents 5(1), 15–20 (2009)
16. Malek, J., Laroussi, M., Derycke, A.: A Multi-Layer Ubiquitous Middleware for Bijective Adaptation between Context and Activity in a Mobile and Collaborative learning. In: The Proceedings of the International Conference on Systems and Networks Communication (ICSNC 2006), vol. 39 (2006)
17. Quay, J.: The importance of context to learning: physical education and outdoor education seeing eye to eye. In: The Proceedings of ACHPER Interactive Health and Physical Education Conference 2002, pp. 1–15 (2002)
18. Wang, Y.-K.: Context Awareness and Adaptation in Mobile Learning. In: The Proceedings of the Second IEEE International Workshop on Wireless and Mobile Technologies in Education (WMTE 2004), pp. 154–158 (2004)
19. Sung, D.-O., Lee, M.-S., Park, J.-H., Park, H.-S., Park, C., Yoo, J.-S., Yoo, K.-H.: Design and Implementation of u-Learning Contents Authoring System based on a Learning Activity. Journal of Korea Contents Association 9(1), 475–483 (2009)
20. Ellis, R.K.: Field Guide to Learning Management Systems, ASTD Learning Circuits (2009), http://www.astd.org/NR/rdonlyres/12ECDB99-3B91-403E-9B15-7E597444645D/23395/LMS_fieldguide_20091.pdf
21. Peter, S.E., Dastbaz, M., Bacon, E.: Personalised e-Learning, Semantic Web and Learning Ontologies. In: The Proceedings of World Conference on Educational Multimedia, Hypermedia and Telecommunications (ED-MEDIA 2008), pp. 1818–1825 (June 2008)
22. Peter, S.E., Bacon, E., Dastbaz, M.: Learning styles, personalisation and adaptable e-learning. In: The Proceedings of the Fourteenth International Conference on Software Process Improvement Research, Education and Training (INSPIRE 2009), pp. 77–87. The British Computer Society (2009)
23. GRAPPLE, http://www.grapple-project.org/
24. Oneto, L., Abel, F., Herder, E., Smits, D.: Making today's Learning Management Systems adaptive. In: Workshop on Learning Management Systems meet Adaptive Environments at EC-TEC 2009, Nice, France (September 2009)
25. XMLHttpRequest, http://en.wikipedia.org/wiki/XMLHttpRequest
26. Kim, M.H., Choi, S.-Y.: An Ontology-Based Adaptive Learning System to Enhance Self-directed Learning. In: Kang, B.-H., Richards, D. (eds.) PKAW 2010. LNCS, vol. 6232, pp. 91–102. Springer, Heidelberg (2010)
27. Evans, S.J., Waller, P.C., Davis, S.: Use of proportional reporting ratios (PRRs) for signal generation from spontaneous adverse drug reaction reports. Pharmacoepidemiol Drug Safe (10), 483–486 (2001)
28. Rothman, K.J., Lanes, S., Sacks, S.T.: The reporting odds ratio and its advantages over the proportional reporting ratio. Pharmacoepidemiol Drug Safe (13), 519–523 (2004)
29. Bate, A., Lindquist, M., Edwards, I.R., Olsson, S., Orre, R., Lansner, A., De Freitas, R.M.: A Bayesian neural network method for adverse drug reaction signal generation. European Journal of Clinical Pharmacology 54(4), 315–321 (1998)

Effects of Knowledge Sharing and Social Presence on the Intention to Continuously Use Social Networking Sites: The Case of Twitter in Korea

Bong-Won Park[1] and Kun Chang Lee[2,*]

[1] Department of Interaction Science, Sungkyunkwan University
Seoul 110-745, Republic of Korea
combio00@naver.com
[2] Professor of MIS and WCU Professor of Creativity Science
SKK Business School and Department of Interaction Science
Sungkyunkwan University
Seoul 110-745, Republic of Korea
kunchanglee@gmail.com, leekc@skku.edu

Abstract. Recent surge of social networking websites in the world supports a widely accepted assumption that people aspires to be recognized online by sharing information with others, perceive enjoyment and keeps to use their social networking site continuously. Different from traditional social networking sites (SNSs) like Cyworld and Facebook, Twitter is famous for its short message and ease of sharing knowledge with others in a prompt manner. Therefore, Twitter is preferred most by many people who seem innovative generically. In this sense, Twitter accumulates its fame as the most influential SNS media among users. However, there is no study to investigate why people holds continuous intention to use the Twitter from the perspective of knowledge-sharing and social presence. To resolve this research issue, this paper adopts six constructs such as personal innovativeness, knowledge-sharing intention, perceived ease of use, perceived enjoyment, social presence, and intention to continuously use. Empirical results with 105 valid questionnaires revealed that the proposed research model is statistically significant, and people's intention to use the Twitter continuously is influenced by social presence, perceived enjoyment, and perceived ease of use.

Keywords: intention to continuously use, Personal innovativeness, Perceived ease of use, knowledge-sharing intention, social presence, perceived enjoyment.

1 Introduction

The Internet is used by many to develop relationships and share information. Recently, to effectively support such interactions, social networking sites such as Cyworld, Facebook, MySpace, and Twitter have been launched. Boyd and Ellison [1] define social networking sites as "web-based services that allow individuals to construct a public or semi-public profile within a bounded system, articulate a list of

---

* Corresponding author.

T.-h. Kim et al. (Eds.): UNESST 2010, CCIS 124, pp. 60–69, 2010.

other users with whom they share a connection, and view and traverse their list of connections and those made by others within the system." In a social networking site (SNS), users post on the site their current feelings, touring information, restaurant menus, and photographs.

These SNSs are popular throughout the world. According to the New York Times, the number of Facebook users in 2010 is estimated over 500 million, compared to the 200 million users of one and a half years previous [2]. However, the fastest growth of an SNS occurred with Twitter from December 2008 to December 2009 [3]. In Twitter, users send/receive messages, or "tweet," by writing a maximum of 140 characters using a PC or smart phone. The number of registered users in Twitter in 2010 is estimated at over 105 million [4]. In Korea, Twitter has become popular since Yuna Kim, a 2010 Olympic champion in women figure's skating, registered for the service. As many Korean celebrities and movie stars are registering for this service, the number of Twitter users is increasing.

Due to the increasing use of SNSs and their popularities with users, many researchers have studied user behavior and adoption of SNSs [5-10]. However, even though new services such as SNSs may attract many users in the beginning, retaining these users is very difficult because of competition from new rival services or the deterioration of a site's attractiveness. Therefore, the more important research topic is the retention of SNS users. Currently, research studies that consider not only continuous use intention, but also user characteristics in relation to SNSs, such as the intent to share knowledge and personal innovativeness, are limited.

In this paper, we focus on the intention to continuously use SNSs and, in particular, the intention to participate in knowledge sharing, personal innovativeness, social presence and the perceived ease of use and perceived enjoyment of these sites.

2   Previous Studies

2.1   Social Networking Sites (SNS)

Three different approaches - surveys, traffic logs, and crawling - have been used to analyze SNS users [5]. In a survey, researchers aim to understand why users use the SNS [6], and why users disclose personal information [7, 8]. In traffic logs, researchers want to know how users behave on the site. For example, Benevenuto et al. [11] found that many users browse friends' pages rather than writing a text/message in online social networks. Burke et al. [12] found that newcomers receiving feedback and having many friends actively engage in a site. In crawling, researchers want to know who contributes the most and which term or topic is the most popular [9, 10].

2.2   Intention to Continuously Use

In information systems, including electronic commerce sites, the intention to continuously use is related to perceived usefulness, satisfaction, confirmation, and loyalty incentives [13, 14]. Kang et al. [15] focused on self-image congruity and regret to analyze continuous use behavior in a SNS. Along these lines, Mäntymäki and Salo [16] analyzed the effects of trust and social presence as they affect continuous use intention. However, Lin et al. [17] stressed perceived playfulness as a factor for ensuring the continued use of a Web portal, and Thong et al. [18] emphasized perceived ease of use and perceived enjoyment as factors in the continued use of mobile internet services. In addition, Hong et al. [19] underscored perceived ease of use as a factor for continued use of mobile Internet services.

From these data, we find that perceived enjoyment (playfulness) and perceived ease of use are more important factors in the use of Web portals or mobile Internet services than they are for information systems including electronic commerce sites, even though perceived usefulness, satisfaction, confirmation, and loyalty incentives are also important. Furthermore, we realize that other factors such as self-image congruity and regret, trust, and social presence should also be considered.

3 Hypothesis Development

3.1 Personal Innovativeness

In explaining the adoption of IT, Agarwal and Karahanna [20] created a new construct called PIIT (personal innovation in the domain of information technology), which describes "the willingness of an individual to try out any new information technology." Even though personal innovativeness is not related to ease of use in the adoption of mobile commerce, it is related to ease of use in PDA acceptance of healthcare professionals [21] and Internet use and adoption by knowledge workers [22].

Twitter is relatively new to Internet users and is increasing rapidly worldwide. In SNSs, innovative persons are typically the first to use the site, added by their typical considerable knowledge of IT. Therefore, a person's perceived ease of use depends on his/her level of innovation. Hence, we form the following hypothesis:

Hypothesis 1: Personal innovativeness in information technology is positively related to perceived ease of use.

3.2 Knowledge-Sharing Intentions

Prior to the introduction of high-speed Internet and mobile/smart phones, "knowledge is shared mainly through person-to-person contacts." [23] However, since the inception of Web 2.0, whose main features are collaboration, participation, and openness, was introduced in 1994, much knowledge has been shared on open websites such as Wikipedia. In addition, when a person interacts with others in SNSs, s/he tends to share a deeper level of information with his/her friends or unknown persons. In this situation, a monetary or tangible reward motivates people to share knowledge. However, some people derive enjoyment from sharing knowledge in online communities without a reward [24].

In Twitter, many people write about experience with or knowledge of recently purchased (used) products (services). In addition, a person can obtain feedback from other people. This response pleases most people. From these facts, we hypothesize that

Hypothesis 2: The intention to share knowledge is positively related to perceived enjoyment.

3.3 Perceived Enjoyment

Davis et al. [25] defined perceived enjoyment with regard to computer usage as "the extent to which the activity of using the computer is perceived to be enjoyable in its own right, apart from any performance consequences that may be anticipated." Agarwal and Karahanna [20] thought that such enjoyment is similar to pleasure and intrinsic interest. This kind of enjoyment is positively related to perceived ease of use in adopting Web-based information systems [26] and positively impacts the intention to use computer software, such as word processing software and business graphics programs [26]. In addition, Lin et al.[17] and Thong et al.[18] found that perceived enjoyment is associated with the intention to continuously use a Web portal or mobile service.

Twitter is a Web-based service and users want to use this site for enjoyment. Henceforth, the following two hypotheses are induced.

> Hypothesis 3a. Perceived enjoyment is positively related to perceived ease of use.
> Hypothesis 3b. Perceived enjoyment is positively related to intention to continuously use a service.

3.4 Social Presence

Social presence is the degree to which a person perceives communication media, such as face-to-face communication, on a socio-emotional level [27]. In other words, it is the degree to which one person experiences the presence of another person. Many prior studies [28, 29] found that this social presence is increased by the provision of graphical product and service information.

As for eldercare, the more a person senses social presence while interacting with a robot or screen agent, the more s/he perceives it to be enjoyable [28]. In the cases of commercial websites, the more the users perceive a high social presence, the higher is their e-loyalty and the better are their attitudes toward the product or service [30]. In SNSs, social presence affects the intention to continuously use products in social virtual worlds [16].

In Twitter, a person is able to receive instant feedback. In other SNSs, a person uploads images related to her/his personal life and comments on the pictures/writing of others. Based on these interactions, users may feel as though they are interacting in person. In this regards, the following hypotheses are derived.

> Hypothesis 4a: Social presence is positively related to perceived enjoyment.
> Hypothesis 4b: Social presence is positively related to intention to continuously use a service.

3.5 Perceived Ease of Use

In the Technology Adoption Model [31], two major constructs, usefulness and ease of use, impact behavioral intention. Recently, many new IT products such as smart phones have been introduced. Ease of use is important in the adoption of these products and services because new and unfamiliar products and services are often considered to be difficult to use. In addition, the relationship between perceived ease of use and intention to continuously use was supported by Thong et al. [18], and Hong et al.[19].

Twitter is a new service for Internet users, and most people are not familiar with it. Therefore, the current and continued use of this service depends on its ease of use. Therefore, we hypothesize as follows:

> Hypothesis 5: Perceived ease of use is positively related to intention to continuously use a service.

4 Empirical Analysis

4.1 Questionnaire Survey and Sample Statistics

Survey items were adapted from previous studies to investigate the relationships among factors that affect the intention to continuously use a service. For example, in the case of personal innovativeness, four survey items were developed based on Agarwal and Prasad [32] and Agarwal and Karahanna [20]. To analyze social presence, four survey items were adopted from Schmitz and Fulk [33] and Short et al. [27]. After creating the questionnaire, we randomly selected a sample of Twitter users in South Korea. The number of initial respondents was 118, which was reduced to 105 after we assessed the response qualities. Of these participants, 57 were male and 48 were female. All respondents were college students in the same university class. To ensure that the data were reliable, respondents received extra credit from a professor.

4.2 Reliability and Confirmatory Factor Analyses

The statistical tools of SPSS 17.0 were used for the preliminary analysis, after which measurement and the structural model were analyzed using the partial least squares (PLS) approach which is useful in analyzing descriptive and predictive relationships [34]. Furthermore, this method is suitable for analyzing data from a small sample (i.e., less than 200 respondents) [35].

Preliminary analysis

Six constructs were used for testing the hypotheses in the research model: personal innovativeness, social presence, perceived enjoyment, intention to continuously use, knowledge-sharing intention, and perceived ease of use. Table 1 shows results from the reliability test. The Cronbach's alpha values for the six constructs, all of which were greater than 0.7, indicate that these items were reliable. Next, principle component factor analysis with varimax rotation was used to analyze the data. The first factor, personal innovativeness, explained 36.0% of the variance; the second factor, social presence, explained 15.3%. On the basis of these results, we concluded that the measurement items were statistically valid.

Table 1. Reliability and Factor Analyses

	Cronbach a	INNO	SP	EN	CU	KS	EU
Innovativeness1		0.931					
Innovativeness2	0.93	0.903					
Innovativeness4		0.875					
Innovativeness3		0.853					
Socialpresence3			0.893				
Socialpresence1	0.90		0.828				
Socialpresence2			0.818				
Socialpresence4			0.678				
Enjoyment1				0.835			
Enjoyment2	0.92			0.783			
Enjoyment3				0.777			
Enjoyment4				0.702			
Continuous use3					0.812		
Continuous use1	0.90				0.799		
Continuous use2					0.797		
Knowsharing1						0.886	
Knowsharing3	0.86					0.873	
Knowsharing2						0.823	
Ease of use1							0.835
Ease of use2	0.75						0.779
Ease of use3							0.763
Eigenvalue		7.564	3.222	2.148	1.705	1.229	1.088
Variance explained		36.017	15.343	10.227	8.117	5.852	5.182
Total variance explained (%)		36.017	51.361	61.587	69.705	75.557	80.739

Note: INNO: Innovativeness, SP: Social presence, EN: Perceived enjoyment, CU: Intention to continuously use, KS: Knowledge-sharing intention, EU: Perceived ease of use.

The measurement model

Confirmatory factor analysis was performed to test our measurement scales with respect to reliability and validity. On the reliability test, a composite reliability greater than 0.7 and an AVE (average variance extracted) greater than 0.5 indicate an adequate fit [36]. On the validity test, the correlation between two factors should be less than the square root of the AVE value of each factor [36]. As shown in Table 2, these data are valid because they satisfy the criteria.

Table 2. Correlations of latent variables and AVEs

Construct	Composite Reliability	INNO	SP	EN	CU	KS	EU
Innovativeness	0.94	0.89					
Social presence	0.93	0.12	0.88				
Perceived Enjoyment	0.94	0.31	0.63	0.90			
Continuous use	0.94	0.28	0.55	0.64	0.91		
Knowledge sharing	0.91	0.23	0.16	0.28	0.23	0.88	
Perceived ease of use	0.86	0.22	0.22	0.33	0.36	0.25	0.82

Note: Values on the underlined diagonal are the square roots of the AVEs.

The structural model

This study's hypotheses were tested using SmartPLS 2.0 with the bootstrapping procedure, and we found that we could accept all of the hypotheses except for that linking personal innovativeness and perceived ease of use. The results indicate that perceived ease of use, perceived enjoyment, and social presence account for 46.9% of the intention to continuously use.

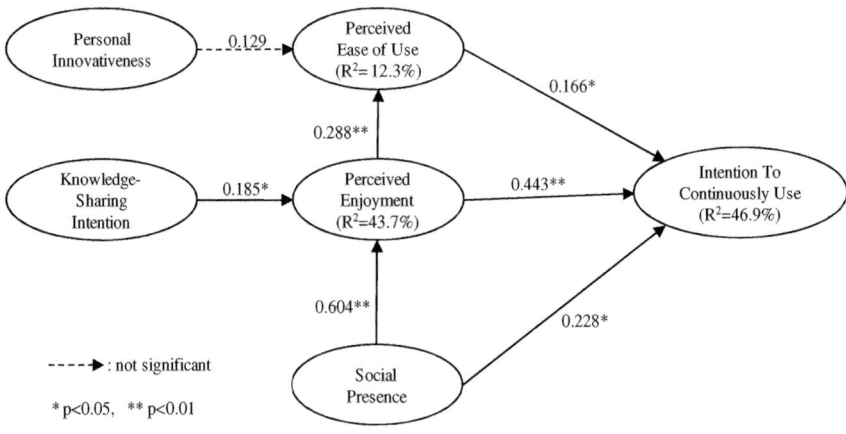

Fig. 1. Results

4.3 Discussion

This paper investigated which personal characteristics are influencing people to continuously use Twitter. Results tell us that the short message nature of Twitter limits people's personal innovativeness to affect the perceived ease of use when using Twitter. Besides, Twitter facilitates knowledge sharing among people due to its short message nature. Such facilitated knowledge sharing attitude on Twitter tends to increase users' perceived enjoyment. This result is backed up by people's altruism on the cyber world [37]. When a person shares her/his knowledge with other people, s/he gets feedback. Through this feedback a person established and builds social relationships. Social bonds motivate a person to share her/his knowledge more actively than before. In addition, a person derives enjoyment from helping other people even though they do not receive a monetary reward. Such altruism is a motive for knowledge sharing [37]. Therefore, a person with knowledge-sharing intention can derive enjoyment from using Twitter much more.

In addition, we found that social presence features of media helped users to continuously use Twitter. Social presence urges users to feel more intimate sense with others. According to Aragon [38], various types of media features such as an immediate response by e-mail, frequent feedback, and humor increase the perception of social presence. Also a sense of social presence increase by allowing users to personalize services [39]. Twitter includes various forms of social presence features such as enabling users to send and check messages through smart phones or other mobile devices, and more personalized and immediate feedback systems. Therefore, social presence features of Twitter increases users' intention to continuously use it.

5 Concluding Remarks

Internet users often want to meet and communicate with other people as they do in the real world. SNSs help meet this need. Until now, many SNSs including Facebook, Cyworld, MySpace, and Twitter have launched. Therefore, an Internet user should select a SNS from many SNSs. Among SNSs, the number of Twitter users is quickly increasing. If a person is not satisfied with a current SNS, s/he will switch other SNSs. Since a person can easily switch from one SNS to another, user retention is an important issue.

In this paper, we analyzed the factors that affect the continuous use of Twitter. To meet this research objective, we applied the PLS procedure. In addition, we selected Korean Twitter users as a sample because many Internet users are already familiar with these kinds of SNSs, and Twitter is increasing in popularity.

From this PLS analysis, we found, first, that perceived ease of use, perceived enjoyment, and social presence are important factors in the intention to continuously use the service. Second, personal innovativeness is not related to perceived ease of use. Third, as a person has the high intention to share knowledge, s/he gets much enjoyment from it. Fourth, the social presence in SNSs is important because it gives enjoyment to users and impacts to continuously use.

This study's results will help not only the Twitter Company, but also other SNSs. On the basis of these results, operators of SNSs should improve factors positively related to user retention.

Acknowledgments. This study was supported by WCU (World Class University) program through the National Research Foundation of Korea funded by the Ministry of Education, Science and Technology (Grant No. R31-2008-000-10062-0).

References

1. Boyd, D.M., Ellison, N.B.: Social network sites: Definition, history, and scholarship. Journal of Computer-Mediated Communication, 13(1) (2007),
   http://jcmc.indiana.edu/vol13/issue1/boyd.ellison.html
2. Helft, M.: Facebook Makes Headway Around the World. The New York Times (2010)
3. Nielson.: Led by Facebook, Twitter, Global Time Spent on Social Media Sites up 82% Year over Year (2010),
   http://blog.nielsen.com/nielsenwire/global/led-by-facebook-twitter-global-time-spent-on-social-media-sites-up-82-year-over-year
4. Niccolai, J.: Biz Stone: Twitter Has 105 Million Users. Macworld (2010),
   http://www.macworld.com/article/150633/2010/04/twitter.html
5. Strufe, T:. Profile Popularity in a Business-oriented Online Social Network. In: SNS 2010 Workshop, Paris, France (2010).

6. Kwon, O., Wen, Y.: An Empirical Study of the Factors Affecting Social Network Service Use. Computers in Human Behavior 26, 254–263 (2010)
7. Fogel, J., Nehmad, E.: Internet Social Network Communities: Risk Taking, Trust, and Privacy Concerns. Computers in Human Behavior 25, 153–160 (2009)
8. Souza, Z.D., Dick, G.N.: Disclosure of Information by Children in Social Networking—Not Just a Case of "You Show Me Yours and I'll Show You Mine". International Journal of Information Management 29, 255–261 (2009)
9. Ebner, M., Reinhardt, W.: Social Networking in Scientific Conferences - Twitter as Tool for Strengthen a Scientific Community. In: Proceedings of the 1st International Workshop on Science 2.0 for TEL at the 4th European Conference on Technology Enhanced Learning (2009)
10. Kwak, H., Lee. C., Park, H., Moon, S.: What Is Twitter, a Social Network or a News Media? In: The Proceedings of the 19th World-Wide Web (WWW) Conference, Raleigh, North Carolina, USA (2010)
11. Benevenuto, F., Rodrigues, T., Cha, M., Almeida, V.: Characterizing User Behavior in Online Social Networks. In: Proceedings of the ACM SIGCOMM Internet Measurement Conference (IMC), pp. 49–62 (2009)
12. Burke, M., Marlow, C., Lento, T.: Feed Me: Motivating Newcomer Contribution in Social Network Sites. Paper presented at ACM CHI 2009: Conference on Human Factors in Computing Systems, Boston, MA (2009)
13. Bhattacherjee, A.: An Empirical Analysis of the Antecedents of Electronic Commerce Service Continuance. Decision Support Systems 32(2), 201–214 (2001a)
14. Bhattacherjee, A.: Understanding Information Systems Continuance: An Expectation-Confirmation Model. MIS Quarterly 25(3), 351–370 (2001b)
15. Kang, Y.S., Hong, S., Lee, H.: Exploring Continued Online Service Usage Behavior: The Roles of Self-Image Congruity and Regret. Computers in Human Behavior 25(1), 111–122 (2009)
16. Mäntymäki, M., Salo, J.: Trust, Social Presence and Customer Loyalty in Social Virtual Worlds. In: 23rd Bled eConference eTrust: Implications for the Individual, Enterprises and Society, Bled, Slovenia (2010)
17. Lin, C.S., Wu, S., Tsai, R.J.: Integrating Perceived Playfulness into Expectation-Confirmation Model for Web Portal Context. Information and Management 42(5), 683–693 (2005)
18. Thong, J.Y.L., Hong, S.-J., Tam, K.Y.: The Effects of Post-Adoption Beliefs on the Expectation–Confirmation Model for Information Technology Continuance. International Journal of Human-Computer Studies 64(9), 799–810 (2006)
19. Hong, S.-J., Thong, J.Y.L., Tam, K.Y.: Understanding Continued Information Technology Usage Behavior: A Comparison of Three Models in the Context of Mobile Internet. Decision Support Systems 42(3), 1819–1834 (2006)
20. Agarwal, R., Karahanna, E.: Time Flies When You're Having Fun: Cognitive Absorption and Beliefs about Information Technology Usage. MIS Quarterly 24(4), 665–694 (2000)
21. Yi, M.Y., Jackson, J.D., Park, J.S., Probst, J.C.: Understanding Information Technology Acceptance by Individual Professionals: Toward an Integrative View. Information & Management 43, 350–363 (2006)
22. Lewis, W., Agarwal, R., Sambamurthy, V.: Sources of Influence on Beliefs about Information Technology Use: An Empirical Study of Knowledge Workers. MIS Quarterly 27(4), 657–678 (2003)
23. Hansen, M.T., Nohria, N.: What's Your Strategy for Managing Knowledge? Harvard Business Review, 106–116 (March-April 1999)

24. Zhaoli, M., Jiong, G.: Knowledge Sharing in Online Communities. In: The 17th European Conference on Information Systems, Verona, Italy (2009)
25. Davis, F.D., Bagozzi, R.P., Warshaw, P.R.: Extrinsic and Intrinsic Motivation to Use Computers in the Workplace. Journal of Applied Social Psychology 22, 1111–1132 (1992)
26. Yi, M.Y., Hwang, Y.: Predicting the Use of Web-based Information Systems: Self-Efficacy, Enjoyment, Learning Goal Orientation, and the Technology Acceptance Model. International Journal of Human-Computer Studies 59, 431–449 (2003)
27. Short, J., Williams, E., Christie, B.: The Social Psychology of Telecommunications. Jone Wiley, London (1976)
28. Heerink, M., Kröse, B., Wielinga, B., Evers, V.: Enjoyment Intention to Use and Actual Use of a Conversational Robot by Elderly People. In: Proceedings of the 3rd ACM/IEEE International Conference on Human Robot Interaction, New York, NY, USA, pp. 113–120 (2008)
29. Steinbrück, U., Schaumburg, H., Duda, S., Kruger, T.: A Picture Says More Than a Thousand Words-Photographs as Trust Builders in E-commerce Web sites. In: Proceedings of CHI, pp. 748–749 (2002)
30. Cyr, D., Hassanein, K., Head, M., Ivanov, A.: The Role of Social Presence in Establishing Loyalty in e-Service Environments. Interacting with Computers 19, 43–56 (2007)
31. Davis, F.D.: Perceived Usefulness, Perceived Ease of Use, and User Acceptance of Information Technology. Management Information Systems Quarterly 13(3), 319–339 (1989)
32. Agarwal, R., Prasad, J.: A Conceptual and Operational Definition of Personal Innovativeness in the Domain of Information Technology. Information Systems Research 9(2), 204–215 (1998)
33. Schmitz, J., Fulk, J.: Organizational Colleagues, Media Richness, and Electronic Mail: A Test of the Social Influence Model of Technology Use. Communication Research 18(4), 487–523 (1991)
34. Sellin, N., Keeves, J.: Path Analysis with Latent Variables. In: Keeves, J.P. (ed.) Educational Research, Methodology, and Measurement: An International Handbook, pp. 633–640. Pergamon, Oxford (1997)
35. Chin, W.W., Newsted, P.R.: Structural Equation Modeling with Small Samples Using Partial Least Squares. In: Hoyle, R.H. (ed.) Statistical Strategies for Small Sample Research, pp. 307–341. Sage, Thousand Oaks (1999)
36. Fornell, C., Larcker, D.: Structural Equation Models with Unobservable Variables and Measurement Error. Journal of Marketing Research 18(1), 39–50 (1981)
37. Hars, A., Ou, S.: Working for Free? Motivations for Participating in Open-Source Projects. International Journal of Electronic Commerce 6(3), 25–39 (2002)
38. Aragon, S.R.: Creating Social Presence in Online Environments. New Directions for Adult and Continuing Education 100, 57–68 (2003)
39. Gefen, D., Straub, D.W.: Consumer Trust in B2C e-Commerce and the Importance of Social Presence: Experiments in e-Products and e-Services. Omega 32(6), 407–424 (2004)

Exploring Individual Creativity from Network Structure Perspective: Comparison of Task Force Team and R&D Team

Kun Chang Lee[1], Seong Wook Chae[2], and Young Wook Seo[3]

[1] Professor, SKK Business School and Department of Interaction Science, Sungkyunkwan University, Seoul 110-745, Republic of Korea
[2] Principal Researcher, National Information Society Agency, Republic of Korea
[3] Researcher, Software Engineering Center at NIPA, Republic of Korea
{kunchanglee, seongwookchae, seoyy123}@gmail.com

Abstract. The objectives of this paper are to empirically investigate the fact that the factors affecting individual creativity differ depending on team characteristics and the fact that its practical implications are plentiful, especially for those who are concerned with how to design team network structures with a bid to motivate individual creativity. From previous studies, this paper suggests crucial factors for facilitating individual creativity: intrinsic motivation, organizational learning culture, and network structure. To maximize practical implications, we divide team characteristics into two types: task force teams and R&D teams. A task force team is organized with a clear mission to be completed within a rather short period. In contrast, an R&D team exists for a long time with numerous projects to finish with various terms and conditions. Empirical results reveal that individual creativity in the task force team should be controlled by adjusting the organizational learning culture and degree centrality, while individual creativity in the R&D team must be administered in a way that the individual's intrinsic motivation is stimulated and encouraged through the use of a structural hole through which external information from outside team is available.

Keywords: Individual creativity, Team characteristics, Intrinsic motivation, Organizational learning culture, Network Structure.

1 Introduction

For the firms struggling to survive in hyper-competitive markets, how to increase individual creativity emerges as an important strategy. Creativity has been receiving great attention from both researchers and practitioners as a last resort available through which firms' competitiveness can be enhanced dramatically.

In firms, individuals work in different types of teams. Creativity can be pursued in an individual perspective (individual creativity), team perspective (team creativity), or organizational perspective (organization creativity). In this paper, the main emphasis is placed on individual creativity. Most firms operate both temporary teams and permanent teams. As an example of ad hoc teams, a task force team (hereafter, TF team)

T.-h. Kim et al. (Eds.): UNESST 2010, CCIS 124, pp. 70–78, 2010.

is typical. Its mission is clear, and team members are usually recruited from other teams who seem to fit the mission. TF teams are supposed to last only temporarily. Meanwhile, an R&D team is an exemplar of a permanent team, and its mission is expected to be pursued long-term. Another point we need to discuss here before presenting research questions is the network structure that is formed by relationships among team members. Also, we need to consider the organizational learning culture, which is believed to influence individuals greatly. However, if individuals have a strong intrinsic motivation to upgrade their own creativity to get their jobs done well, their individual creativity is also changed favorably.

Then research questions become clear. (1) Are the organizational learning culture and individual's intrinsic motivation making significant influences on individual creativity? (2) Do network structures, such as degree centrality and structural hole, affect individual creativity? (3) How do the team characteristics of a TF team and an R&D team moderate the relationship between individual creativity and its antecedents, such as intrinsic motivation, organizational learning culture, and network structures?

2 Theoretical Background

2.1 Creativity

Creativity is a series of processes that is capable of inducing innovative results based on the ability to create something new and innovative [1]. Creativity does not happen inside people's heads, but in the interaction between a person's thoughts and a socio-cultural context. Creativity can be viewed as a systemic rather than an individual phenomenon [2]. In this sense, individual creativity is related to team characteristics because team characteristics can be regarded as a kind of working environment where individuals reveal their creativity. Team characteristics are the subset of the characteristics of the context in which an individual works. For example, there are two types of teams, temporary teams and permanent teams, in most firms. A TF team is a typical temporary team, and an R&D team is a permanent team. The objective of an R&D team is to achieve scientific improvement and enhancement of products and technology, not focusing on ordinal and formal work. Therefore, employees' creativity is essential for R&D teams, and such creativity contributes to the organization's competitive edge by creating new knowledge and developing it into concrete ideas. Moreover, it is important to create an environment where each individual's various creative ideas can be harmonized. On the contrary, SI (System Integration) companies are facing severely tough requirements from clients to submit highly creative proposals. These companies create TF teams whose mission is very clear. TF team members who seem to fit the mission are usually recruited from other teams. A proposal TF team usually consists of about 10 members and is supposed to last only temporarily. Essentially, it has unique team characteristics that are required for obtaining short-term creativity under the time pressure.

2.2 Social Network Perspective

The social network perspective draws on the patterns of interactions and exchanges within social units in which an actor is embedded to explain outcomes experienced by the actor [3]. In this perspective, an employee's position in a social network is linked to performance [4]. The structure of social interactions enhances or constrains access to valued resources. In research using social networks, the relative merits of different network patterns as determinants of network outcomes have long been debated [5, 6]. Debate has particularly focused on two network patterns, network closure and structural holes. *Network closure* [6] refers to a pattern of dense, mutually interconnected ties among the members of a network. A network rich in *structural holes* [5] is one in which the different parts of the network are largely disconnected but bridged by a few nodes, which have the potential to act as brokers.

Network density or social "closure" inside a group indicates the likely absence of "structural holes," and is thought to foster identification with the group and a level of mutual trust, which facilitates exchange and collective action [6]. Density thus enables the joining of individual interests for the pursuit of common initiatives. Tsai (2000) found that teams with high network degree centrality can increase their accessibilities to information quality, which enables them to be able to easily apply the knowledge and activities of other teams dealing with similar complex tasks [7]. Centrality describes the consideration of an actor's position relative to the entire social network. Although social network literature defines centrality in a various ways, such as degree, betweenness, and closeness [8], we have chosen degree centrality. Meanwhile, the concept of structural holes helps to explain how certain team members who span boundaries can play a key role in recombinant activity. In a team network where everyone is connected to everyone else, there are no structural holes [5]. The underlying mechanism posited by Burt (1992) is that actors in a network rich in structural holes will be able to access novel information from remote parts of the network, and exploit that information to their advantage [5]. An individual who spans a structural hole benefits by brokering and controlling flow of information between the unconnected individuals.

3 Research Hypotheses

Individual creativity is believed to develop differently according to the individual's position in the network and other behavioral factors, such as intrinsic motivation and organizational learning culture. Accordingly, a research model was organized as shown in Fig. 1, where network structure represents degree centrality and structural holes, and behavioral factors encompass intrinsic motivation and organizational learning culture. Further, since we are planning to compare R&D teams with TF teams, "team characteristics" is used as a moderating variable.

There are two types of motivation based on different causes that give rise to an event. Intrinsic motivation refers to the motivational state in which an individual is attracted to their work in and of itself, not due to any external outcomes that might result from task engagement [9]. On the other hand, extrinsic motivation is derived from external pressures or constraints. Research on creativity has found that individuals will be most creative when they are primarily intrinsically motivated, rather than extrinsically motivated by expected evaluation, dictates from superiors, or

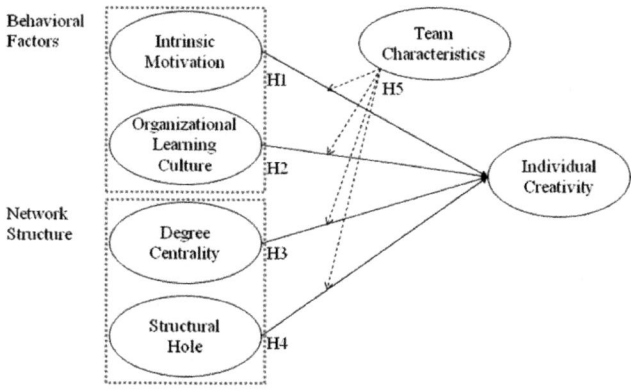

Fig. 1. Research model

the promise of rewards [10]. Moreover, intrinsic motivation is the motivation to work because the activity is interesting and personally satisfying. Thus,

H1: Intrinsic motivation will positively influence individual creativity

Senge (1990) defined organizational learning as "a continuous testing of experience and its transformation into knowledge available to whole organization and relevant to their mission" ([11] p. 6). It is viewed as one that has capacity for integrating people and structure to move an organization in the direction of continuous learning and change. Thus, learning organization involves an environment in which organizational learning is structured, so that teamwork, collaboration, creativity, and knowledge processes have a collective meaning and value. Organizational learning culture, by definition, refers to an organization skilled at creating, acquiring, and transferring knowledge, and at modifying its behavior to reflect new knowledge and insights [12]. Accordingly, we propose:

H2: Organizational learning culture will positively influence individual creativity

A number of prior studies based on social network theory have used cross-sectional data to understand the influence of network structure on creativity and organizational effectiveness [13]. The relationship between network position and creativity at work is influenced by certain contextual characteristics, such as diversity relative to the network, cultural norms, and tightness of the symbolic structures. Degree centrality explains the extent of individuals' communication activity [8]. Individuals who have a high degree of centrality are likely to hold positions of prominence that are character-ized by high communication and knowledge exchange activities, increased access to resources and information, and by a high potential to create new linkages that enhance social capital and organizational capabilities [7]. Individuals with a lower degree of centrality generally hold peripheral network positions that are not conducive to high volumes of communication [8]. In a directed information network, it is necessary to consider the "direction" of the relations. In-degree indicates the extent to which an individual serves as a knowledge source or advisor to other team members. Individuals with high in-degree centrality are sought after, thus enabling them to build up a diverse set of resources, skills, and knowledge. Thus, the higher an individual's in-degree centrality, the greater his creativity, which yields the following hypothesis:

H3: Degree centrality will positively influence individual creativity

The concept of structural holes is that the extent to which an actor in a network has access to unconnected non-redundant contacts impacts the actor's information benefits [5]. Therefore, it helps to explain how certain individuals who span boundaries can play key roles in recombinant activity. In the context of task force and R&D teams, a structural hole would be an intermediary between team members that are themselves not connected. The more structural holes an individual spans, the fewer his redundant contacts. This means that he is able to have more chances to obtain various amounts of information, assisting individual creativity. Hence,

H4: Structural holes will positively influence individual creativity

According to previous studies, intrinsic motivation, organizational learning culture, and network structure are the crucial factors that influence individual creativity. As stated above, creativity does not happen inside people's heads, but in the interaction between a person's thoughts and a socio-cultural context [2]. Creativity can be viewed as a systemic rather than an individual phenomenon. Therefore, the strength of influence on individual creativity depends on team characteristics and its environment [14].

Mostly, an R&D team is required to show innovative performances for which it plays an essential role in obtaining novel information by interacting with other people who have different experiences, skills, and knowledge. Especially, they have to concentrate on not losing their novelty and diversity of ideas, which can disappear as time goes on, in order to perform continuing novel creativity as is required for a stable department in an organization. To maintain their novelty, it is important to develop relationships with externally disconnected groups and to gain access to a broader array of ideas and opportunities. Those kinds of efforts can be facilitated by each individual's motivation. In particular, individuals bridging structural holes may be able to access resources from unique parts of their network or may hear about cutting-edge technologies and opportunities more quickly than others not so positioned [15].

Meanwhile, a TF team is naturally composed of team members with heterogeneous backgrounds, such as education, tenure, gender, experience, etc. Therefore, those TF team members must be controlled in line with a set of specific rules, so that the aspired level of team performance can be obtained. Accordingly, it leads to the assumption that organizational learning culture plays a much more crucial role on the TF team than the R&D team. Moreover, mutual trust and extreme focus on cooperation are emphasized on the TF team, putting weight to degree centrality from the network perspective. Based on such arguments, a hypothesis about team characteristics is suggested as follows.

H5: Team characteristics will moderate the relationship between individual creativity and its antecedents, such as intrinsic motivation, organizational learning culture, and network structure.

4 Experiments

4.1 Measurement and Survey

All items used to measure the non-network related construct (intrinsic motivation, organizational learning culture, and individual creativity) were adapted from reliable literature and measured on a 7-point, Likert-type scale. Network structure measures (degree centrality and structural hole) were calculated from the survey results that show the network relationships between team members. Measurement of structural hole is calculated by dyadic constraint [5]. For the sake of the survey, seven TF teams with 74 members were selected from three SI companies as were six R&D teams with 63 members from 6 companies. Therefore, 137 valid questionnaires were collected. 80.3% of the respondents were male, and 19.0% were female; 51.8% were in their thirties.

4.2 Results

By referring to SmartPLS version 2.0, Partial least square (PLS) was used for measurement validation and testing the structural model shown in Fig. 1. Network structure for the study was calculated using UCINET 6.1. The individual item reliabilities, composite reliabilities (0.882~0.953), Cronbach's alphas (0.799~0.935), and average variances extracted (0.715~0.839) by the constructs for each team indicated that they had acceptable levels of convergent validity and reliability. For discriminant validity to be significant, the AVE from the construct should be greater than the variance shared between the construct and other constructs in the model. In all cases, the AVE for each construct was larger than the correlation of that construct with all other constructs in the model. Therefore, structural model can be calculated as shown in Fig. 2.

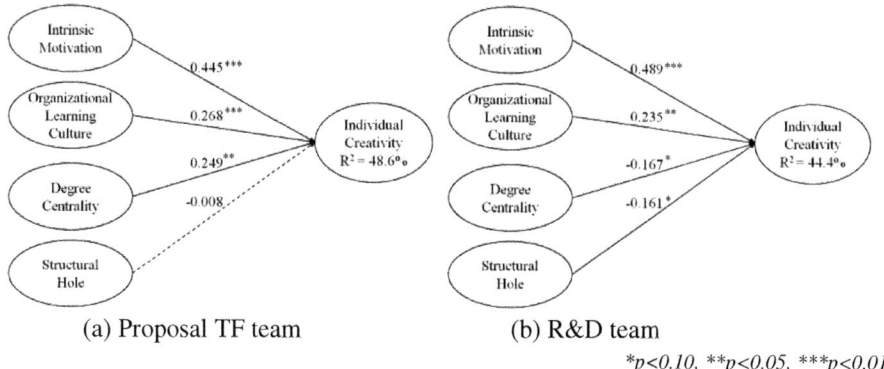

(a) Proposal TF team   (b) R&D team

*p<0.10, **p<0.05, ***p<0.01

Fig. 2. Path Estimate by PLS Analysis

First, as hypothesized, intrinsic motivation has a significant influence on individual creativity for both TF teams (b=0.445, p<0.01) and R&D teams (b=0.489, p<0.01), validating H1. Second, the coefficient between organizational learning culture and individual creativity was significant for both TF teams (b=0.268, p<0.01) and R&D teams (b=0.235, p<0.01), thus supporting hypothesis H2. Third, degree centrality has a significant positive impact on individual creativity for TF teams (b=0.249, p<0.05) but has a negative influence on it in case of R&D teams (b=-0.167, p<0.10), thus partially supporting H3. Finally, structural holes affect individual creativity significantly for TF teams (b=-0.008, n/s) and R&D teams (b=-0.161, p<0.10). H4 is also partially supported.

In terms of the moderating effect, the analysis revealed that team characteristics moderated the relationship between individual creativity and intrinsic motivation ($t_{spooled}$ = 2.148), organizational learning culture ($t_{spooled}$ = 1.674), degree centrality ($t_{spooled}$ = 21.426), and structural holes ($t_{spooled}$ = 6.586). Thus, H5 is supported.

5   Discussion and Conclusion

This study has several key findings that are validated by empirical studies with two different team characteristics (TF teams and R&D teams). First, the results confirm the significant influence of behavioural factors, such as intrinsic motivation and organizational learning culture, on individual creativity. Second, by showing the impact of both network structures and behavioural factors on individual creativity, this study contributes to the creativity literature that is provided with the integrative study approach. Finally, the relationship between individual creativity and its antecedents is moderated by team characteristics. In terms of behavioral factors, organizational learning culture affects individual creativity significantly in the case of TF teams while intrinsic motivation has a significant influence on individual creativity for the R&D teams. Additionally, from the perspective of network structures, degree centrality influences individual creativity significantly in the case of TF teams. This is comparable with the fact that structural holes have a significant impact on individual creativity for the R&D teams.

This paper's primary contribution is to introduce team characteristics as key moderating variables in a model that explains the revelation of individual creativity. Comparing the TF team with the R&D team, we found very interesting results regarding the influence of network structure on individual creativity. Degree centrality shows a significant influence on individual creativity even under a 10% significance level. However, H3 is supported for the TF team where short-term performance is emphasized. This pressure of short-term accomplishments catalyzes degree centrality among team members. In contrast, H3 is not supported in R&D teams where relatively long-term performance is weighted, resulting in a loose network relationship emphasizing structural holes. Such an assumption that the degree of influence of network structure on individual creativity is different depending on team characteristics was tested rigorously by using team characteristics as a moderating variable. Moreover, by viewing the revelation of individual creativity as being from behavioural factors, this study introduces a set of practical implications. Organizational learning culture should be built in such a way that individual creativity can grow quickly in a rather short period for the TF team. Since time is tight, reasonable compensation policies, leader's initiatives, and learning culture formation should be done in a short period, so that mutual trust is quickly built among members and necessary knowledge and information can be rapidly learned. Meanwhile, for R&D teams, the permanent teams, it should be kept in mind that the degree of each individual employee's intrinsic motivation in their job determines the level of individual creativity. It is not easy for employees to concentrate on retaining their novelty and diversity of ideas. Therefore, the team ought to consider motivating their employees intrinsically to encourage each member's efforts to maintain their novelty. Attempting to explain and predict revelation of individual creativity in an organization without understanding the moderating role of team characteristics and their nature is likely to result in theories that are incomplete and potentially misleading.

In summary, individual creativity on the TF team should be controlled by adjusting the organizational learning culture and degree centrality because the TF team exists temporarily until their assigned mission is finished, and therefore, each individual ought to focus heavily on their works garnering all kinds of available information. On the contrary, empirical results show that indvidiual creativity on the R&D team must be administered in a way that stimulates individual's intirnisic motivations and encourages the use of structural holes through which external information is available.

Studying creativity in an R&D context that needs to be concerned with the individual level, team level, and organizational level, which are all interconnected within a wider social system, is a possible area for future research.

Acknowledgment. This research was supported by the World Class University (WCU) program through the National Research Foundation of Korea, funded by the Ministry of Education, Science and Technology, Republic of Korea (Grant No. R31-2008-000-10062-0).

References

1. Amabile, T.M.: A model of creativity and innovation in organizations. Research in Organizational Behavior 10, 123–167 (1988)
2. Csikszentmihályi, M.: The Domain of Creativity. In: Runco, M.A., Albert, R.S. (eds.) Theories of Creativity, pp. 190–212. Sage, Newbury Park (1990)
3. Borgatti, S.P., Foster, P.C.: The Network Paradigm in Organizational Research: A Review and Typology. Journal of Management 29, 991–1013 (2003)
4. Ahuja, M.K., Galletta, D.F., Carley, K.M.: Individual Centrality and Performance in Virtual R&D Groups: An Empirical Study. Management Science 49, 21–39 (2003)
5. Burt, R.S.: Structural holes: The social structure of competition. Harvard University Press, Cambridge (1992)
6. Coleman, J.S.: Social capital in the creation of human capital. American Journal of Sociology 94(supplement), 95–120 (1988)
7. Tsai, W.: Social Capital, Strategic Relatedness and the Formation of Intra-Organizational Linkages. Strategic Management Journal 21, 925–939 (2000)
8. Freeman, L.C.: Centrality in Social Networks: Conceptual Clarification. Social Networks 1, 215–239 (1979)

9. Deci, E.L., Ryan, R.M.: Intrinsic Motivation and Self Determination in Human Behavior. Plenum Press, New York (1985)
10. Amabile, T.M.: Managing creativity in organizations: on doing what you love and loving what you do. California Management Review 40, 39–58 (1997)
11. Senge, P.M.: The Fifth Discipline: The Art and Practice of the Learning Organization, Doubleday, New York (1990)
12. Garvin, D.A.: Building a learning organization. Harvard Business Review 71, 78–91 (1993)
13. Song, S., Nerur, S., Teng, J.: An Exploratory Study on the Roles of Network Structure and Knowledge Processing Operation in Work Unit Knowledge Management. The DATA BASE for Advances in Information Systems 38, 8–26 (2007)
14. Woodman, R.W., Sawyer, J.E., Griffin, R.W.: Toward a Theory of Organizational Creativity. The Academy of Management Review 18, 293–321 (1993)
15. Uzzi, B.: The Sources and Consequences of Embeddedness for the Economic Performance of Organizations: The network effect. American Sociological Review 61, 674–698 (1996)
16. Borgatti, S.: Creating Knowledge: Network Structure and Innovation (2005), http://www.socialnetworkanalysis.com/knowledge_creation.htm

Webpage Segments Classification
with Incremental Knowledge Acquisition

Wei Guo[1], Yang Sok Kim[2], and Byeong Ho Kang[1]

[1] University of Tasmania, Sandy Bay,
Tasmania, Australia
[2] University of New South Wales, Sydney,
New South Wales, Australia

Abstract. This paper suggests an incremental information extraction method for social network analysis of web publications. For this purpose, we employed an incremental knowledge acquisition method, called MCRDR (Multiple Classification Ripple-Down Rules), to classify web page segments. Our experimental results show that our MCRDR-based web page segments classification system successfully supports easy acquisition and maintenance of information extraction rules.

Keywords: Information extraction, social networks, knowledge acquisition.

1 Introduction

Many web applications are developed to help the user to find or browse information effectively. For example, search engines can propose a list of webpages that the user might be interested in response to the keywords entered by the user, and web monitoring applications can gather newly uploaded information from the chosen webpages and report it promptly. Modern web pages are usually very complex, because they are often organized to represent different information to the users in a single page. On the one hand, this is useful, because it is attractive, atheistic, and convenient for the users. On the other hand it might cause negative effects on the web applications. The web pages might contain many "noise" such as navigation, decoration, interaction and other special words include the copyrights and contact information which is harmful to the retrieval performance [1].

Most webpages are divided into segments according to their structure and the segments contain various types of information, including target information that the user interest in. The segment classification aims to classify segments with their structural attributes to identify specific information types of a given webpage. Easy maintenance of the classification knowledge is essential for the segment classification, because there are changes in the webpages of interest or changes of classification scenarios. Even though this requirement is important, there is limited research on adaptive classification method [2-5].

We propose an incremental knowledge-based webpage segment classification method, which employs an incremental knowledge acquisition method called MCRDR

T.-h. Kim et al. (Eds.): UNESST 2010, CCIS 124, pp. 79–87, 2010.
© Springer-Verlag Berlin Heidelberg 2010

(Multiple Classification Ripple-Down Rules) to implement the webpage segment classifier. The method supports web page segment classification and easy maintenance for the classification knowledge. Experiments were conducted to evaluate the following issues: Firstly we examined whether or not our method can be used to deal with webpage segment classification problem. Secondly, we also evaluated whether or not our method successfully supports easy maintenance of the segment classification knowledge to manage different segments. The following contents are organized as follows: Section 2 summarizes previous studies, including webpage segmentation and classification approaches. Section 3 explains our method for the webpage segment classification problem. Section 4 describes experimental design and Section 5 experimental results. Our conclusion and further study will be discussed in Section 6.

2   Related Studies

Webpages are usually presented in a "human-oriented way". Human can easily distinguish different segments in a webpage by understanding of content, or by discerning visual elements, but it is not easy for computers to understand webpages. Web information extraction research aims to extract specific information from the given webpage. Web Information Extraction (IE) research is grouped into two approaches, the structure or position-based IE and ontology-based IE [2]. The ontology-based IE uses domain knowledge, such as relationships, lexical appearance, and context keywords, to describe data. Even though this approach is inherently resilient and general, it requires that extracting information can be fully described using page-independent features. However, not all interesting information is necessarily meet this requirement [5-6]. The structure-based IE [4, 7-9] relies on inherent structural features of HTML documents, such as informative content blocks [8, 10-14] and content template [15-18]. Basically, structure-based extraction tools use a HTML parser to construct a parsing tree and extraction rules are written to locate specific information based on the parse-tree hierarchy. The structure-based extraction is very accurate, but it frequently fails. It is necessary to maintain extraction rules to ensure the performance of the IE systems. There is limited research on this issue. For the adaptive capability, whereas some is based on machine learning techniques[5], others rely on knowledge acquisition methods [2].

We use structure-based IE method and employ MCRDR (Multiple Classification Ripple-Down Rules) method to manage structural changes incrementally. The MCRDR method is an enhanced version of RDR [19-22]. It is not only preserves the benefits and fundamental RDR idea but also has the ability to produce multiple classifications for a given case. It is also powerful in single classification domain, because it has been proved to allow coverage of the domain quicker than RDR [23]. MCRDR supports error-driven knowledge acquisition and each rule is acquired to remedy error [24]. MCRDR has been used in personalized web document classification domain. The results of the experiments in the study shows the good performance of MCRDR based document classifier and the approach of using MCRDR in web document classification are recommended [25]. We view MCRDR is appropriate for our study, because it ensures incremental knowledge acquisition by the domain users, and overcomes knowledge acquisition problem with exception-based rule acquisition.

3   Incremental Webpage Segment Classification System

Our Incremental Webpage Segment Classification System (IWSCS) was implemented to classify segments of webpages incrementally based on MCRDR. IWSCS retrieves the corresponding webpages from the given URLs and generates small blocks, called segments. We used "<div>" tag for this purpose, because modern webpages usually use this tag to make segments with CSS style definition. IWSCS extracts various attributes such as "id" and "class" of a <div> tag, number of hyperlinks in the segments, and other structural characteristics. Each segment is stored into a database as a case for further processing with the extracted attributes as well as the whole copy of HTML source code of the cases.

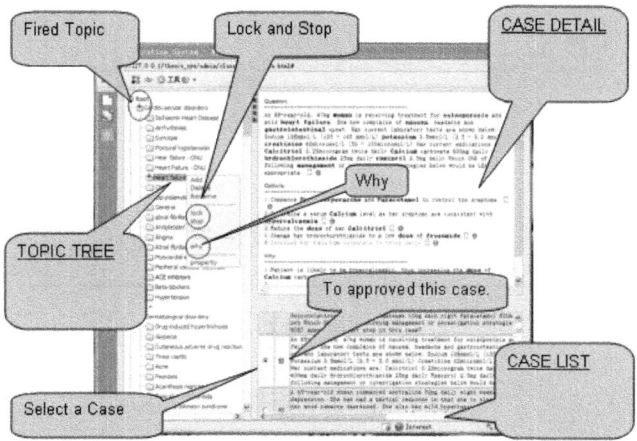

Fig. 1. Main Interface of IWSCS

Fig. 1 illustrates the main interface of IWSCS, which is divided into three main areas – the topic tree, the case viewer, and the case list viewer. The user can select any cases in the case list views, which displays available cases. When the user selects a case from the case list, the system displays details of the chosen case in the case viewer as illustrated in Fig. 2. The system is not only displays the attributes of a case, but also shows how does this case looks like when it was in a webpage. This feature is helpful to the user, as human can easily distinguish the content in web page and to make rules for the segment classification.

When the user selects a case from the case list, the system also displays the fired topic types in the topic tree as illustrated in Fig. 3 (a). If the user satisfies the suggestion by the system, he/she approves classification by click the approve button on the case in the case list. If the system does not provide recommendation or provide wrong suggestion, the user can initiate the knowledge acquisition. Fig. 3 (b) illustrates how to add conditions to the rule. The user can select an attributes, type in condition words in the text field and select the relationship between the attribute and condition words. The generated rules are stored to database for further process.

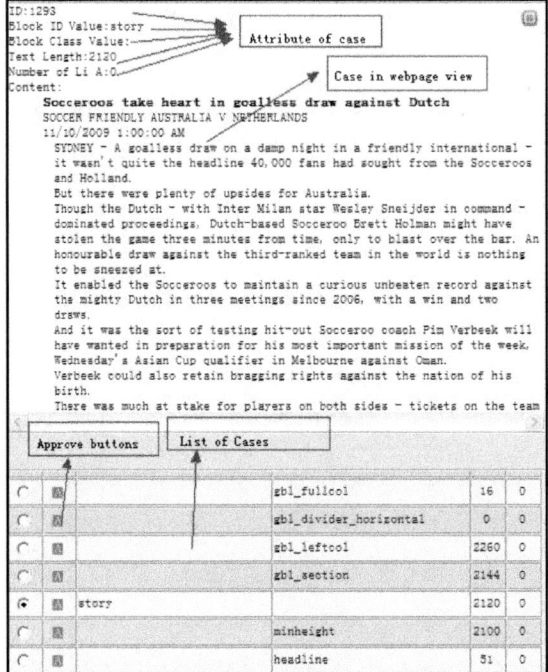

Fig. 2. Main Interface of IWSCS

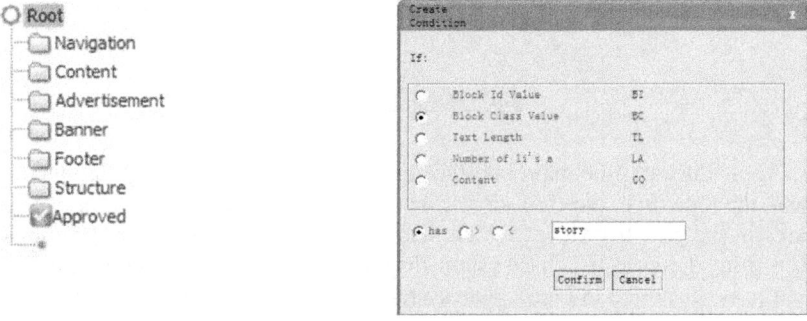

(a) The Topic Tree   (b) The Condition Editor

Fig. 3. The Topic Tree and the Condition Editor of IWSCS

4 Experimental Design

The experiment was designed to evaluate whether or not our IWSCS successfully manage webpage segment classification problem incrementally. For this purpose, our system is tested in an incremental case environment. Different cases extracted from different webpages are more likely have different attribute values, and these attributes will be used to create webpage segment classification rules. At the beginning of the experiment, IWSCS contains no rules or topic classifications. There is no external expert involved in this experiment, because there are no specific requirements of knowledge for domain. Anyone who is familiar with HTML programming or web-page design could be able to produce adequate rules to classify webpage segments based on their knowledge and experience. The system also provides a friendly inter-face to display cases, including attributes and content of a given case. The feature allows the tester to make a judgment easily and allow the tester to write a rule easily. In addition, the system also provides a function to allow the tester to switch the cur-rent case to other classified case to make a comparison. Every action on IWSCS dur-ing the experiment such as rule creation and classification recommend approval will be stored in to the database with a timestamp. Finally, the data will be used to analyze knowledge acquisition results in the following aspects:

(1) Growth of Knowledge Base: This analysis was designed to discover rule creation trend. During the experiment, the actions of the tester were recorded and analysed to discover how many cases had been approved by the tester and how many rules were in the knowledge when the tester was moving to next case.
(2) Time Spend: This analysis was designed to find out how much time the tester spent to add rules. This experiment can be used to demonstrate whether or not knowledge base is easy to maintain by using our IWSCS. This experiment result is calculated based on the timestamps, which was recorded when the tester ap-proved a case or added a rule each time.
(3) Classifications per Case: This analysis was used to indentify how many classes were assigned to each case at end of the experiment. This experiment demonstrates whether or not multiple classifications are necessary for segments classification.
(4) Growth of Mistakes: This analysis was designed to analyse incorrect classifica-tion trends. It is expected that the number of mistakes will generated when more cases are added into knowledge base. Aim of this analysis is to examine how well IWSCS manage misclassified cases.
(5) Correct Classifications: This analysis was designed to find out how correctly IWSCS classified cases during the experiment period. The result of this analysis presents performance of IWSCS.

5   Experiment Results

5.1   Growth of Knowledge Base

The number of rules is illustrated in Fig. 4., where horizontal axis represents the num-ber of cases classified and the vertical axis represents the number of rules. Although the number of rules increased in a fluctuant way, it shows that knowledge base in-crease is slow down when more cases were added. This means IWSCS is able to classify more cases correctly without adding rules to the knowledge base.

5.2   Time Spend

Fig. 5 shows that time spent increase lineally as more cases were classified by the tester. Average time spent per case is only about 18 second. In a generally the time

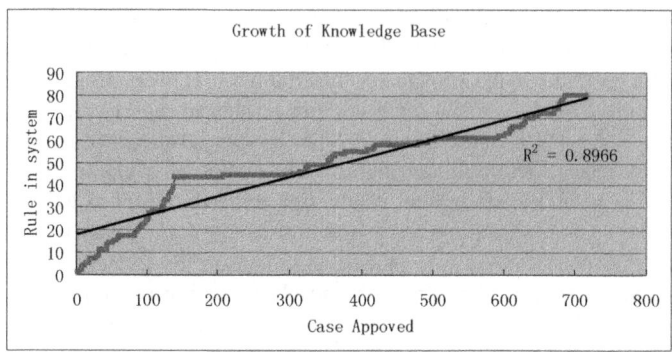

Fig. 4. Growth of Knowledge Base

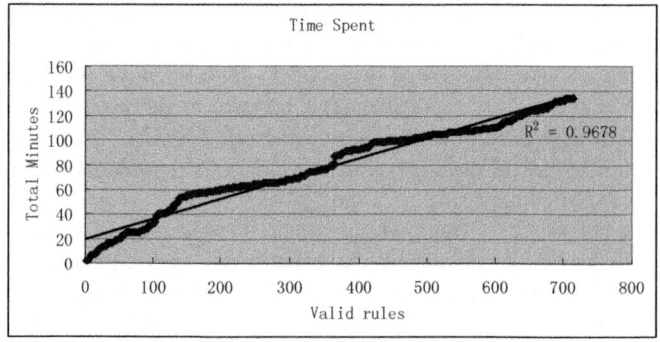

Fig. 5. Time Spend

spend trend become flatten during the experiment, which means less time was spent on cases, because the system acquired enough knowledge to make suggestions and they are directly approved by the tester.

5.3 Classifications per Case

Many cases belong to more than one classification as illustrated Fig. 6. This result supports that multiple classification is reasonable. However, it is notable that some cases were not classified any categories, because the classification categories did not cover all possible categories in the web pages.

5.4 Growth of Mistakes

Obviously, the tester is expected to make more mistakes if more cases were analyzed. However, the growth of mistake was slow down as illustrated in Fig. 7. This supports that our system seems to be a good at assisting the tester to detect and correct his previous mistakes. Although mistakes cannot be avoided, it is useful if the system supports easy correction mechanism.

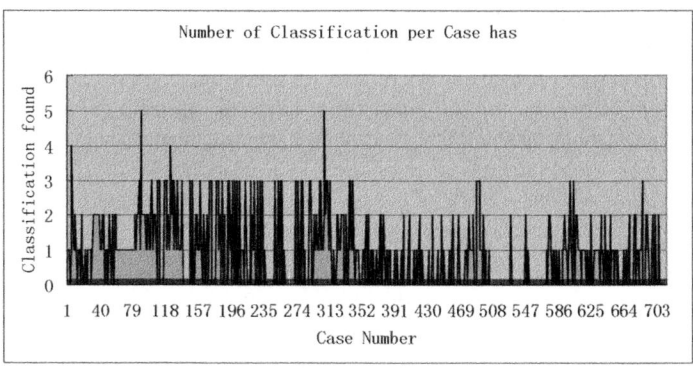

Fig. 6. Classifications per Case

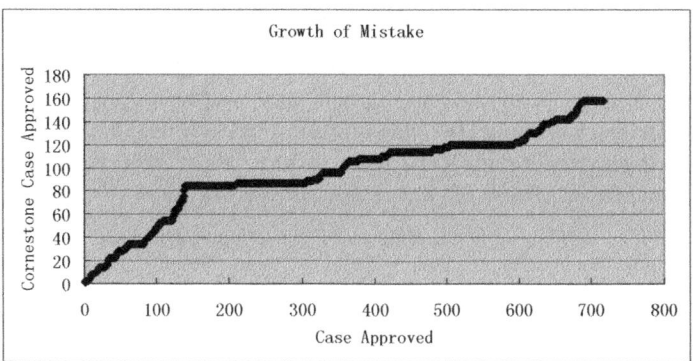

Fig. 7. Growth of Mistakes

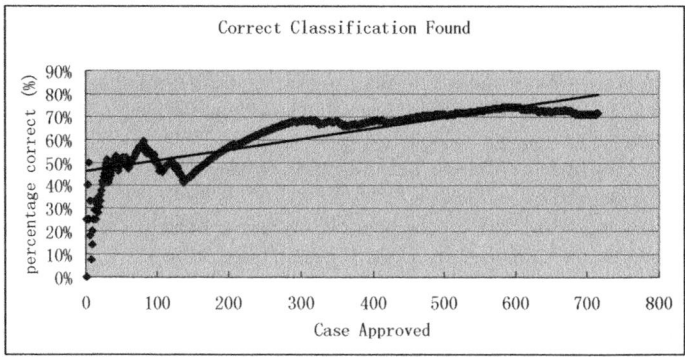

Fig. 8. Correct Classification Found

5.5   Correct Classifications

Fig. 8 illustrates how many percent of the conclusions for each case suggested by the system is approved as correct classification by the tester. At the beginning of the experiment, correct suggestion percentage is unstable, but it went steady after approximately 150 cases had been classified. This means that IWSCS requires a learning phase to produce more accurate results. In addition, correct classification seems relatively high percentage within short time, since the trend-line has reached about 80% correct classification toward at the end of experiment period.

6 Conclusions

Incremental classification of the webpage segments is essential for information extraction, as there are different types of webpages exist and they change over time. We proposed an incremental segments classification system using MCRDR to resolve this problem. We conducted an experiment with different webpage data set to evaluate whether our system successfully support easy rule acquisition. Our experimental results shows that our system is suitable to classify webpage segments from different web pages, and this system is also able to provide the reason why a conclusion was made. The system is very easy to use, because the time spent test result shows the tester only spent about 18 seconds to classify a case, and the whole classification time is only about 2 hours. In addition, the classification performance is promising because the system has reached about 80% classification success rate at the end of experiment. In addition, this system seems to be very useful to assist the experts to correct their previous mistakes while ensuring consistency of classification.

References

1. Yu, S., Cai, D., Wen, J.-R., Ma, W.-Y.: Improving Pseudo-Relevance Feedback in Web Information Retrieval Using Web Page Segmentation (2003)
2. Gregg, D.G., Walczak, S.: Adaptive Web Information Extraction. Commun. ACM. 49(5), 78–84 (2006)
3. Kushmerick, N., Thomas, B.: Adaptive Information Extraction: Core Technologies for Information Agents. In: Intelligent Information Agents. Agentlink Perspective, pp. 79–103 (2003)
4. Kang, J., Choi, J.: Recognising Informative Web Page Blocks Using Visual Segmentation for Efficient Information Extraction. Journal of Universal Computer Science 14(11), 1893–1910 (2008)
5. Turmo, J., Ageno, A., Catala, N.: Adaptive Information Extraction. ACM Comput. Surv. 38(2), 4 (2006)
6. Kushmerick, N., Weld, D.S., Doorenbos, R.: Wrapper Induction for Information Extraction. In: IJCAI 1997. Proceedings of the Fifteenth International Joint Conference on Artificial Intelligence, pp. 729–735 (1997)
7. Chidlovskii, B.: Information Extraction from Tree Documents by Learning Substree Delimiters. In: Workshop on Information Integration on the Web in 18th International Joint Conference on Artificial Intelligence (2003)
8. Debnath, S., Mitra, P., Giles, C.L.: Automatic Extraction of Informative Blocks from Webpages. In: 2005 ACM Symposium on Applied Computing, pp. 1722–1726. ACM Press, New York (2005)

9. Gupta, S., Kaiser, G., Neistadt, D., Grimm, P.: Dom-Based Content Extraction of Html Documents. In: International World Wide Web Conference, pp. 207–214. ACM Press, New York (2003)
10. Lin, S.-H., Ho, J.-M.: Discovering Informative Content Blocks from Web Documents. In: SIGKDD 2002, Edmonton, Albert, Canada, (2002)
11. Pasternack, J., Roth, D.: Extracting Article Text from the Web with Maximum Subsequence Segmentation. In: Proceedings of the 18th International Conference on World Wide Web, pp. 971–980. ACM, Madrid (2009)
12. Gottron, T.: Combining Content Extraction Heuristics: The <I>Combine</I> System. In: Proceedings of the 10th International Conference on Information Integration and Web-based Applications & Services, pp. 591–595. ACM, Linz (2008)
13. Song, R., Liu, H., Wen, J.-R., Ma, W.-Y.: Learning Block Importance Models for Web Pages. In: 13th International Conference on World Wide Web, pp. 203–211. ACM Press, New York (2004)
14. Song, R., Liu, H., Wen, J.-R., Ma, W.-Y.: Learning Important Models for Web Page Blocks Based on Layout and Content Analysis. SIGKDD Explor. Newsl. 6(2), 14–23 (2004)
15. Bar-Yossef, Z., Rajagopalan, S.: Template Detection Via Data Mining and Its Applications. In: WWW 2002, Honolulu, Hawaii, USA, (2002)
16. Chakrabarti, D., Kumar, R., Punera, K.: Page-Level Template Detection Via Isotonic Smoothing. In: Proceedings of the 16th international conference on World Wide Web, pp. 61–70. ACM, Banff (2007)
17. Vieira, K., da Costa Carvalho, A., Berlt, K., de Moura, E., da Silva, A., Freire, J.: On Finding Templates on Web Collections. World Wide Web 12(2), 171–211 (2009)
18. Wang, Y., Fang, B., Cheng, X., Guo, L., Xu, H.: Incremental Web Page Template Detection. In: Proceeding of the 17th international conference on World Wide Web, pp. 1247–1248. ACM, Beijing (2008)
19. Compton, P., Edwards, G., Kang, B., Lazarus, L., Malor, R., Menzies, T., Preston, P., Srinivasan, A., Sammut, C.: Ripple Down Rules: Possibilities and Limitations. In: 6th Bannf AAAI Knowledge Acquisition for Knowledge Based Systems Workshop, Banff, Canada, pp. 6-1–6-20 (1991)
20. Compton, P., Edwards, G., Kang, B., Lazarus, L., Malor, R., Preston, P., Srinivasan, A.: Ripple Down Rules: Turning Knowledge Acquisition into Knowledge Maintenance. Artificial Intelligence in Medicine 4(6), 463–475 (1992)
21. Compton, P., Jansen, R.: A Philosophical Basis for Knowledge Acquisition. Knowledge Acquisition 2(3), 241–258 (1990)
22. Compton, P., Kang, B., Preston, P., Mulholland, M.: Knowledge Acquisition without Analysis. In: Aussenac, N., Boy, G.A., Ganascia, J.-G., Kodratoff, Y., Linster, M., Gaines, B.R. (eds.) EKAW 1993. LNCS, vol. 723, pp. 277–299. Springer, Heidelberg (1993)
23. Kang, B.H., Gambetta, W., Compton, P.: Verification and Validation with Ripple-Down Rules. International Journal of Human-Computer Studies 44(2), 257–269 (1996)
24. Kang, B., Compton, P., Preston, P.: Multiple Classification Ripple Down Rules: Evaluation and Possibilities. In: 9th AAAI-Sponsored Banff Knowledge Acquisition for Knowledge-Based Systems Workshop, Banff, Canada, University of Calgary (1995)
25. Park, S.S., Kim, Y.S., Kang, B.H.: Web Document Classification: Managing Context Change. In: IADIS International Conference WWW/Internet 2004, Madrid, Spain, pp. 143–151 (2004)

Multi Agent System Based Path Optimization Service for Mobile Robot*

Huyn Kim and TaeChoong Chung

Department of Computer Engineering, School of Electronics and Information,
Kyunghee University,
South Korea
{Kimhyun,tcchung}@khu.ac.kr

Abstract. If a person drives a optimization route recommended by his navigation, considering the person has specific driving habits and propensity and there are many circumstances changes, it is said that the route recommended by a navigation is not optimized.

The prey pursuit problem has being put to use in multi-agents researches with the food chain system using multi agents in the virtual grid space. In this paper, we suggest the limitless space just like reality and the new algorithm to explain reality far enough than the existing grid space.

Keywords: multi agent, prey pursuit problem, personalization, optimized path, dynamic environment.

1 Introduction

In this paper, we propose the route recommendation system which is a part of personalizing information method.

Personalizing information service, providing the optimization information to users, is the core technology of ubiquitous, and it is required to get profiles based on individual Characteristics. There are many generative methods of personal profiles, such as the method of data retrieval accumulating user's activity data(migratory routes, movements, manipulations), and the method of recommendation utilizing data of existing users who have similar propensities. Each of all drivers has specific characteristics, such as a person who insists on driving in first lane or right turn, and a person who misses the recommended route with low concentration on his navigation.

It's not an useful way for users to get the average shortest route that agents analyze routes based on existing services from navigation, and also it doesn't consider environment variables concerning solutions. In the reality, they are environment variables to decide an optimization route that are frequent changes or driving environments, and specific personal driving habits.

---

* This research was supported by Basic Science Research Program though the National Research Foundation of korea(NRF) funded by the Ministry of Education, Science and Technology(grant number)"2010-0012609.

T.-h. Kim et al. (Eds.): UNESST 2010, CCIS 124, pp. 88–94, 2010.

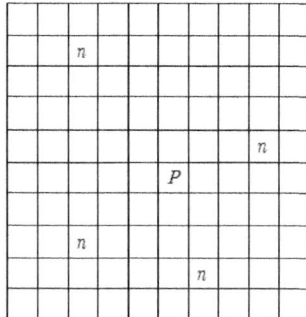

Fig. 1. Prey pursuit problem

Currently it's possible both-way data transmission and reception by the generation of communication technology and computer high technology, in this paper, we suggest the heuristic approach for the providing system of personal optimization route with considering a variety of environment variables. Let's set the dynamic environment information is n's agents and the prey(target, result), that agents seek, is P. And we propose the heuristic approach based on experiments that n is track down and capture P.[1,2,3,7,8]

It starts from the researches about multi-agents developed for satisfying user's needs and solving their problems. Therefore multi-agent system cooperated agents is suggested to find solutions for complicated problems which can't be solved by a single agent. M. Benda proposed the prey pursuit problem to express complicate reality as a typical experiment model of the efficient multi-agent system, and it is a research about capture 1 target by 4 independent agents in the limited grid space.[2]

The basic experiments environment of the prey pursuit problem is that there are 4 agents and 1 target and agents capture the target through cooperation between them.[3] The prey is a target what agents reach, and it's the goal of multi-agent research that each agents reach the target efficiently through the lowest cost. But previous experiment environment is restricted by a space of **n*n** leading a lack of reality and is solved the problems by only capture prey of agents.

In this paper, we suggest a new experiment environment, the circular grid space, trying to express the reality similarly. Also we express relation of agents and agents, prey and agents to the direction vector so that we make a new heuristic approach concerning distance, location and directivity.

2 Background

2.1 Grid Space of Circular Type That Considers the Actuality World

The experiment environment of general prey pursuit problem is restricted space that all sides are blocked, and when prey was driven to one direction, imperfection capture can happen. Even if strategy to capture effectively was developed, restricted space and imperfection capture were still lacked actuality and efficiency[4,5,6,7].

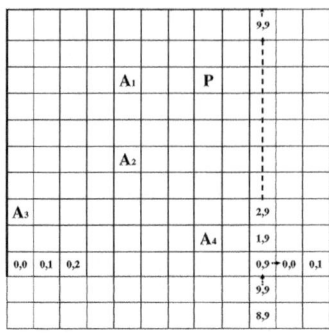

Fig. 2. Grid Space of Circular Type

For this reason, we proposed continuous grid space of circular type that reflects the actuality to differ with general experiment environment, show Figure.1. It is work from infinite space that agent captures prey in the actuality world. But, in case of transport speed of prey is same with agent from infinite space, if agents have gathered to one direction and prey runs away only to one direction, capture is impossible. We consider problems that can appear from these infinite space, made continuous grid space of circular type. That is, from grid space between (0,0) and (0,9), we make (0,9) that right is blocked by circular state and do (0,9) and (0,0) adjoin.

For example, top, bottom, right and left of (3,3) are (2,3), (4,3), (3,2) and (3,4) respectively. but top, bottom, right and left of (0,0) become (9,0), (1,0), (0,9) and (0,1). Therefore, in case of transport speed of prey is same with agent, capture is possible because it is multi agent system. Also, we wish to give prey ability that can get away from agent and prove efficiency of new capture strategy.

2.2 Capture Strategy of Prey Using Direction Vector

When prey moves to agent's opposite direction in infinite space, capture is impossible. As grid space of circular type is endless circular environment similar to infinite space, it is hard to capture by general strategy. Therefore, we suggest new strategy that express distance relation between prey and agent by direction vector.

Agent confirms position of other agent and prey, and moves to the capture direction. Prey calculates distance relation with agent to get away from agent and move from all agents to the farthest space.

If transfer speed of prey is same with agent and prey moves faster than agents, we may know that capture is fairly difficult.

Agent need strategy that achieve capture effectively and prey need strategy that can have the ability that recognize neighborhood state space and get away from agent. We introduced direction vector to make these strategies. The strategy is made by vector that reflects distance with agents and prey, distance relation between agents.

A. Escape direction vector of prey from agents

Prey(P) moves to opposite direction of agents to get away from agent(A_i), as distance between agents and prey is near, transfer direction vector of prey grows. Prey gets away from agents using resultant vector of Eq.1.

$$\overrightarrow{PE} = \overrightarrow{A_1E} + \overrightarrow{A_2E} + \overrightarrow{A_3E} + \overrightarrow{A_4E} \tag{1}$$
$$= \sum_i \overrightarrow{A_iE}$$
$$\Rightarrow \left| \overrightarrow{A_iE} \right| = \frac{1}{(Px - A_ix)^2 + (Py - A_iy)^2}$$

B. Transfer direction vector of agents to capture prey

The direction vector($\overrightarrow{A_iP}$) that agent(A_i) moves to prey(P) reflects distance with prey and agent. The size of direction vector($\overrightarrow{A_iP}$) between each agent and prey is inversely proportional to the distance between prey and each agent. But, the problem of collision between agent happens at transport process of agents. We made vector function that consider distance relation between agent and agents to solve this problem with (Eq.2). This is vector that grow to opposite direction as is near with other agents. The repulsion vector($\overrightarrow{RA_i}$) value of agent(A_i) is expressed to total sum of direction vector between each agent.

$$\overrightarrow{RA}_i = \sum_{j \ne i} \overrightarrow{A_jA_i}$$
$$\Rightarrow \left| \overrightarrow{A_jA_i} \right| = \frac{1}{(A_jx - A_ix)^2 + (A_jy - A_iy)^2} \tag{2}$$

Here, $\overrightarrow{A_jA_i}$ is direction vector between agent($\overrightarrow{A_j}$) and agent($\overrightarrow{A_i}$). This grows to opposite direction as distance between agents is short. The size of direction vector($\overrightarrow{A_jA_i}$) between agent and other agents is inversely proportional to the distance between agents. There is effect that this become more distant between agents. Therefore, we can solve the problem of collision between agents. Transfer direction vector($\overrightarrow{VA_i}$) of agent is an resultant vector of $\overrightarrow{A_iP}$ and $\overrightarrow{RA_i}$ with Eq.3.

$$\overrightarrow{VA}_i = \overrightarrow{A_iP} + \overrightarrow{RA}_i \tag{3}$$

when we produced transfer direction vector($\overrightarrow{VA_i}$) of agent, applied weighted value to $\overrightarrow{A_iP}$ and $\overrightarrow{RA_i}$ with Eq.4. We decide that it is suitable that agents move to a direction according to weighted value(α, β). ($\alpha > \beta$, because it is important more than prevention of collision between agents that go toward prey)

$$\overrightarrow{VA_i} = \alpha \cdot \overrightarrow{A_iP} + \beta \cdot \overrightarrow{RA_i} \tag{4}$$

Prey and agents may not move. It is a selection method that is in place. Agents need not to move if transfer direction is worse than current position. This problem can be solved using $\overrightarrow{VA_i}$ value. Agents move to next position if conflict happens.

Figure.4 is transfer strategy using direction vector and Figure.3 is prey pursuit problem algorithm that uses direction vector.

3 Estimation

Usually, the performance evaluation is based on success rate of capture and the number of each agent's state transition in prey pursuit problem.

In this paper, we wish to capture 100% and collision escaping strategy between agents by standard of estimation through presenting grid space of circular type newly. Also, this experiment environment removes element that is imperfection capture considering actuality, and initial position of prey and agents are given randomly, and we did perfection capture of prey on end condition.

Examining experiment result of Table.1, we could prove the efficiency of algorithm that considers direction vector by weighted values(α, β) of prey and agents.

```
/* Initialization phase */
Set an initial position for prey and 4 agents position.
/* Main algorithm */
Loop
        1. Initialize weighted values α and β for agents
    α : agent to prey , β : agent to other agent
        2. Prey applies the prey escape vector PE using
(Eq.1) to choose position to escape from each agents.
        3. Agents(A_i) applies the vector RA_i using (Eq.2) to
prevent conflict with each agents.
4.Applies weighted value α and β to (Eq.3), and Agents(A_i)
applies the real moving vector VA_i using (Eq.4) to move the
position to capture prey
```

Fig. 3. Prey Pursuit Problem Algorithm

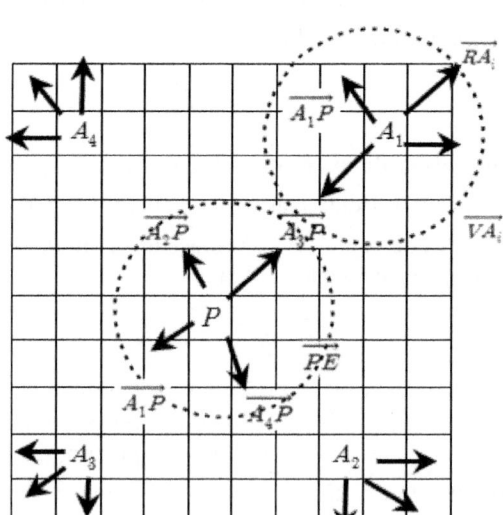

Fig. 4. Transfer strategy using direction vector

We could see various results by size of grid space. When α value is more than 4 from 30×30 grid space and more than 0.7, 0.1 from Table 1, effective state transition and 100% capture were seen (1000th) . We are find the **impotent α is impotent in this paper.**

Table 2 is a comparative table. That is make a comparative study of original method effect of agent control strategy and reinforcement learning strategy in the new environment.[5,6,7,8,9,10]

Table 1. The result of prey pursuit problem on the weighted value

(α)	(β)	30×30		50×50		100×100	
		Capture probability	State transition	Capture probability	State transition	Capture probability	State transition
0.1	0.1	3%	107	1%	230	0.2%	872
0.2	0.1	42%	98	19%	251	8%	864
0.3	0.1	55%	91	26%	223	11%	820
0.4	0.1	78%	79	32%	210	23%	795
0.5	0.1	84%	67	54%	182	31%	757
0.6	0.1	92%	69	62%	171	42%	693
0.7	0.1	100%	63	75%	144	50%	610
0.8	0.1	100%	64	81%	130	62%	625
0.9	0.1	100%	61	92%	128	69%	612
1	0.1	100%	62	100%	111	75%	602

Table 2. Applied Original strategy in the new environment

Grid Space of Circular Type	50×50	
effect of agent control strategy	*Capture probability*	6.2%
	State transition	56.4%
reinforcement learning strategy	*Capture probability*	34%
	State transition	24.1%

4   Conclusion and Future Work

Now, various experiments on multi agent system are carried out. The prey pursuit problem is using much within this various experiments. The reason is that prey pursuit problem was expressed most similarly with the actuality world. However, we can know that an experiment that is achieved in limited grid space differs much with the actuality world. The actuality world is environment of infinity space. We need to achieve more researches through experiment environment that can express the so complex and various actuality world. The grid space of circular type that is proposed in this paper is continuous space that express the actuality world similarly.

We can prove prevention of collision between agents and efficient capture through heuristic using direction vector in this new experiment environment. Also, through capture strategy that uses proposed direction vector, we can verify the efficiency in random arrangement state.

But, because probability of prey capture is low in specific situation(that initial position is assigned to one direction), we more research that can solve this. And we will need more research about agent system that can be applied to new environment.

References

1. Kim, S., Kim, B., Yoon, B.: Multi-agent Coordination Strategy using Reinforcement Learning. In: The Proceedings of the 22nd KIPS Fall Conference, vol. 7-2, pp. 285–288 (2000)
2. Stone, P., Veloso, M.: Multiagent System : A Survey from a Machine Learning, Technical Report CMU-CS-97-193, The University of Carnegie Mellon (December 1997)
3. Haynes, T., Sen, S.: Evolving behavioral strategies in predators and prey. In: Weiband, G., Sen, S. (eds.) Adaptation and Learning in Muiltiagent Systems. Springer, Berlin (1996)
4. Sen, S., Sekaran, M., Hale, J.: Learning to coordinate without sharing information. In: National Conference on Artificial Intelligence, pp. 426–431 (July 1994)
5. Stephens, L.M., Merx, M.B.: The effect og agent control strategy on the performance of a DAI pursuit problem. In: Proceeding of the 1990 Distributed AI Workshop (October 1990)
6. de Jong, E.: Multi-Agent Coordination by Communication of Evaluation. In: Boman, M., Van de Velde, W. (eds.) MAAMAW 1997. LNCS, vol. 1237. Springer, Heidelberg (1997)
7. Lee, H., Kim, B.: Multiagent Control Strategy using Reinforcement Learning. The KIPS Transactions 10-B 3. 2003.6
8. Levy, R., Rosenschein, J.S.: A game thoretic approach to the pursuit problem. In: Working Papers of the 11th International Workshop on Distributed Atrificial Intelligence (February 1992)
9. Cammarata, S., McArthur, D., Steeb, R.: Strategies of Cooperation in Distributed Problem Solving. In: Proceedings of Eighth International Joint Conference on Artificial Intelligence, Karlsruhe West Germany (August 1993)
10. Stephens, L.M., Merx, M.B.: The effect of agent control strategy on the performance of a DAI pursuit problem. In: Proceeding of the 1990 Distributed AI Workshop (October 1990)

In-depth Evaluation of Content-Based Phishing Detection to Clarify Its Strengths and Limitations

Koichiro Komiyama[1], Toshinori Seko[1], Yusuke Ichinose[1], Kei Kato[2],
Kohei Kawano[2], and Hiroshi Yoshiura[2]

[1] JPCERT Coordination Center,
3-17 Kandanishiki-chou, Chiyoda-ku, Tokyo, Japan
`koichiro.komiyama@jpcert.or.jp`
[2] Graduate school of Electro-Communications, University of Electro-Communications,
1-5-1 Chofugaoka, Chofu, Tokyo, 182-8585 Japan
`yoshiura@hc.uec.ac.jp`

Abstract. Zhang et al. proposed a method for content-based phishing detection (CBD) and reported its high performance in detecting phishing sites written in English. However, the evaluations of the CBD method performed by Zhang et al. and others were small-scale and simply measured the detection and error rates, i.e, they did not analyze the causes of the detection errors. Moreover, the effectiveness of the CBD method with non-English sites, such as Japanese and Chinese language sites, has never been tested. This paper reports our in-depth evaluation and analysis of the CBD method using 843 actual phishing sites (including 475 English and 368 Japanese sites), and explains both the strengths of the CBD method and its limitations. Our work provides a base for using the CBD method in the real world.

Keywords: Phishing attack, Network security, web.

1 Introduction

Phishing is a fraudulent activity in which the perpetrator creates a website that mimics a legitimate website, such as that of a financial institution, in an effort to obtain the personal information of people who believe they are accessing the legitimate site. It has become prevalent in the U.S., and is now increasingly common in other countries such as Japan.

In contrast to most methods of phishing detection [1,2,3], which are based on blacklists and whitelists of websites, the content-based phishing detection (CBD) method developed by Zhang et al. [4] extracts keywords from a suspect website, uses them in an Internet search to identify the original legitimate site, and compares the suspect site with the original site. It uses neither whitelists nor blacklists, eliminating the need to maintain such lists. The experimental evaluation performed by Zhang et al. [4] showed that the CBD method has a 95% accuracy rate in detecting phishing sites. There are, however, some issues regarding its effectiveness:

T.-h. Kim et al. (Eds.): UNESST 2010, CCIS 124, pp. 95–106, 2010.

- The evaluations performed by Zhang et al. and others [5] used only 100–200 Websites. They simply measured the detection and error rates—they did not analyze the causes of the detection errors.
- The CBD method was applied only to websites written in English—its effectiveness with non-English sites, such as Japanese and Chinese sites, was not tested.
- The algorithm used may not be effective for websites with little text.
- The false positive rate is high—it often judges legitimate sites as phishing sites.

We addressed the first and second issues using 475 English and 368 Japanese phishing sites found in the wild. All these sites were taken from JPCERT/CC's phishing data repository that contains files from live phishing sites. Our findings also shed light on the third and fourth issues.

Section 2 of this paper surveys previous methods for detecting phishing. It also describes the basic CBD algorithm, evaluations previously performed, and previous methods to improve the basic CBD method. Section 3 describes our implementation of CBD and a preliminary evaluation using it. Section 4 describes CBD improvements we made. Section 5 describes our main findings that demonstrate the effectiveness of CBD to both English and Japanese sites, while also showing its limitations. Section 6 concludes the paper.

2 Related Work

2.1 Overview

The most commonly used phishing detection methods use a blacklist of known phishing sites. These methods do not cause false positives as long as the list is correct. However, phishing sites are not recognized until they are added to the list, and phishing sites have an average lifetime of only 3.1 days [6]. Blacklist-based methods thus have an inadequate detection rate (i.e., true positive rate). Moreover, the list requires regular maintenance. The performance of the blacklist-based methods can be improved by using complementary heuristics, as exemplified by anti-phishing toolbars such as SpoofGuard [1] and Netcraft [2].

Whitelist-based methods, in contrast, use a list of sites that are known to be legitimate. These methods have a 100% true positive rate as long as the list is correct, but the false positive rate is high because all legitimate sites cannot be included in the list. Moreover, the whitelist-based methods also require the continuous maintenance of the list. The method developed by Cao et al. [3] automatically learns a whitelist for each user using a Bayesian classifier so that it contains the sites regularly logged in by the user. A potential problem with this method is that the listed sites can change over time (e.g., their IP address might change), leading to false positives.

A third type of method uses heuristics to improve performance. These heuristics are based on observations such as that phishing sites are likely to have recently registered domain names and to use IP-based URLs. Such methods typically identify heuristics and tune them using learning with training samples. For example, logistic regression [7], a decision tree [8], and a support vector machine [9] have been used for the learning method. One problem with heuristics methods is that they must continuously learn new heuristics to keep up with new types of phishing sites. They do this by continuously collecting new website samples. Another problem is that phishers can circumvent such methods once these heuristics are known. For example, the heuristic that phishing sites tend to use recently registered domains can be circumvented by renting a cheap domain, holding it for a sufficiently long time, and then using it for phishing.

The content-based detection (CBD) method developed by Zhang et al. [4] assumes that there is text-level similarity between a phishing site and the corresponding legitimate site. It uses neither blacklists nor whitelists and does not need training. It is difficult to circumvent because users will be suspicious if the phishing site is not similar to the legitimate site. Since it relies on a very simple and general assumption, i.e., there is similarity between the phishing and legitimate sites, it can be used in combination with other methods. Although it has some obvious strength, the effectiveness of the CBD method has not been evaluated in depth. The evaluation reported here aims to overcome this deficiency.

Methods similar to CBD make use of visual similarity between phishing and legitimate sites [10, 11]. Another type of phishing detection method is identity-based; i.e., such methods estimate the identity (i.e., brand name) that the suspect site falsely uses [12, 13]. One such method [13] searches the Internet using the set of two keywords, the domain name of the targeted brand and the domain name of the suspect site. If no site is found, i.e., the targeted brand and the suspect site are not related, the method judges the suspect site to be phishing.

2.2 Content-Based Detection Method

Algorithm. The CBD algorithm has three steps (see Fig. 1)
Step 1: Extract N keywords from a suspect website using a standard method (e.g., TF-IDF).
Step 2: Search the Internet using the same N keywords. The original legitimate website is assumed to be included in the top M results returned.
Step 3: If the suspect site matches one of the top M retrievals, it is judged legitimate; otherwise, it is judged phishing. They are considered matching if their domains are the same.

Previous evaluation. Zhang et al. used 100 legitimate sites to estimate the true positive rate of detection and 100 phishing sites to estimate the false positive rate [4]. All the sample sites were written in English. Five keywords (N) were extracted in Step 1, and M was set to 30 in Step 2.Their evaluation showed that CBD method had a high true positive detection rate as well as a high false positive detection rate of 30%.

2.3 Problems with Content-Based Methods

As mentioned in the introduction, there are some issues with content-based methods.

- The evaluation by Zhang et al. used 100 phishing and 100 legitimate sites. Those by Nakayama [5] used 172 phishing and 172 legitimate sites. These evaluations simply measured the detection and false positive rates; they did not analyze the causes of the detection errors.

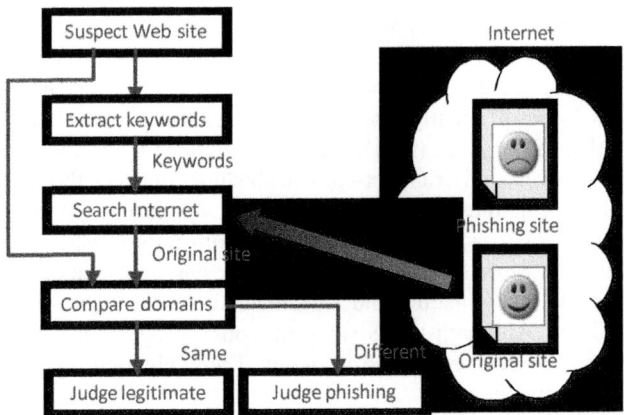

Fig. 1. Algorithm of content-based method

- Content-based methods have been applied only to Websites written in English; their effectiveness for non-English sites, such as Japanese and Chinese sites, has not been evaluated.
- The algorithm may not be effective for Websites that have little text.
- Despite the improvements described in Section 2.2, they still have high false positive rates.

We specifically addressed the first and second issues. We also shed some light on the third and fourth issues by analyzing why some legitimate sites were not retrieved in the detection process.

3   Preliminary Evaluation

3.1   Implementation

We implemented the CBD method for both English and Japanese Websites. The system implemented for English sites was the same as that described by Zhang et al. except for the use of Yahoo API instead of Google API and some details that they did not address: extraction of text content from HTML files and morphological analysis of the text. Our system extracted the text content by using regular expressions and replaced HTML tags with spaces. The system implemented for Japanese sites was the same except that it used MeCab [14] for the morphological analysis. We also implemented a dispatcher that infers the language used in the target Website and passes the site data to either the English or Japanese system accordingly. Lingua:: Language Guesser [15] was used to infer the language. We used 7 sleds to execute our system, leading to average one second of judge time on a personal computer with 2.4GHz dual CPUs and a 4.0GB main memory.

3.2   Procedure

Among the four modes of Zhang's evaluations mentioned in Section 2.2, Basic TF-IDF evaluated the performance of CBD while other three modes evaluated effects of heuristics, such as ZMP. Because our purpose was to evaluate CBD, not evaluate heuristics, we used Basic TF-IDF mode.

We applied the system to 17 actual phishing sites written in English and to 10 actual Japanese phishing sites. Out of these 27 sites, our system correctly judged 24 as phishing, did not judge 2 because no potential original sites were retrieved, and misjudged one site as legitimate.

3.3 Misjudgment

The one phishing site misjudged as legitimate was itself retrieved and included in the top 30 retrievals. This is because it had existed for a long time and was ranked high by the search engine. This exemplifies a serious limitation of CBD: detection will likely fail if the phishing site has a long life span and is ranked high. This limitation can only be overcome by shutting down phishing sites before they become old and highly ranked.

3.4 Failure in Retrieving Legitimate Sites

The legitimate sites were identified (i.e., included in the top 30 retrievals) for 17 of the 24 sites that were correctly judged as phishing. Those for the remaining seven sites also judged as phishing were not identified because none of the retrieved sites matched the suspect site. The original site was not retrieved for the one phishing site that was misjudged Neither the original nor other irrelevant sites was retrieved for the two phishing sites that were not judged. In short, the legitimate sites were not correctly retrieved for ten sites.

These retrieval failures suggest a risk of false positives if the system is applied to legitimate sites. We therefore analyzed these retrieval failures and identified five causes. Because the causes overlapped, i.e., a retrieval failure could have more than one cause, the total is greater than ten.

HTML parsing (two websites). A failure in HTML parsing produced keywords that did not appear in the Web text. For example, "<font>F</font>orgot" was divided into two words, "F" and "orget," and "orget" was selected as a keyword. In another case, the Web content expression was not in accordance with HTML expression rules. For example, "<" and ">" were used in tag strings. These irregular expressions were not correctly parsed.

Morphological analysis of diacritical marks (one website). Tree-Tagger, the English morphological analyzer, cannot correctly analyze character strings that contain diacritical marks such as those used in "español" and "français." For example, "español" was divided into two words, "espa" and "ol."

Phishing sites containing little text (two websites). One phishing site contained only frame tags and linked to URLs. The other site contained mostly images and had little text. The system could not extract keywords from either site. A similar problem would occur with a page containing only a URL transition (used in old pages to transit to a new page).

Phishing sites containing no identifying words (three web sites). These sites were those of companies whose names were combinations of very common words, e.g., "Bank of America." Any single word (e.g., "Bank," and "America") in the site text was not unique and thus not a useful keyword for retrieving the original site.

Phishing sites different from the original (four web sites). Some phishing sites contained character strings that were similar to but different in code from strings in the legitimate sites. For example, one site used "YAH00!" (with zeros instead of "O's"). The three other sites used hosting services. Advertising words were added to their pages by the services, and these words were selected as the keywords. Such keywords are useless for retrieving the legitimate sites.

4 Improvements

We improved our system to overcome some of the limitations described in Section 3.4.

HTML parsing. We modified our parser so that it took into account the inline and block attributes of the HTML language and so that it could handle the irregular expressions that often appeared. We also implemented another parser using Lynx [16] rendering software. The text rendered by Lynx was used as the parsing result.

Morphological analysis of diacritical marks. We modified the morphological analyzer so that it removed words containing diacritical marks and replaced them with similar words, e.g., "español" was replaced with "espanol."

Phishing sites containing little text. The system was extended to recognize the patterns of frame-tag pages and to check the frame content pages instead of the tag pages. The problem with redirect pages was overcome by having the system check the destination pages. If the suspect page was neither a frame tag nor a redirect page and contained little text, the system used the words in the title of the suspect page as key words.

Table 1. Parsing HTML and treating diacritical marks

		Parsing HTML	
		Use regular expressions	Use Lynx
Treating diacritical marks	Do nothing	1	4
	Remove word	2	5
	Replace word	3	6

Our system had two alternative operation modes for HTML parsing (using regular expressions or Lynx) and three for treating diacritical marks (doing nothing, removing words containing diacritical marks, or replacing the words with similar words). There were thus six alternative operation modes, as shown in Table 1.

5 Evaluation

5.1 Procedure

We applied our improved system (described in Section 4) to 843 actual phishing sites (475 English and 368 Japanese). The operation mode was Basic TF-IDF because of the reason mentioned in Section 3.2. We use two metrics: the true positive rate and the original site retrieval rate, i.e., the number of times the original site was included in the top 30 retrievals against the total number of searches.

We used the second metric because failure in retrieving legitimate sites suggests that there would be false positives when checking legitimate sites.

5.2 True Positive Rates

- The true positive rate for the English phishing sites was 96.4%, i.e., 458 out of 475. The previously reported high performance of the CBD method in detecting English phishing sites was therefore confirmed by this larger scale evaluation.
- Seventeen English phishing sites were misjudged. One of these sites was included in the top 30 retrievals and was thus judged legitimate. No potential legitimate sites were retrieved for the other 15, so the system did not judge them.
- The true positive rate for the Japanese phishing sites was 99.7%, i.e., 367 out of 368. This shows that the CBD method also has high performance in detecting Japanese phishing sites.
- One Japanese phishing site was not judged because no potential legitimate sites were retrieved for this site. The granularity of disclosure control should not be the whole text but the words in the text. Thus, any word that could reveal private information should be detected.

5.3 Legitimate Site Retrieval Rate

We tested the performance of the six alternative operation modes (see Table 1) for parsing and treating diacritical marks.

Treating diacritical marks. As shown in Fig. 2, removing words contained diacritical marks was the best alternative, and replacement was worse than doing nothing.

HTML parsing. HTML parsing using Lynx was less effective than using regular expressions for retrieving the legitimate sites. This was because Lynx output strings that were not included in the text but were generated by Lynx in place of images and tags ([INLINE], [EMBED], [BUTTON], etc.). These strings were sometimes selected as keywords, leading to retrieval failure. Figure 3 shows the relation between the results of using regular expressions and using Lynx when removing words contained diacritical marks. Since the Lynx result did not completely overlap the regular expression result, the retrieval rate could be increased by also using Lynx (from 83.6 to 87.9%).

Effects of other techniques
– Frame-tag and transition pages
   Two of the 843 sites were frame-tag and transition sites. The legitimate sites were correctly retrieved by using the techniques for phishing sites containing little text described in Section 4.1.
– Title keywords
   Our system used the words in the suspect page title as keywords when the page included less than seven words. Seven pages met this condition. All of them mostly consisted of images. The legitimate sites were correctly retrieved for six of them while only one was retrieved when the title words were not used as keywords.

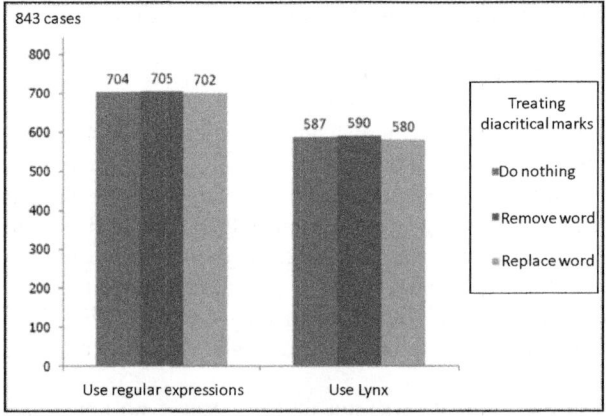

Fig. 2. Original site retrieval rate

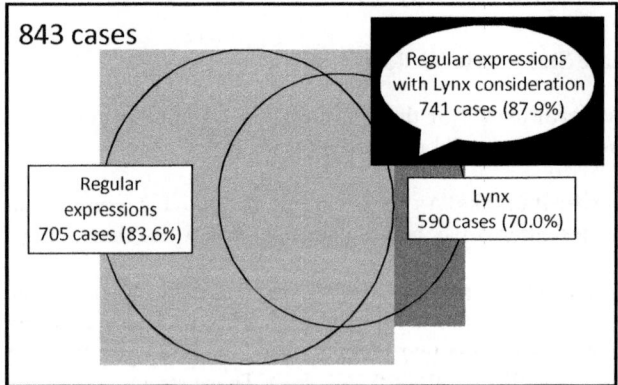

Fig. 3. Identifying original sites by using regular expressions and Lynx

5.4   Causes of Failure in Retrieving Original Sites

The original site was not identified for 102 of the 843 sites. Our analysis identified seven reasons for this.

Login page characteristics (37 websites). Some online banking login pages could not be retrieved because these pages used robots.txt and meta tags. For other login pages, words that are peculiar to login pages, i.e., examples of IDs and passwords, were selected as keywords. These keywords matched only the login pages, which were ranked low by the search engine, and did not match other pages in the same domain, which were ranked higher. Thus, using these keywords resulted in neither these login pages nor pages in the same domain being included in the top 30 retrievals. This use of inappropriate keywords could be prevented by using the domain-keyword method [5] described in Section 2.2; i.e., extract keywords from not only from the target page but also from the surrounding pages.

Phishing site containing no peculiar words (22 websites). As explained in the item 4 of Section 3.4, peculiar words were not selected as keywords for Websites of the companies such as "Bank of America" whose names consisted of only common words. Another example is "Alliance & Leicester" in Britain, where "Leicester" is a well-known address.

Phishing site with frequently changing text (four websites). Pages on online shopping sites, such as eBay and Amazon, have text parts that are changed frequently (e.g., those showing new goods). Some keywords that were selected from these parts had just appeared there and were not yet registered in the search engine's index, so using these keywords resulted in a retrieval failure. This problem could be solved by using the time-invariant-keyword method [5] described in Section 2.2.

Very minor website (one website). Appropriate keywords were extracted, but the legitimate site was not retrieved because it was a minor page and thus ranked low by the search engine.

Failure in Japanese morphological analysis (one website). Morphological analysis failed for a Japanese phishing site that contained colloquial expressions. Appropriate keywords were thus not extracted. Morphological analysis fails more frequently for Japanese than for English because words in a Japanese sentence are not divided by spaces—they are written continuously. Other languages such as Chinese have the same characteristic, so they would have the same problem with morphological analysis.

Phishing site different from legitimate site (67 websites)
- As described in the item 5 of Section 3.4, some phishing sites contained character strings that were similar to but different in code from strings in the legitimate sites. The legitimate sites were not retrieved when these character strings were selected as keywords.
- The legitimate site changed after it had been mimicked by the phishing site. The text in the phishing site was therefore different from that in the legitimate one. The

keywords extracted from the phishing site were thus useless in retrieving the legitimate site.
- Some phishing sites did not mimic a legitimate site; instead, they were created from scratch. For example, one phishing site had a page containing a bank's questionnaire and stated that the bank would send a reward to anyone who answered the questions. The bank site did not have a corresponding, legitimate page.

None of these three cases suggests that false positives will occur when the suspect site is a legitimate website. That is, similar-appearance strings appear only on phishing sites, an old page that has been mimicked will not be found on a legitimate site, and phishing sites created from scratch cannot be legitimate sites.

The first of the failure reasons (login pages characteristics) suggests that false positives will occur when the system is used for legitimate login pages, but this can be avoided by using the domain-keyword method. The third reason (frequently changing text) suggests that false positives will occur, but this can be avoided by using the time-invariant-keyword method. The sixth reason (a phishing site different from the legitimate site) does not suggest false positives.

Therefore, there are three essential problems with the CBD method in terms of false positives.

- The problem of judging a legitimate site with no identifying words as phishing (the second reason of failure) can be addressed by extending the keyword extraction algorithm to accept a word sequence as a keyword. Although possible, this is not a trivial task because there are many sub-tasks: determining the maximum length for such sequences, determining how to select keywords from a set of sequences having different lengths, determining how to avoid increasing the processing time, etc.
- The problem of handling minor legitimate sites can be addressed by increasing M, but the trade-off between this and misjudgment must be considered.
- The problem of handling colloquial expressions can be addressed by improving the morphological analysis, which is not a trivial task.

6 Conclusion

We have implemented and evaluated content-based phishing detection for Websites written in either English or Japanese. The large-scale evaluation clarified the strengths and limitations of the CBD method.

- The previously reported high performance of the CBD method in detecting English phishing sites was confirmed (96.4% detection rate).
- The CBD method was shown to also have high performance in detecting Japanese phishing sites (99.7% detection rate).
- The CBD method has trouble detecting phishing sites that are long lived and thus ranked high by search engines as they appear like legitimate sites in search results. A solution to this problem is to detect phishing sites quickly before the search engines rank them high. Automatic detection and quick takedown are thus critically important.
- The CBD method may produce false positives when it checks a legitimate Website containing no peculiar words or that is a very minor Website. It may also produce

false positives for legitimate Japanese sites that have colloquial expressions. This language-rooted problem would occur not only for Japanese but also for other languages that are more difficult to analyze morphologically than English, such as
- languages that are more difficult to analyze morphologically than English, such as Chinese.

We also suggested methods for selecting more appropriate keywords so as to reduce the false positive rate.

- Use of the Lynx rendering software with the HTML parsing method would improve the handling of irregular but frequent HTML expressions. Removing words with diacritical marks would reduce the number of inappropriate keywords. Use of this improved parsing would increase the retrieval rate of the original site to 87.9%.
- Use of frame tags and transition pages to check the frame content and the destination pages would increase the original site retrieval rate. With this method, two additional original sites were retrieved.

Our work provides bases for using the CBD method in the real world.

References

1. SpoofGuard, http://crypto.stanford.edu/SpoofGuard/
2. Netcraft, http://news.netcraft.com/
3. Cao, Y., Han, W., Le, Y.: Anti-phishing based on automated individual white-list. In: Proceedings of the 4th ACM workshop on Digital identity management, pp. 51–60 (2008)
4. Zhang, Y., Hong, J., Cranor, L.: acontent-based approach to detecting phishing websites. In: Proceedings of the 16th International Conference on World Wide Web (WWW 2007), pp. 639–648 (2007)
5. Nakayama, S., Echizen, I., Yoshiura, H.: Preventing False Positives in Content-Based Phishing Detection. In: Proceedings of 5th IEEE International Conference on Intelligent Information Hiding and Multimedia Signal Processing, pp. 48–51 (2009)
6. APWG :Phishing Activity Trends Report for the Month of (January 2008), http://www.antiphishing.org/reports/apwg_report_jan_2008.pdf
7. Garera, S., Provos, N., Chew, M., Rubin, A.: A framework for detection and measurement of phishing attacks. In: Proceedings of the 2007 ACM Workshop on Recurring Malcode, pp. 1–8 (2007)
8. Ludl, C., McAllister, S., Kirda, E., Kruegel, C.: On the effectiveness of techniques to detect phishing sites. In: Hämmerli, B.M., Sommer, R. (eds.) DIMVA 2007. LNCS, vol. 4579, pp. 20–39. Springer, Heidelberg (2007)
9. Ma, J., Saul, L., Savage, S., Voelker, G.: Beyond blacklists: learning to detect malicious web sites from suspicious URLs. In: Proceedings of the 15th ACM SIGKDD International Conference on Knowledge Discovery and Data Mining, pp. 1245–1254 (2009)
10. Dhamija, R., Tygar, J.: The battle against phishing: Dynamic security skins. In: Proceedings of the 2005 Symposium on Usable Privacy and Security (SOUPS 2005), pp.77–88 (2005)
11. Liu, W., Deng, X., Huang, G., Fu, A.: An Antiphishing Strategy Based on Visual Similarity Assessment. IEEE Internet Computing 10(2), 58–65 (2006)
12. Pan, Y., Ding, X.: Anomaly based web phishing page detection. In: Proceedings of the 22nd Annual Computer Security Applications Conference (ACSAC 2006), pp. 381–392 (2006)

13. Xiang, G., Hong, J.: A hybrid phish detection approach by identity discovery and keywords retrieval. In: Proceedings of the 18th International Conference on World Wide Web, pp. 571–580 (2009)
14. MeCab : Yet Another Part-of-Speech and Morphological Analyzer, http://mecab.sourceforge.net/
15. Lynx for Win32 (by patakuti): Project Home Page, http://lynx-win32-pata.sourceforge.jp/
16. Lingua::LanguageGuesser, http://gensen.dl.itc.u-tokyo.ac.jp/LanguageGuesser/LanguageGuesser_ja.html

Tool for Collecting Spatial Data with Google Maps API

S. Choimeun[1], N. Phumejaya[1], S. Pomnakchim[1], and C. Chantrapornchai[2]

[1] Computer Program, Faculty of Science, Nakorn Pathom Rajabhat University, Thailand
[2] Department of Computing, Faculty of Science, Silpakorn University,
Nakorn Pathom, Thailand
ctana@su.ac.th

Abstract. In this paper, we develop tool for collecting spatial data based on Google Maps API. The tool is implemented using AJAX and XML technology. It helps marking the maps in various forms. Then, after the users define the regions in the maps, the associated data can be described and stored in the database. The data can be further analyzed and displayed in the GIS. The tool supports the KML and NMA files where the user specification can be export and the offline data in such a form can be imported to the system as well. We demonstrate a case of using the tool to collect the spatial data in agriculture area.

Keywords: Google Maps API, Spatial data, AJAX, XML, NMEA.

1 Introduction

The popularity in GIS applications leads to development in various GIS tools. The software helps manage geographical information in many ways such as collecting associated data for landmark in traveling and directions. Google maps become popular tools which provide maps as well as tools for user data. With its open technology, the users can share information, ideas, or develop their owns applications using Google maps API [3].

Also, there are others GIS technology. Though they are powerful, some of them are commercials which are still expensive. To develop applications based on them will be costly and complex.

Various applications are developed based on Google Maps such as the work by NECTEC [2]. This work proposed a way to estimate the travel time in Bangkok using Google Maps. The work by WLHP [9] presented a GIS application to display pollution. Hrvoje Podnar et.al. [1] visualize the students population using Google Maps. Shinji Kobayashi et.al. [6] use Google Maps to refer the patients to the nearest hospitals. Bruce A. Ralston [8] presents a tool to generate areas using KML for population survey in the United States.

In this work, we take advantage of the Google Maps API , including the online maps, and geographical coordinates. We develop the tools to record GIS data from various sources such as user inputs, and from KML as well as NMA formats. Then, the data is recorded in the database for further development in GIS applications.

T.-h. Kim et al. (Eds.): UNESST 2010, CCIS 124, pp. 107–113, 2010.
© Springer-Verlag Berlin Heidelberg 2010

2 Backgrounds

In this section, we briefly describe the necessary backgrounds in GIS technology as it is related to our work.

Geographical information systems are the systems which take advantages of spatial data and define the relationships to the interest issues. The information may be the home address, for example, which is mapped to the spatial data such as the latitude and longitude. Then the database further stores more information about the address.

The important part in developing the GIS applications is the data capture and storage. The data which includes the spatial coordinate and associative database needs to be provided in any valid means. The spatial data may be imported from interactive equipments or files. Then the coordinate is converted appropriately. Many applications are available to help import data such as ArcInfo (http://www.esri.com/software/arcgis/arcinfo/index.html), ArcView (http://www.esri.com/software/arcview/index.html), Mapinfo (http://www.mapinfo.com), ERDAS (http://www.erdas.com) etc. After that, the associated database is imported by any normal program. To store spatial information, it is common that the vector format is used. The storage may keep only points, lines, or areas [3].

Google Maps [5] is an open technology that provides maps. The user can use the web browser to look at the maps. Several convenient tools are built-in such as zooming in and out, marking, view satellite data, etc. While Google maps provide map information, Google Earth [4] is a software to view satellite data in high resolutions. It can save the data in KML file. The KML file is extended from XML which is used to describe the data[11-12]. The KML file can be used together with the Google as shown in Figure 1. Besides the KML file, NMEA 0183 is a standard for GPS data. It is the protocol used by GPS producers to communicate with other devices [13]. In this work, we also consider to import data from GPS device as well.

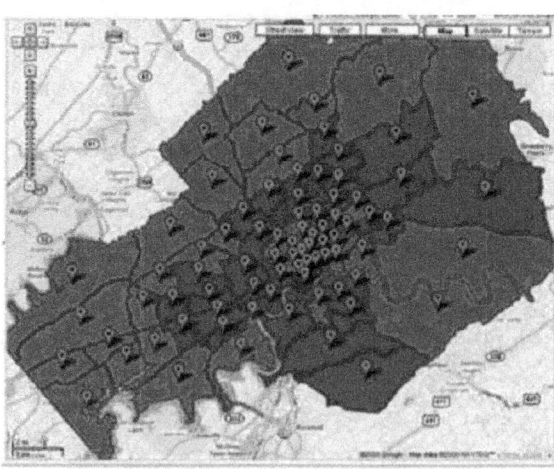

Fig. 1. KML used in Google Maps [8]

3 Tool Architecture

In the development tool, it contains 5 modules as in Figure 2.

1. User module: it is to communicate with the users by importing or exporting spatial data in NMA files or KML files, or by user input specification.
2. GPS module: it is used to store data from GPS devices and convert NMA files to XML files for display.
3. Converter module: it is to convert KML files to XML files for the display purpose.
4. Presentation module: it takes the spatial data in the database table and convert to XML for display. When converted to XML, we also tag whether it is a point, line or area.
5. Drawing model: it will take the XML files from other modules to overlay on Google Maps in various forms according to the coordinate specified in the database.

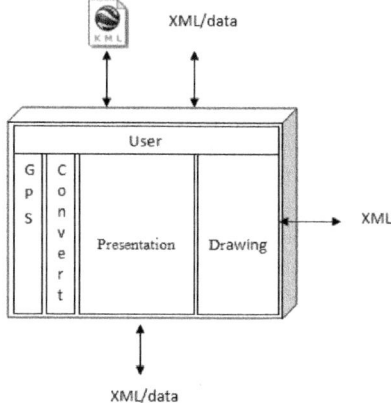

Fig. 2. Architecture of the tool

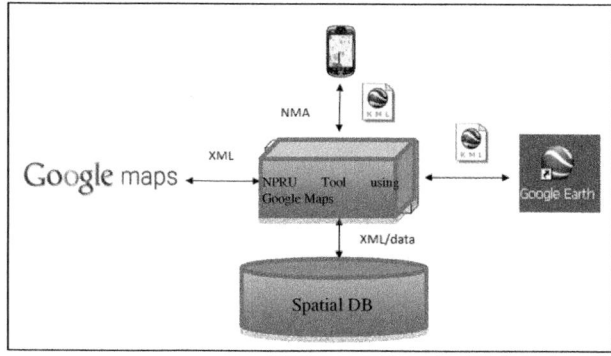

Fig. 3. Overview of the tool interaction

Figure 3 presents how the tool interacts to the other parts. It will invoke the online map from Google Maps and use XML to creates markup. It communicates with Google Earth using KML files. It also reads the data from to the GPS receivers via NMA files.

4 Results and Discussion

Our developed tool is called NPRU tool. We test the usability of the tool for each function as shown in Table 1. It is seen that the user can specify using points, lines and areas. These inputs support the functions specified in each column.

Table 1. Functionality of the tool

Function	Add	Delete	Update	Save	Import	Export	Display	Symbol	Attributes	Data
points	☑	☑	☑	☑	☑	☑	☑	☑	☑	☑
lines	☑	☑	☑	☑	☑	☑	☑		☑	☑
area	☑	☑	☑	☑	☑	☑	☑		☑	☑

The comparison of our tool and others are shown in Table 2. Column "Network connection" means the tools required network connection or not. Column "Satellite View" implies the tool can show satellite view. Column "Data Format" implies the data format that is supported by the tools. Column "GPS Support" implies the tool can read data from GPS or not. It is seen that our tool is capable about the same as Google Maps except that we are interested in the support of KML and data can store locally where it can be manipulated easily.

Table 2. Comparsion of the tools

Tool	Network Connection	Satellite View	Data Format	GPS support (NMA)
Google Maps	100%	Yes	RSS, data stored on google server	Mobile support, Yes
ArcGIS	Some	Plugin	.SHP,db,*KML	Yes
MapInfo	Some	Plugin	.SHP,db,*KML	Yes
Google Earth	Some	Yes	KML, KMZ	No
Point Asia	100%	Selective	Cannot record	Yes
NPRU	**100%**	**Yes**	**KML, data stored in database**	**Yes**

We use our tool to develop GIS for agriculture in Nakorn Pathom area. In the area, it is the province that contains 25 sub-district and 217 villages.

Figures 4-5 show the user interface where a user can overlay on the Google Maps. The user uses the provided drawing tools to create the overlays. The coordinates are extracted from the Google Maps and stored in the database. Figure 6 displays the coordinate displayed from the database.

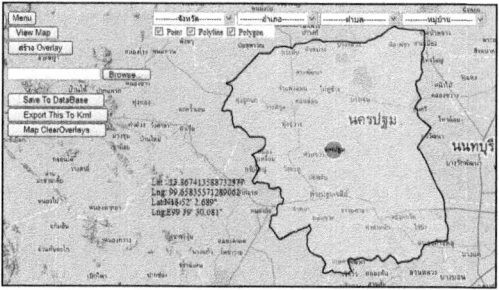

Fig. 4. Defining regions

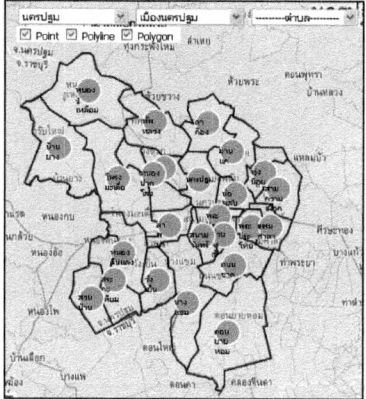

Fig. 5. Define sub-regions

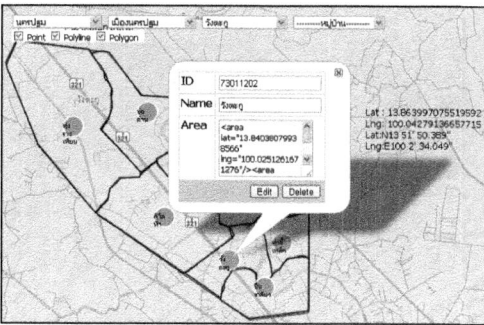

Fig. 6. Coordinate display

From the tool, the satellite view can be shown Figure 7. The user can create his own database to store their local data. In the application, we are interested in the agriculture product in the area. The production data are given in the database. Then, it can be linked and displayed in many ways. Figure 8 shows the production by regions. Figure 9 shows the production by types.

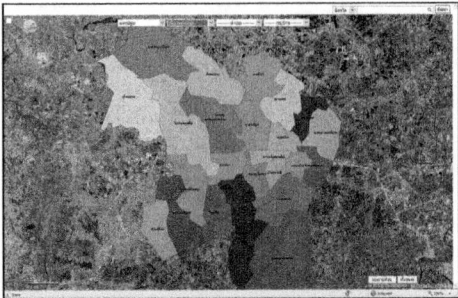

Fig. 7. Satellite view overlays

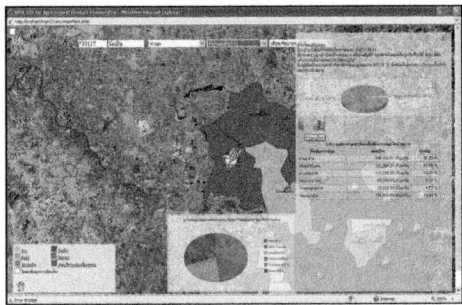

Fig. 8. Production by regions

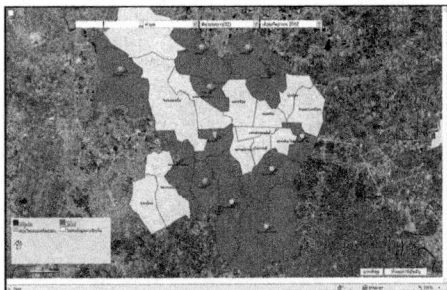

Fig. 9. Production by types

5   Conclusion

In this paper, we present a tool to help gather the GIS data. We take advantages of Google Maps so that we can define coordinates in various forms. Also, the spatial data can be gathered from user input, GPS receivers, or Google Earth. Thus, the tool can import the data from these sources using the KML or NMA format. We compare the functionality of the tools and demonstrate the usage of the tool to develop the agriculture application.   In the future, the tool will be revised accordingly: display geographical coordinates in many forms, communicate with the GPS device to get the coordinate online and exports the data for into local database for future uses.

Acknowledgments. The research is supported in part by NPRU research funding, and SURDI from Silpakorn University, Thailand. We also would like to thank National Agriculture Department, Thailand for the data.

References

1. Adam, H.P., Workman, G.R., Chan, J.: Geospatial visualization of student population using Google Maps. In: CSC: Northeastern Conference, pp. 175–181 (2009)
2. Bangkok University, Travel time estimation using Google Map and ITS in Bangkok, `http://wiki.nectec.or.th/bu/ITM532Students_2009/ApiruckButla Report`
3. Chang, K.J.: Introduction to Geographic Information Systems, pp. 2–3. McGraw-Hill, New York (2002)
4. Google Inc., Google Earth, Google Inc. (1998), `http://earth.google.com/download-earth.html`
5. Google Inc., Google Maps API Concepts, Google Inc(1998), `http://code.google.com/intl/th/apis/maps/`
6. Kobayashi, S., et al.: A Geographical Information System Using the Google Map API for Guidance to Referral Hospitals. Journal of Medical Systems, doi:DOI:10.1007/s10916-009-9335-0
7. Kott, B.: Green Business Operations (London) and Simon Ilyushchenko, Site Reliability Engineer (Mountain View), `http://google-latlong.blogspot.com/2009/07/ visualizing-greenhouse-gas-emissions.html`
8. Ralston, B.A., Streufert, J.A.: Efficient Generation of Area Thematic Maps in KML. In: Proceedings of the 16th ACM SIGSPATIAL International Conference on Advances in Geographic Information System, pp. 517–518 (2008)
9. West London Housing Partnership, EST, WLHP Measure Map, `http://wlhpmeasuremap.aeasolutions.co.uk/map/index`
10. `http://www.gisthai.org/about-gis/gis.html`
11. `http://earth.google.com/intl/th/userguide/v4/index.html#gett ing_to_knowdocumentation/javascript/v2/basics.html`
12. `http://earth.google.com/intl/th/userguide/v4/ug_kml.html`
13. `http://www.navy.mi.th/elecwww/magaz/magazine/no13/7.pdf`

Promotion Assistance Tool for Mobile Phone Users

P. Intraprasert, N. Jatikul, and C. Chantrapornchai

Department of Computing, Faculty of Science
Silpakorn University
Nakorn Pathom, Thailand 73000
ctana@su.ac.th

Abstract. In this paper, we propose an application tool to help analyze the usage of a mobile phone for a typical user. From the past usage, the tool can analyze the promotion that is suitable for the user which may save the total expense. The application consists of both client and server side. On the server side, the information for each promotion package for a phone operator is stored as well as the usage database for each client. The client side is a user interface for both phone operators and users to enter their information. The analysis engine are based on KNN, ANN, decision tree and Naïve Bayes models. For comparison, it is shown that KNN and decision outperforms the others.

Keywords: Mobile phone usage analysis, Phone promotion package, KNN, ANN, Decision tree, Naïve Bayes.

1 Introduction

Nowadays, mobile phones are commonly used for not only voice communications, but also others such as watching movies, listening to the music, surfing the Internet, SMS, etc. There exists several phone operators in the country. Each of them provides many promotion monthly packages for the phone user. Each user needs to decide whether the package is suitable for him/her.

Based on the information previously recorded, it is possible to analyze the usage. Then the cost of the monthly payment if the package were selected is presumed. In this work, we propose an application which helps the phone users as well as the phone operators to decide the right package. The application consists of the server side which stores usage and promotion database. The client side is just only the web applications for user interface. The analysis engine is based on three models: KNN, ANN and Naïve Bayes. From the three different models and the experiment data, it is shown that KNN and decision tree performs better than the others. The error in the prediction is 0.2%

Several phone operators propose the promotion package for their users. For example, [5,7] proposes a web application which suggest the package for the users. They consider the specific usage records and suggest the supplementary package only dealing SMS, MMS and EDGE/GPRS. They do not take all the types of usages due to their policy.

T.-h. Kim et al. (Eds.): UNESST 2010, CCIS 124, pp. 114–124, 2010.

Data mining technique is commonly used for knowledge management. [3] uses Naïve Bayes for the knowledge management in the restaurant and bakery business. In particular, the technique is used for information classification in the organization. In [4], ANN technique is used to analyze the risk factors in money saving for Thai people in rural area. The technique is able to extract factors that are important to the money saving behavior. In [1], data mining technique is used to predict the purchasing, inventory and selling. Association rules are applied for classification in this case.

This paper is organized as following. Section 2 presents some backgrounds on data mining, decision tree, ANN, KNN and Naïve Bayes. Section 3 applies the techniques to analyze the phone usage behavior. Section 4 presents the experimental results comparing the performance of these techniques. Section 5 presents the whole application. Section 6 concludes the paper.

2 Backgrounds

Data mining is the process that takes large amount of data and analyzes them to find hidden relations or patterns. It is applied in many areas including business, science, medical, etc. It is usually important when especially when building decision support systems.

Knowledge discovery is a way to features of the data. It takes several steps starting data selection, preprocessing, data transformation, data mining, and result analysis. In steps data transformation and data mining, the data is probably changed in to some form using algorithms and data mining techniques are applied. Many artificial intelligent techniques are important in data mining to look for some properties of the data.

A decision tree shows alternatives. At each node a decision needs to be made. For classification, the tree contains nodes which represents features. The leaf nodes represent the classification.

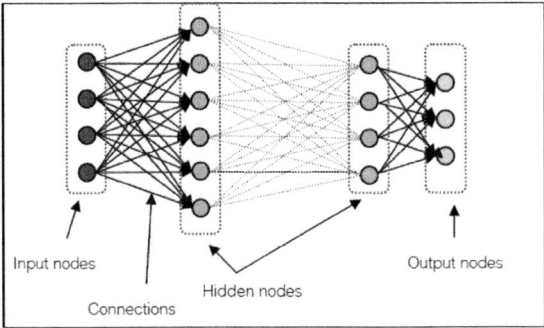

Fig. 1. Artificial Neural Network structure

From Figure 1, Artificial Neural Network (ANN) has three layers: input layer, hidden layers and output layer[6]. Input layer takes input to the network. The input is assumed to be preprocessed. Hidden layers connect the input layer to the output layer. There may be many hidden layers. The output layer computes the output of each node using the following function.

$$y_i = f(w_i^1 x_1 + w_i^2 x_2 + w_i^3 x_3 + \cdots + w_i^m x_m)$$
$$= f(\sum_j w_i^j x_j) \tag{1}$$

where x_{ij} is the input from other nodes and w_{ij} is the weight for each connection.

Learning for the ANN can be supervised or unsupervised. The network can be either feedforward or feedback network.

For Naïve Bayes, we base the prediction on the probability. We compute the probability of being in each class. Assume that each feature used to compute is independent. We pick the class that has the highest probability.

```
=== Model information ===

Filename:       J48_D52014.model
Scheme:         weka.classifiers.trees.J48 -C 0.25 -M 2
Relation:       whatever
Attributes:     4
                time
                network_destination
                unit
                type

=== Classifier model ===

J48 pruned tree
------------------

network_destination = AIS: TM (153.0)
network_destination = TRU: TM (18.0)
network_destination = DTC
|   time <= 10
|   |   unit <= 2.33: TM (19.0/3.0)
|   |   unit > 2.33: TS (3.0)
|   time > 10: TM (122.0/3.0)
network_destination = OTH: TM (7.0/1.0)
network_destination = GPS: GM (16.0)
network_destination = SMS: SM (6.0/3.0)
network_destination = HUT: TM (0.0)
network_destination = CAT: TM (0.0)
network_destination = DTA: TM (0.0)
network_destination = CP: TM (0.0)
network_destination = DM: TM (0.0)
network_destination = ACS: TM (0.0)
network_destination = DPC: TM (1.0)
network_destination = MMS: TM (0.0)
network_destination = DOW: TM (0.0)

Number of Leaves  :      17

Size of the tree :      20
```

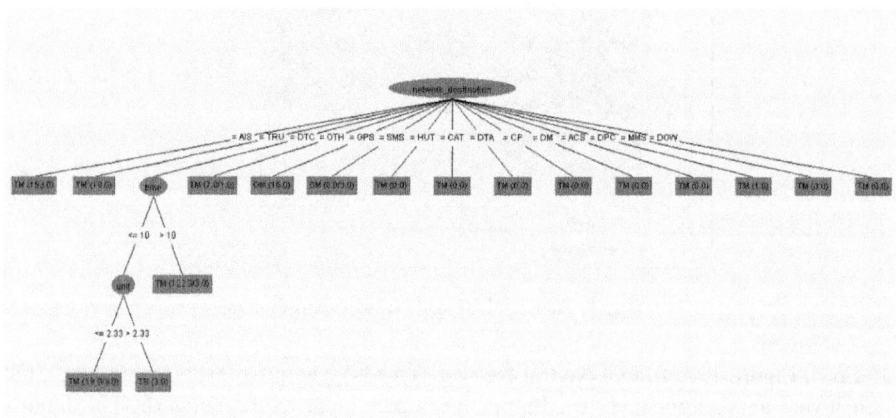

Fig. 2. Decision tree

$$P(a_1, a_2, \dots, a_n|v_j) \;=\; \prod_{i=1}^{n} P(a_i \mid v_j) \tag{2}$$

where Π is the production of $P(a_i|v_j)$ and a_i is the feature.

K-nearest neighbour (KNN) measures the closeness of the groups. It groups the data that are close together K items. The distance between items is measured using the Euclidian distance.

$$dist(x_i, x_j) = \sqrt{\sum_{k=1}^{n}(x_{i,k} - x_{j,k})^2} \tag{3}$$

where $dist(x_i,x_j)$ is the distance between and x_i, and x_j, n is the total samples, x_i, and k is the feature k of x_i sample. Then we pick the K nearest neighbour for each group.

3   Usage Modeling Samples

We take the sample data from users and their promotions. The model learns the behaviors of the users using such a promotion. We select user data from several phone operators. The following features are extracted: outgoing call time and network operator destination. Then types of usages in the supplement service are considered: SMS, MMS, downloading, voting, voice mail, special number calling, and automatic response. Then, we have implemented three models for the usage behavior of a user: decision tree, ANN, KNN and Naïve Bayes respectively.

Figures 2-5 shows the models and their characteristics obtained using the decision tree, Naïve Bayes, KNN, and ANN respectively.

```
=== Model information ===

Filename:      Bayes_D52014.model
Scheme:        weka.classifiers.bayes.NaiveBayes
Relation:      whatever
Attributes:    4
               time
               network_destination
               unit
               type

=== Classifier model ===

Naive Bayes Classifier

                         Class
Attribute                 TM       VM       TS       GP       SM       CP       SR       DM       GM       MM       VO
                        (0.88)   (0.01)   (0.02)    (0)    (0.01)    (0)    (0.01)    (0)    (0.05)    (0)      (0)
-------------------------------------------------------------------------------------------------------------------------
time
  mean                 15.1304  15.3333  10.483       0   18.619       0   18.619       0  16.9077       0        0
  std. dev.             4.3402   1.7885   2.9188  0.1825   3.2243  0.1825   3.2243  0.1825   3.3751  0.1825   0.1825
  weight sum              313        3        7       0        3       0        3       0       16       0        0
  precision            1.0952   1.0952   1.0952  1.0952   1.0952  1.0952   1.0952  1.0952   1.0952  1.0952   1.0952

network_destination
  AIS                   154.0      1.0      1.0     1.0      1.0     1.0      1.0     1.0      1.0     1.0      1.0
  TRU                    19.0      1.0      1.0     1.0      1.0     1.0      1.0     1.0      1.0     1.0      1.0
  DTC                   136.0      4.0      7.0     1.0      1.0     1.0      1.0     1.0      1.0     1.0      1.0
  OTH                     7.0      1.0      2.0     1.0      1.0     1.0      1.0     1.0      1.0     1.0      1.0
  GPS                     1.0      1.0      1.0     1.0      1.0     1.0      1.0     1.0     17.0     1.0      1.0
  SMS                     1.0      1.0      1.0     1.0      4.0     1.0      4.0     1.0      1.0     1.0      1.0
  HUT                     1.0      1.0      1.0     1.0      1.0     1.0      1.0     1.0      1.0     1.0      1.0
  CAT                     1.0      1.0      1.0     1.0      1.0     1.0      1.0     1.0      1.0     1.0      1.0
  DTA                     1.0      1.0      1.0     1.0      1.0     1.0      1.0     1.0      1.0     1.0      1.0
  CP                      1.0      1.0      1.0     1.0      1.0     1.0      1.0     1.0      1.0     1.0      1.0
  DM                      1.0      1.0      1.0     1.0      1.0     1.0      1.0     1.0      1.0     1.0      1.0
  ACS                     1.0      1.0      1.0     1.0      1.0     1.0      1.0     1.0      1.0     1.0      1.0
  DPC                     2.0      1.0      1.0     1.0      1.0     1.0      1.0     1.0      1.0     1.0      1.0
  MMS                     1.0      1.0      1.0     1.0      1.0     1.0      1.0     1.0      1.0     1.0      1.0
  DOW                     1.0      1.0      1.0     1.0      1.0     1.0      1.0     1.0      1.0     1.0      1.0
  [total]               328.0     18.0     22.0    15.0     18.0    15.0     18.0    15.0     31.0    15.0     15.0

unit
  mean                  1.887   0.9604   3.1555       0   0.9604       0   0.9604       0   0.5002       0        0
  std. dev.            2.0155   0.1601   1.9691  0.1601   0.1601  0.1601   0.1601  0.1601   0.3903  0.1601   0.1601
  weight sum              313        3        7       0        3       0        3       0       16       0        0
  precision            0.9604   0.9604   0.9604  0.9604   0.9604  0.9604   0.9604  0.9604   0.9604  0.9604   0.9604
```

Fig. 3. Naïve Bayes

```
=== Model information ===

Filename:      KNN10_D52014.model
Scheme:        weka.classifiers.lazy.IBk -K 10 -W 0 -A "weka.core.neighboursearch.LinearNNSearch
               -A \"weka.core.EuclideanDistance -R first-last\""
Relation:      whatever
Attributes:    4
               time
               network_destination
               unit
               type

=== Classifier model ===

IB1 instance-based classifier
using 10 nearest neighbour(s) for classification
```

Fig. 4. KNN

```
=== Model information ===

Filename:      Nerual_D52014.model
Scheme:        weka.classifiers.functions.MultilayerPerceptron -L 0.3 -M 0.2 -N 500 -V 0 -S 0 -E 20 -H a
Relation:      whatever
Attributes:    4
               time
               network_destination
               unit
               type

=== Classifier model ===

Sigmoid Node 0
    Inputs    Weights
    Threshold    -5.0146123681137205
    Node 11    -2.0004038927928005
    Node 12    4.425250788419373
    Node 13    1.8863874024145924
    Node 14    0.5387650625837604
    Node 15    2.945415846583079
    Node 16    0.5514386639764549
    Node 17    1.7792516823668003
    Node 18    1.3439322324579692
    Node 19    0.3990409992728165
    Node 20    -0.2633959382242593
    Node 21    -4.612280495940129
    Node 22    2.347485354179846
    Node 23    1.620971992978221
    Node 24    1.1589096199799356
Sigmoid Node 1
    Inputs    Weights
    Threshold    -1.906926556436067
    Node 11    -1.1857036846971907
    Node 12    0.028999755880157962
    Node 13    -0.32024013707799726
    Node 14    -0.5748457750317433
    Node 15    -0.026708383778953557
    Node 16    0.0623228620058279
    Node 17    -0.06053535565032244
    Node 18    -0.03388984571016932
    Node 19    -0.022323417494817966
    Node 20    -0.7782429516394246
    Node 21    -0.8588153207077339
    Node 22    -0.6368436372336976
    Node 23    -0.089886583739161629
    Node 24    -0.17977681390169367
Sigmoid Node 2
    Inputs    Weights
    Threshold    -1.2574778054409332
    Node 11    -1.5410399722809045
    Node 12    0.25830705502127477
    Node 13    -2.7669148576316123
    Node 14    -1.6253898873079935
    Node 15    0.46181993999207605
    Node 16    0.7795541782421587
    Node 17    -0.4800918763254508
    Node 18    0.01945216576025389
    Node 19    0.683395538014334 5
    Node 20    -1.8870673502894135
    Node 21    1.4366278682148648
    Node 22    -3.1615987758619477
    Node 23    -0.6538858403376574
    Node 24    -0.6956571286414347
Sigmoid Node 3
```

Fig. 5. ANN

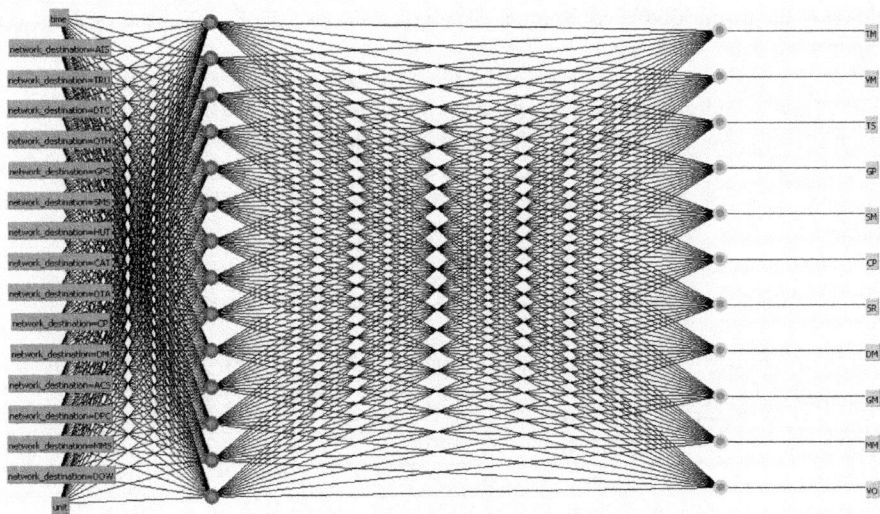

Fig. 5. (*continued*)

4 Model Comparison and Measurement

From the test data, we obtain at least three-month usage records for each user. Then the promotion model is built for a variety of users. For KNN case, we test various K values to find out which K value gives the highest correctness. In Figure 6, rows

K	1	2	3	4	5	6	7	8	9	10	11
D52008	98.39%	98.45%	98.39%	98.45%	98.45%	98.45%	98.45%	98.45%	98.45%	98.45%	98.45%
D52014	95.65%	95.65%	95.94%	95.36%	95.36%	95.36%	95.36%	95.36%	95.36%	95.36%	95.36%
D52017	98.77%	98.52%	98.52%	98.52%	98.52%	98.52%	98.52%	98.52%	98.52%	98.52%	98.52%
D52018	96.41%	96.62%	96.66%	96.91%	96.80%	96.84%	96.76%	96.69%	96.73%	96.80%	96.80%
D52019	86.67%	86.91%	87.65%	88.40%	88.89%	90.62%	90.86%	91.11%	90.37%	90.62%	90.37%
D52020	77.71%	77.65%	77.65%	77.65%	77.41%	77.41%	77.47%	77.71%	77.71%	77.71%	77.71%
D52022	98.91%	98.87%	98.87%	98.87%	98.87%	98.87%	98.87%	98.87%	98.87%	98.87%	98.87%
D52023	81.92%	83.05%	81.92%	81.92%	81.92%	81.36%	81.36%	80.79%	81.36%	81.36%	81.36%
G52001	99.80%	99.67%	99.67%	99.71%	99.67%	99.71%	99.71%	99.71%	99.71%	99.71%	99.71%
G52003	99.96%	99.96%	99.96%	99.96%	99.96%	99.96%	99.96%	99.96%	99.96%	99.96%	99.96%
G52009	97.61%	98.01%	97.61%	97.61%	97.61%	97.61%	97.61%	97.61%	97.61%	97.61%	97.61%
G52010	99.53%	99.53%	99.53%	99.53%	99.53%	99.53%	99.53%	99.53%	99.53%	99.53%	99.53%
G52012	97.88%	98.06%	98.06%	98.06%	98.06%	98.06%	98.06%	98.06%	98.06%	98.06%	98.06%
G52013	99.23%	99.23%	99.23%	99.23%	99.23%	99.23%	99.23%	99.23%	99.23%	99.23%	99.23%
G52014	99.02%	99.02%	99.02%	99.02%	99.02%	99.02%	99.02%	99.02%	99.02%	99.02%	99.02%
Means	95.16%	95.28%	95.25%	95.28%	95.29%	95.37%	95.38%	95.37%	95.37%	95.39%	95.37%

Fig. 6. A proper K value for KNN

contains the promotion model name. The figure shows that K=10 is the best for our experiment data.

For training, we train the promotion model based on the users using that promotion. Then we obtain the model for each promotion. For a specific user, various models are tried for a user to see which model gives the good correctness. If two models give the same correctness, we select the model that gives the least cost per month. For example, user A's data is applied against all the four models. The result is shown in Table 1.

Table 1. Comparison of the correctness of a user data using various models

Promotion model	Decision Tree	K-nearest Neighbor	Naive Bayes Classifier	Artificial Neural Network
D52008	79.6813%	79.6813%	79.6813%	79.6813%
D52014	96.9456%	96.9456%	77.4236%	91.8991%
D52017	69.0571%	69.0571%	69.0571%	79.6813%
G52001	**98.008%**	**98.008%**	90.3054%	97.6096%
G52003	69.0571%	69.0571%	69.1899%	69.0571%
G52009	**98.008%**	**98.008%**	96.9456%	97.6096%

It is shown that G52001 and G52009 for decision tree and KNN give the better correctness (98.008%). Then we take both promotion information and applied to the usage data to compute the cost if the user uses the promotion.

For example, if the user data is as following.

Table 2. Example usage data

Type of usage	Unit
Outgoing calls	240 mins
SMS	19 msgs
MMS	1 msg
GPRS	214 mins

Model G52001, the promotion is : basic monthly rate 200 baht, free calls every network 200 minutes, extra minute is 1.50 baht/min, SMS costs 2 baht/msg, MMS costs 6 baht per message, and GPRS cost 1 baht per minute. This cost 554.26 baht per month including 7% VAT compared to Model G52009, which costs 331.7 baht/month. Thus, G52009 is suitable for the user.

5   Application Systems

We develop the application which integrates the database of promotions and users' usage data together.

Register
Login
Client
DataBase
WEKA
Use weka to cluster data
Server

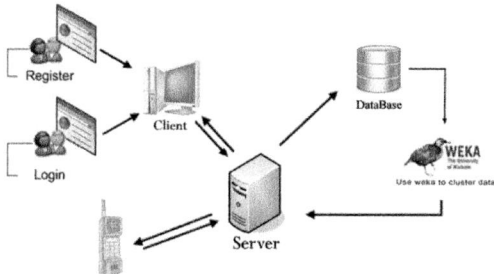

Fig. 7. Architecture of the application

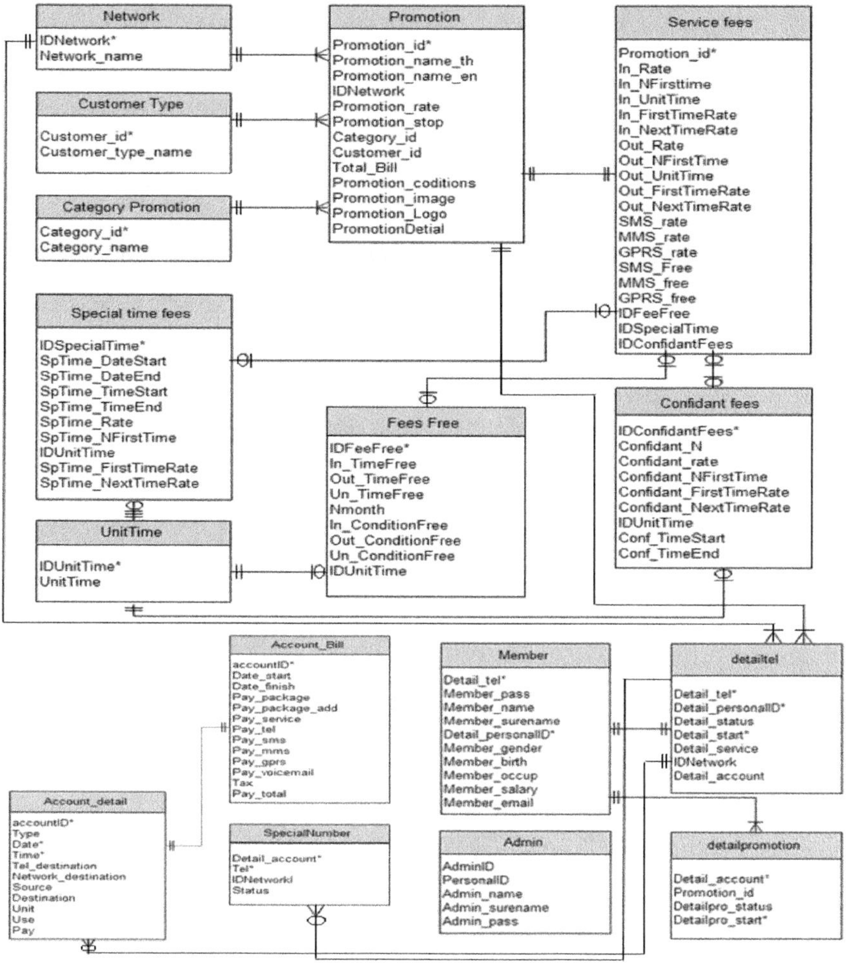

Network
IDNetwork*
Network_name
Promotion
Promotion_id*
Promotion_name_th
Promotion_name_en
IDNetwork
Promotion_rate
Promotion_stop
Category_id
Customer_id
Total_Bill
Promotion_coditions
Promotion_image
Promotion_Logo
PromotionDetial
Service fees
Promotion_id*
In_Rate
In_NFirsttime
In_UnitTime
In_FirstTimeRate
In_NextTimeRate
Out_Rate
Out_NFirstTime
Out_UnitTime
Out_FirstTimeRate
Out_NextTimeRate
SMS_rate
MMS_rate
GPRS_rate
SMS_Free
MMS_free
GPRS_free
IDFeeFree
IDSpecialTime
IDConfidantFees
Customer Type
Customer_id*
Customer_type_name
Category Promotion
Category_id*
Category_name
Special time fees
IDSpecialTime*
SpTime_DateStart
SpTime_DateEnd
SpTime_TimeStart
SpTime_TimeEnd
SpTime_Rate
SpTime_NFirstTime
IDUnitTime
SpTime_FirstTimeRate
SpTime_NextTimeRate
Fees Free
IDFeeFree*
In_TimeFree
Out_TimeFree
Un_TimeFree
Nmonth
In_ConditionFree
Out_ConditionFree
Un_ConditionFree
IDUnitTime
Confidant fees
IDConfidantFees*
Confidant_N
Confidant_rate
Confidant_NFirstTime
Confidant_FirstTimeRate
Confidant_NextTimeRate
IDUnitTime
Conf_TimeStart
Conf_TimeEnd
UnitTime
IDUnitTime*
UnitTime
Account_Bill
accountID*
Date_start
Date_finish
Pay_package
Pay_package_add
Pay_service
Pay_tel
Pay_sms
Pay_mms
Pay_gprs
Pay_voicemail
Tax
Pay_total
Member
Detail_tel*
Member_pass
Member_name
Member_surename
Detail_personalID*
Member_gender
Member_birth
Member_occup
Member_salary
Member_email
detailtel
Detail_tel*
Detail_personalID*
Detail_status
Detail_start*
Detail_service
IDNetwork
Detail_account
Account_detail
accountID*
Type
Date*
Time*
Tel_destination
Network_destination
Source
Destination
Unit
Use
Pay
SpecialNumber
Detail_account*
Tel*
IDNetworkI
Status
Admin
AdminID
PersonalID
Admin_name
Admin_surename
Admin_pass
detailpromotion
Detail_account*
Promotion_id
Detailpro_status
Detailpro_start*

Fig. 8. ER diagram for storing usage and promotion information

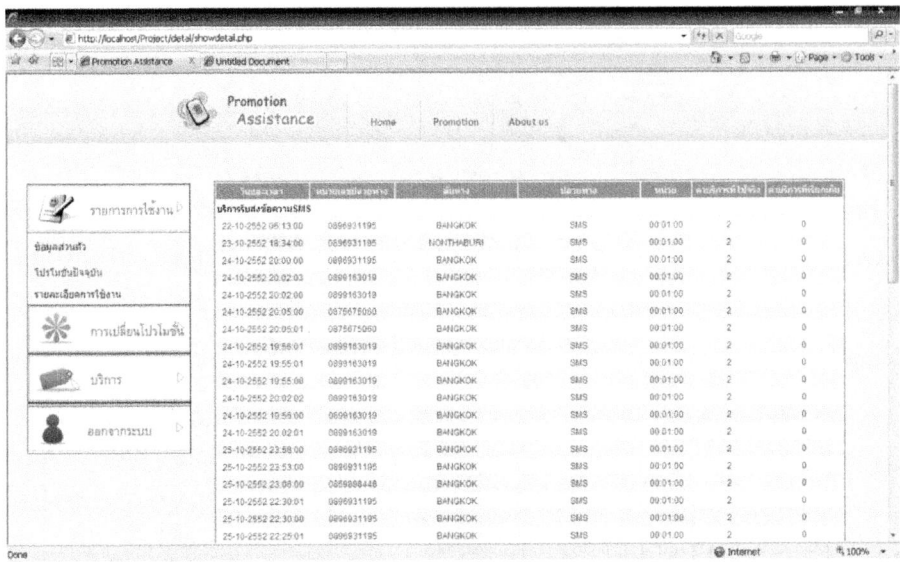

Fig. 9. The user can view their current usage by month

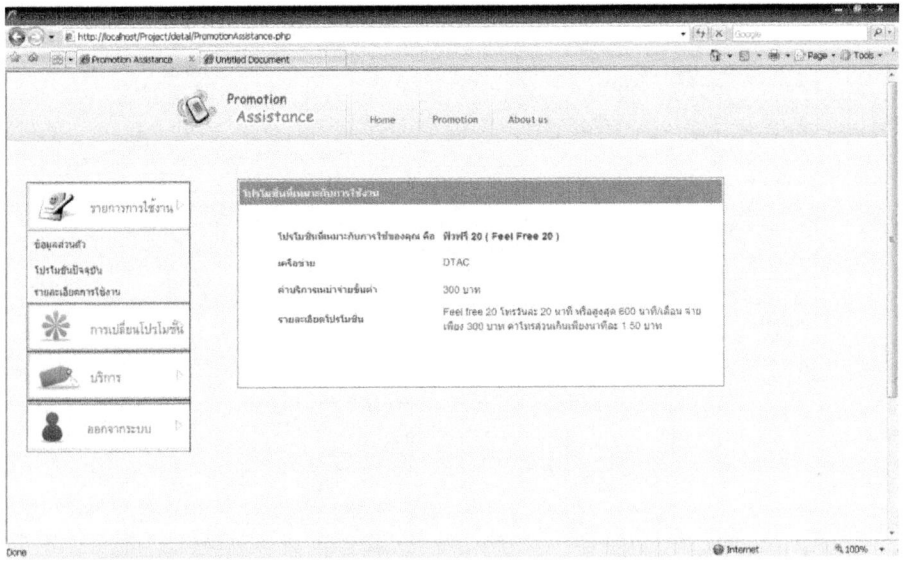

Fig. 10. The proper promotion is introduced to a user

In Figure 7 the server stores database containing the usage records and promotions. Weka [8] is used to analyze the usage data and predict the expense. The user logons to the system for recording the usage, view current available promotion and his promotion. After analyzing, if the change of promotion saves costs, the system sends the SMS message alert to him to suggest the promotion.

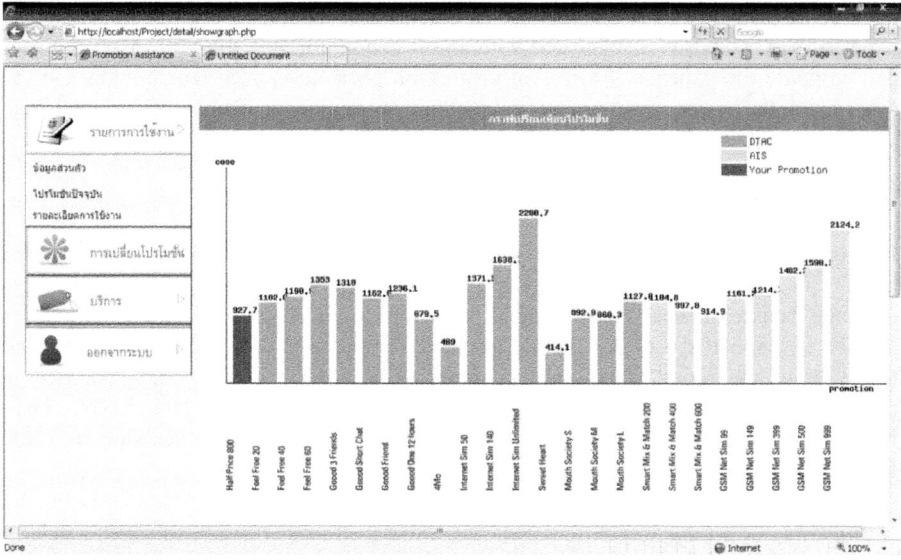

Fig. 11. The user can compare the expense of using various promotions

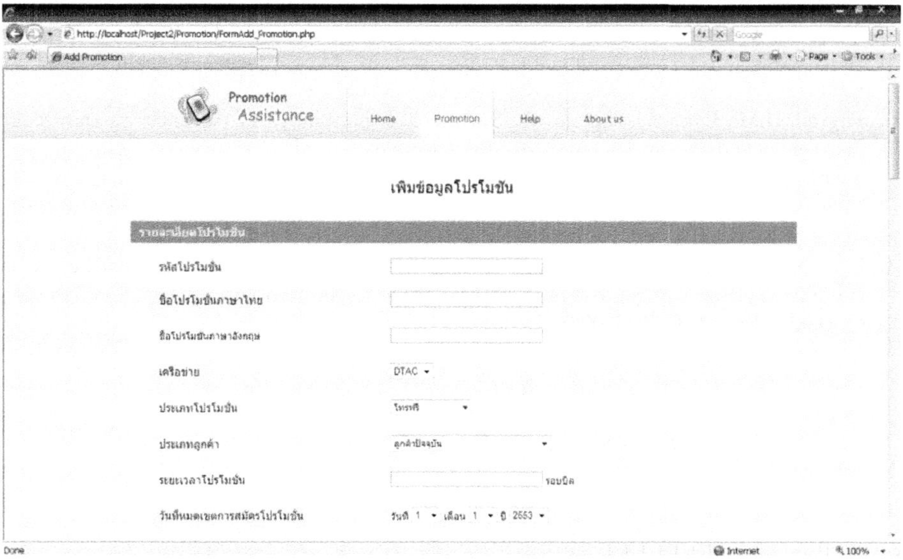

Fig. 12. The phone operator can update their current promotion

We design several tables in the database to store information about usage and promotion as shown in Figure 8. The tables includes promotions and fees, member and payment records, current promotion he/she uses.

On the web client, the user needs to login to the system. Their usage records are stored and can be viewed as in Figure 9. Periodically, the usage data is analyzed against the previous models. Then the calculation for the expense for each promotion is performed. The user is suggested with a new promotion in Figure 10. Also, the user can compare the expense if different promotion package is used (Figure 11). On the other hand, the phone operator can update their promotions periodically (Figure 12).

6   Conclusion

In this paper, we propose an application which help suggest a proper promotion for mobile phone users. The applications take advantage of data mining technique. Lots of usage data are analyzed and models for each promotion are extracted. The model is applied to a specific user data to suggest whether the user should change the promotion to save the monthly expense. Features of user data are extracted and used in modeling. We study 4 techniques for modeling the promotion: ANN, KNN, Naïve Bayes and decision tree. From the experiments, it is shown that decision tree and KNN performed better compared to ANN and Naïve Bayes.

In the future, when more usage data is stored, the system can automatically update or improve the stored model. Also, when looking at certain group of user's data, a new promotion can be suggested to the system to promote a group of user.

References

1. Jirapaisarnkul, C.: Data mining for selling analysis, Master thesis, Sripatum University (2004)
2. Fayyad, U.M., Piatetsky-Shapiro, G., Smyth, P., Uthurusamy, R.: Advances in knowledge discovery and data mining. AAAI/MIT Press (1996)
3. Saenghamud, P., et al.: A Development of Information Technology System for Knowledge Management by Naive Bayesian incase in Restaurant and Bakery Business. In: Proceedings of the 1st NCTechED, pp. 14–21 (2008)
4. Pornpacharapong, V.: Risk Factors Affecting Money Saving Behavior of Thai People in Rural Area using Artificial Neural Networks. In: Proceedings of the 5th Operation Research Conference, pp. 284–289 (2008)
5. http://www.gsmadvance.ais.co.th/th/mixandmatch_detail.html
6. http://bc.siamu.ac.th/superman/137-411/ pdf%5CNeuralNetwork.pdf
7. http://www.ais.co.th
8. http://www.cs.waikato.ac.nz/ml/weka/

An Approach to Filtering Duplicate RFID Data Streams

Hairulnizam Mahdin[1] and Jemal Abawajy[2]

[1] Faculty of Comp. Sc. & Info. Tech,
University of Tun Hussein Onn Malaysia, Johor, Malaysia
hairuln@uthm.edu.my
[2] School of Information Technology
Deakin University,
Victoria, Australia
jemal@deakin.edu.au

Abstract. In a system where distributed network of Radio Frequency Identification (RFID) readers are used to collaboratively collect data from tagged objects, a scheme that detects and eliminates redundant data streams is required. To address this problem, we propose an approach that is based on Bloom filter to detect duplicate readings and filter redundant RFID data streams. We have evaluated the performance of the proposed approach and compared it with existing approaches. The experimental results demonstrate that the proposed approach provides superior performance as compared to the baseline approaches.

1 Introduction

RFID technology enables capturing large volumes of data at high speed and can be used for identifying, locating, tracking and monitoring physical objects without line of sight. This capability makes RFID technology desirable for many applications such as supply chain management. Large-scale RFID-enabled systems are composed of multiple networked RFID readers and physically distributed tags, the middleware software that processes and manages the information gathered, and the enterprise applications that implements the enterprise business logic, and the enterprise database management systems.

In this paper, we address the problem of detecting and eliminating redundant data streams in a system where distributed network of RFID readers are used to collaboratively collect data from tagged objects. This is important as multiple readers are used in many applications for a variety of reasons such as to increase the reading reliability [1]; to read objects passing through different doors at warehouse [2]; in supply chain [3] and object's location sensing [4]. However, reading tagged objects by multiple readers could create duplicate readings when multiple readers read the same tagged object simultaneously. The problem of duplicate reading is common in RFID and an approach that efficiently detect duplicate readings is required [5].

In this paper, we propose an approach that is based on Bloom filter [6] for detecting and filtering redundant data from RFID data streams. The performance of the proposed approach is studied and the experimental results demonstrate that the

T.-h. Kim et al. (Eds.): UNESST 2010, CCIS 124, pp. 125–133, 2010.
© Springer-Verlag Berlin Heidelberg 2010

proposed approach provides superior performance as compared to the baseline approaches.

The rest of the paper is organized as follows. Section 2 presents the related work. Section 3 explains the proposed algorithms in detail. Section 4 presents the performance analysis of the proposed algorithm. We use the sliding windows-based approach in [7] as well as the approach proposed in [8] to compare the performance of the proposed algorithm. We also discuss the results. The conclusion is presented in Section 6.

2   Related Works

Figure 1 shows RFID-enabled system of interest. The system is assumed to contain multiple networked RFID readers (i.e., $reader_1$, $reader_i$, $reader_n$) deployed to collaboratively collect data from tagged objects. In this paper, we focus on passive RFID tag. These tags are widely used especially in supply chain because of its cheap prices. The RFID readers query tags to obtain data and forward the resulting information through the middleware to the backend applications or database servers. The applications then respond to these events and orchestrate corresponding actions such as ordering additional products, sending theft alerts, raising alarms regarding harmful chemicals or replacing fragile components before failure.

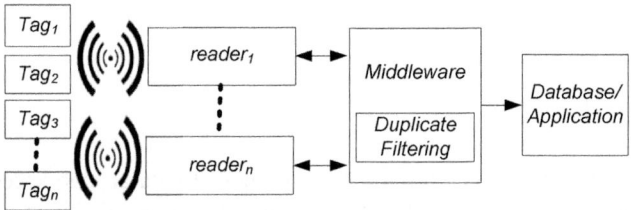

Fig. 1. RFID-enabled system architecture

In RFID-enabled systems, a reading can be defined as duplicate if it is repeated and did not give new information to the system. Redundant readings are useless and should be removed from the data stream without affecting the system. RFID data duplication problem can be discussed at data level or reader level [5]. Duplicate reading at a reader level occurs when an object is covered by more than one reader. In contrast, duplicate reading at data level occurs when RFID readers can repeat reading of the same object as long as the object is within its read range.

In this paper, we focus on reader level data duplicate filtering problem. There are many approaches proposed to filter data level duplicate reading [7][8][9][10][11]. An approach that uses a sliding window to group a number of readings and compare them with each other is discussed in [7]. Only single occurrence from a number of similar readings will be output from that particular window. Another way to remove data level duplicate readings is by using query [9][10]. Query is imposed on the database records to retain only single reading that will represent the others in the given time frame. In [11], new record is made up to represent all other similar reading by specifying the initial and last time of detection. An approach that deferred reading output is discussed in [9][10][11]. This approaches is not suitable for use with applications that demand real time processing.

There are also several approaches proposed in the literature to filter reader level RFID data duplicates. An approach based on a radio frequency absorbing material to controls the RFID propagation from dispersing to neighboring reader's area is discussed in [2]. The material is placed between readers to prevent a reader from reading neighboring tags. However, this solution is not feasible in most application because of design constraint and its high cost. Another approach based on complex computations for detecting the location of the tags from the reader is discussed in [12]. Our aim is to identify which reader should preserve the readings so every reader will only report on their own objects.

Approaches that explore the Bloom filter [6] for filtering duplicate data in RFID has recently emerged in the literature [8][13]. An approach that used the original Bloom filter to remove the duplicate is discussed in [8]. The main idea of the standard Bloom Filter (BF) is to represent an element in a form of positive counter in a bit array of size m using k number of hash functions. All bits in BF are initially set to 0 and will be replaced by 1 when it is hashed by the elements. To test whether an element is a member of a set, the element will be run through the same hash functions used to insert the elements into the array. The element is said to be the member of the set if all the bits in which the element was mapped to is positive. For each new element, the corresponding k bits in the array are set to 1.

Two approaches were proposed in [8]: eager and lazy approach that use Bloom filter to filter duplicate data. Generally, when a new reading comes at local reader, it will be inserted in the Bloom filter. The filter then will be sent to the central filter for update. Central filter is coordinating readings from all the readers under its network. In eager approach, the copy of the Bloom filter will be sent to every other reader to avoid the same reading from entering through them again. However it is too costly to update all the reader every time new reading arrives. In lazy approach, only reader that sends new reading will have new copy of the Bloom filter from the central filter. In our approach, we focus only filtering at the central filter to preserve the reading only to the authorized reader. The work in [14] filters duplicate readings at a single reader. In contrast, the work presented in this paper takes into account multiple distributed RFID readers. Thus our work can be considered as complement to these previous works.

The proposed algorithm is based on the Counting Bloom filter [15], which was introduced to allow counting and deleting operations that cannot be performed with the standard Bloom Filter [6]. In the proposed approach, if the new readings on the same object from different readers have a higher number from the previous reader, the new reading will replace the old reading in the filter. In this paper, we model the relation between the reader read rate and the distance between the reader and the tag based on the work of [16]. The reader detection range can be classified as a major detection region and a minor detection region. Tags read inside the major detection area will have about 95% read rate while the tag read in the minor detection region will have about 5% read rate [16].

3 RFID Data Stream Filtering Scheme

Double Comparison Bloom Filter (DCBF) uses CBF1 and CBF2 filters to represent the count of the readings and the reader identification (RID) respectively. Fig. 2 shows the pseudo-code of the DCBF algorithm. The input to the DCBF is the reading count for each tag (C), the tag identification (TID) and the reader identification (RID). The reading count (C) is needed to compare which reader (based on RID) have the higher reading on the tag (identify through TID).

In step 1, reading count for each tag is done at each reader and is sent with the TID and the RID to the global filter which will run this algorithm. For step 2-8, each incoming TID will be hashed and checked on its condition. If the hashed counter have 0 values or smaller than C, or RID is the same in CBF2 hashed counter, the position will be retained in an array named CounterNum. If one of the hashed counters did not satisfy the condition in step 4, the algorithm will exit (step 7) from all loop and start back to step 1 to receive new reading. If all hashed counters satisfy the condition in step 4, step 10-14 is carried out where the new value of C is stored in the CBF1 counter and RID in CBF2 counter.

```
Algorithm DCBF
INPUT: C, RID, TID
BEGIN
1: FOR (each incoming TID)  DO
2:      FOR (i=1 TO k)  DO
3:          Pos ← Hashᵢ(TID)
4:          IF (CBF1 [Pos] == 0) | | (C > CBF1[Pos]) | | (RID > CBF2[Pos]) THEN
5:              CounterNum [i] ← Pos
6:          ELSE
7:              EXIT
8:          ENDIF
9:      ENDFOR
10:     FOR (i=1 TO k)  DO
11:         Pos ← CounterNum [i]
12:         CBF1 [Pos] ← C
13:         CBF2 [Pos] ← RID
14:     ENDFOR
15: END FOR
END DCBF
```

Fig. 2. Double Comparison Bloom Filter Algorithm

We give example of inserting values in DCBF from the hashing process. Let say we have tag 1 from reader 1 with reading counts of 30. Tag 1 is hashed 3 times and the first hashed return 0, the second hash return 1 and the third hash return 3. The value of 30 will be inserted to these hashed counters in CBF1 and CBF2 as shown in Table 1.

Table 1. The condition of CBF after tag 1 is hashed 3 times

CBF1	30	30	0	30	0	0
CBF2	1	1	0	1	0	0
Counter positions	[0]	[1]	[2]	[3]	[4]	[5]

To have the complete views, here is another example how DCBF works. Initially, all the counters in both filters are set to 0. When new reading record arrives, CBF will only insert the count of the reading if the count is higher than current hashed counters values. For each time a reading is inserted into CBF, it means at that time the reader has the highest reading on that tag.

For example refer to table 2 and Fig. 3. Table 1 list the readings on tag 1 and tag 2 by two readers which are R1 and R2. Each reader will send the number of readings on their tag for every 100secs to the global filter. Initially all counters both CBF1 and CBF2 are set to 0 as shown in Fig. 3(a). At time 100, R1 sends reading on tag 1 which is 12. The tag 1 is hashed k times and will be inserted in filters since there were no other readings previously.

Table 2. Reading on tag A1 by different reader

Time	Reader ID	Tag ID	Count of readings
100	R1	1	12
100	R2	1	3
200	R1	2	3
200	R2	2	10

All the hashed counters (shaded boxes) in CBF1 will be given value of 12 to represent the number of count while hashed counters in CBF2 is given value 1 to represent the reader ID as shown in Fig. 3(b). Then reading on tag 1 by R2 arrived with number of readings 3. Tag 1 is hashed and returns the same counters like the previous reading. However this reading will be ignored by the filter because the number of readings by R2 on tag 1 is lower than the previous (Fig. 3(c)).

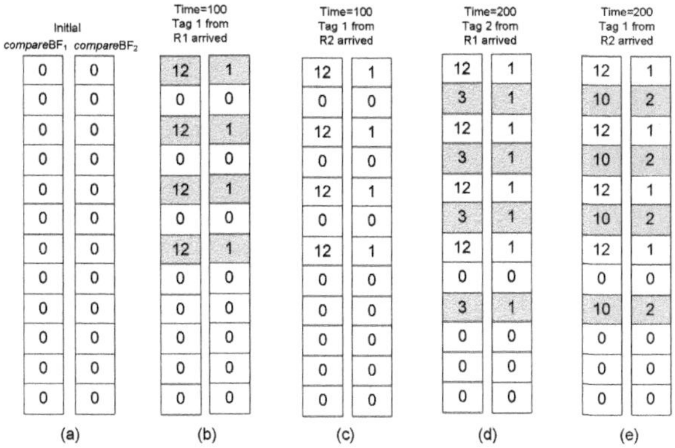

Fig. 3. The state of CBF1 and CBF2 based readings in Table 1

We need to keep track on how many tagged objects that each reader has. Based on table 2, at time 100, R1 has one object while R2 has none. At time 200, R1 arrived with reading on tag 2 with number of readings 3. Tag 2 will be inserted in the filters since all the hashed counters returns 0 which means this is the new reading for tag 2

(Fig. 3(d)). Now R1 has 2 objects (including tag 1). When reading from R2 arrives, it also reads tag 2 but with the higher reading than R1 did. The algorithm will insert the new number of readings on tag 2 by R2 in the filter and remove the previous reading of tag 2 by R1 (Fig. 3(e)). By storing the reader ID the filter can answer the query to which reader that a tag is belong to.

4   Performance Analysis

In this section, we present the performance analysis of the proposed algorithm. We will first discuss the experimental setup. We then discuss the results of the experiments.

4.1   Experimental Setup

As in [16] and [17], we generated the data streams using Binomial distribution. We use the sliding windows-based approach the Baseline algorithm [7] and the original Bloom filter [8] to compare the performance of the proposed algorithm.

4.2   Analysis of False Positive Rate

In this experiment, we want to analyse the false positive rate (FPR) of DCBF. A false positive will occurs in DCBF when a reading is detected incorrectly as a duplicate in the same window. We perform this experiment to find out the ratio of array size m to the number of readings n along with number of hash functions k that will return the lowest FPR. The result from this experiment will be used to set the parameters in the next experiments.

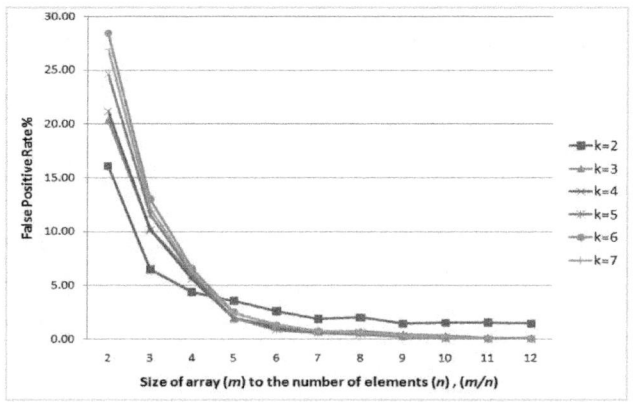

Fig. 4. False positive rate in DCBF

Result for the first experiment is shown in Fig. 4. DCBF is run under different number of hash functions with varied ratio on number of readings n to the array m. From Fig. 4 we can see that FPR rate reaching almost zero when the number of hash function is more than 4 and the size of n is 1/9 to the size of m. Based on this result we will run DCBF on next experiments with 7 hash functions and set the size of m 9 times bigger than number of elements n to get the best results.

4.3 Comparative Analysis of the Algorithms

In this experiment, we investigated the rate of incorrect filtering by DCBF, Baseline and Bloom filter. Incorrect filtering means that the tag with lower reading count failed to be filtered and have been inserted into the filter. For this experiment we generate 200 tags readings for 2 readers. The number of overlapped readings will be varied from 5% to 50% for each data sets. Tag that located in the major detection region will have 80% read rate while minor detection region will have 20% read rate. The reading cycle will be repeated for 10 times. The overlapped readings were scattered randomly in the data stream.

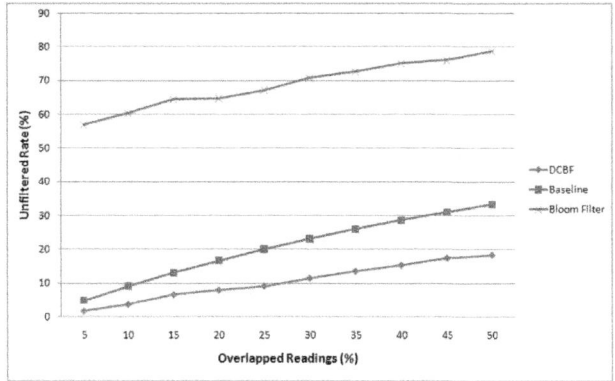

Fig. 5. Percentage of unfiltered duplicate readings

Results on Fig. 5 shows that DCBF performs better than Baseline and Bloom filter to filter the duplicate readings. DCBF has the lowest unfiltered reading rates among the other algorithms. The highest is the Bloom filter [8]. This is because Bloom filter could not stored the data on the number of readings and reader ID which is needed to perform this task correctly. For sliding windows approach they have problem to filter correctly when duplicate readings are scattered in the data stream. The RFID readings can be scattered and non-continuos due to the outside interference and signal weakness. When the readings are scattered there are readings that cannot be compared with each other while it is need to be done to filter the duplicate. This left some duplicate readings in the windows.

4.4 Execution Time

In this experiment, we measure the execution time of DCBF, Baseline and Bloom filter to perform the filtering tasks. The data set generated have different number of reading arrivals per cycle is set to 20, 40, 80, 160, 320, 640 and 1280.

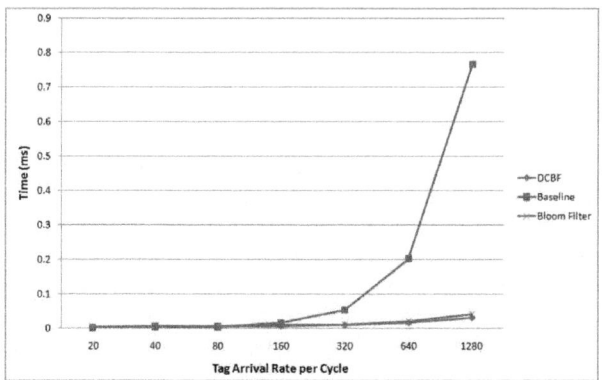

Fig. 6. Time execution comparison to filter the duplicate readings

From Fig. 6, DCBF perform better in terms of time execution than Baseline. Baseline which is based on sliding windows approach takes more time to execute especially when the reading getting high arrival rate per cycle. This is because it has to go through along the windows that become bigger with the increase of tag arrival rate for each new coming reading. This is different from DCBF where the arrival rate does not have exponential effect on its time processing. Unlike Baseline, DCBF does not have to go through along the windows to check for the duplication. Its only need to hash the tag ID to check whether it is a duplicate reading or not. For Bloom filter the performance is same like DCBF. However as the previous result shows it has very high unfiltered duplicates which make it is not suitable to perform this task.

5 Conclusions

In this paper, we studied the problem of RFID data duplicate problem and proposed a new approach that is based on Bloom filter ideas. We compared the performance of the proposed approach with several existing approaches. The results show that proposed approach has low false rate and best execution time as compared to the existing approaches.

References

1. Pupunwiwat, P., Bela, S.: Location Filtering and Duplication Elimination for RFID Data Streams. In: International Journal of Principles and Applications of Information Science and Technology, vol. 1(1) (December 2007)
2. Leong, K.S., Ng, M.L., Grasso, A.R., Cole, P.H.: Synchronization of RFID readers for dense RFID reader environments. In: Proceedings of the 2006 International Symposium on Applications and the Internet Workshops (SAINT 2006), pp. 48–51 (2006)
3. Martinez-Sala, A.S., Egea-Lopez, E., Garcia-Sanchez, F., Garcia-Haro, J.: Tracking of Returnable Packaging and Transport Units with active RFID in the grocery supply chain. Computers in Industry 60(3), 161–171 (2009)

4. Ko, C.-H.: RFID 3D location sensing algorithms. Automation in Construction. Building Information Modelling and Collaborative Working Environments 19(5), 588–595 (2010)
5. Derakhshan, R., Orlowska, M., Li, X.: RFID Data Management: Challenges and Opportunities. In: IEEE International Conference on RFID, pp. 175–182 (2007)
6. Bloom, B.: Space/time tradeoffs in hash coding with allowable errors. Commun. ACM 13(7), 422–426 (1970)
7. Bai, Y., Wang, F., Liu, P.: Efficiently Filtering RFID Data Streams. In: CleanDB Workshop, pp. 50–57 (2006)
8. Wang, X., Zhang, Q., Jia, Y.: Efficiently Filtering Duplicates over Distributed Data Streams. In: International Conference on Computer Science and Software Engineering, Wuhan, Hubei, pp. 631–634 (2008)
9. Jeffery, S.R., Alonso, G., Franklin, M.J., Hong, W., Widom, J.: A Pipelined Framework for Online Cleaning of Sensor Data Streams. In: Proceedings of the 22nd International Conference on Data Engineering (ICDE 2006), p. 140 (2006)
10. Rao, J., Doraiswamy, S., Thakkar, H., Colby, L.S.: A Deferred Cleansing Method For RFID Data Analytics. In: Int. Conf. on Very Large DataBases (VLDB 2006), pp. 175–186 (2006)
11. Gonzalez, H., Han, J., Li, X., Klabjan, D.: Warehousing and analysing massive RFID data sets. In: Proc. of the International Conference on Data Engineering (ICDE 2006), pp. 1–10 (2006)
12. Song, J., Hass, C.T., Caldas, C.H.: A Proximity-Based Method for Locating RFID Tagged Objects. Adv. Eng. Inform 21, 367–376 (2007)
13. Shen, H., Zhang, Y.: Improved approximate detection of duplicates for data streams over sliding windows. Journal Of Computer Science And Technology 23(6), 973–987 (2008)
14. Mahdin, H., Abawajy, J.: An Approach to Filtering RFID Data Streams. In: 10th International Symposium on Pervasive Systems, Algorithms, and Networks, pp. 742–746 (2009)
15. Fan, L., Cao, P., Almeida, J.: Broder A Z. Summary cache: A Scalable Wide-Area Web Cache Sharing Protocol. IEEE/ACM Trans. Networking 8(3), 281–293 (2000)
16. Jeffery, S.R., Garofalakis, M., Franklin, M.J.: Adaptive cleaning for RFID data streams. In: Proceedings of the 32nd International Conference on Very Large Databases, pp. 163–174 (2006)
17. Chen, W.-T.: An accurate tag estimate method for improving the performance of an RFID anticollision algorithm based on dynamic frame length ALOHA. In: Chen, W.-T. (ed.) IEICE Trans. on Automatic Science and Engineering, pp. 9–15 (2009)

Developing Personal Learning Environments Based on Calm Technologies

Jinan Fiaidhi

Department of Computer Science, Lakehead University
955 Oliver Road, Thunder Bay, Ontario P7B 5E1, Canada
jinan.fiaidhi@lakeheadu.ca

Abstract. Educational technology is constantly evolving and growing, and it is inevitable that this progression will continually offer new and interesting advances in our world. The instigation of calm technologies for the delivery of education is another new approach now emerging. Calm technology aims to reduce the "excitement" of information overload by letting the learner select what information is at the center of their attention and what information need to be at the peripheral. In this paper we report on the adaptation of calm technologies in an educational setting with emphasis on the needs to cater the preferences of the individual learner to respond to the challenge of providing truly learner-centered, accessible, personalized and flexible learning. Central to calm computing vision is the notion of representing learning objects as widgets, harvesting widgets from the periphery based on semantic wikis as well as widgets garbage collection from the virtual/central learning memory.

1 Introduction

The need for computing in support of education continues to escalate. Until recently, everyone assumed that educational computing required desktop computers. Today wireless-enabled laptops, PDAs, iPads and Smart phones make it possible for students to use their time more efficiently, access databases and information from the Internet, and work collaboratively. Through this flexible learning approach, students can succeed in selectively incorporating critical input from their peers and instructor, then revising their documents based on their own interpretation of facts and theory. This technology will soon give students full-time access to computation and wireless connectivity, while expanding where educational computing can take place to the home and field. This is an important equity issue because these computers will provide much of the educational benefit of more expensive computers in an inexpensive format that has many advantages over desktops. Connectivity for these devices will soon be the norm rather than the exception. As they become more functional and more connected, the possibility for completely new and unforeseen application increases. However, the conventional learning packages use some legacy Web-based distant learning software (e.g. Blackboard, WebCT, WebFuse, CoSE, TopClass, WebEx, VNC, SCORM, and Tango) that luck portability, ubiquity and scalability as well as it does not support collaborative composition of new learning materials. It is of

T.-h. Kim et al. (Eds.): UNESST 2010, CCIS 124, pp. 134–146, 2010.

substantial benefit to learners with ubiquitous devices if we can have an integrated collaboration environment over the Internet, enabling users to compose their own personal learning environment. Actually, the emerging paradigm of Web 2.0 is transforming traditional Internet from a mass media to a social media mode. In Web 2.0, applications are delivered through Web browsers and they are responsive to users through rich application interfaces, often including pre-built application components or service widgets. Mashups are the essence of such applications. A mashup is an application that combines content from more than one source into an integrated experience. Today mashups are very common as the new authoring tools and middlewares are being developed that will produce new applications and services without much programming. As tools and middleware like these become more robust, we will see increasing use of mashups in teaching and learning. There are many mashup applications, such as Yahoo! Pipes[1], Google Earth[2], Video Mash-Up[3] and News Mash-Up[4]. However, how to mash up information effectively is a challenging issue. For this reason, the 2008 Horizon report [1] classifies mashups into three categories with increasing level of semantics awareness. Figure 1 illustrates them.

Fig. 1. Mashups Semantic Awareness Categories

Whatever a mashup category is, it boils down to the following architectural issues [2]:

- Accessibility to the existing enterprise services and data/content repositories
- The ability to perform Web-based mashup assembly and use (using SaaS style)
- Availability of user-friendly assembly models
- Availability of mashup management and maintenance module

Mashup services must be based on some sort of content aggregation technologies. The traditional content aggregation technology was until recently based on Portals and Portlets. Portals are designed as an extension to traditional dynamic Web applications, in which the process of converting data content into marked-up Web pages is split into two phases - generation of markup "fragments" and aggregation of the fragments into pages. Each markup fragment is generated by a "portlet", and the portal combines them into a single Web page. Portlets may be hosted locally on the portal server or

---

[1] http://pipes.yahoo.com/pipes
[2] http://earth.google.com
[3] www.wikieducator.org
[4] www.feedchronicle.com

remotely on another server. However, the portal technology is about server-side, pres-
entation-tier aggregation and it cannot be used easily to drive more robust forms of
application integration. Mashup services are more loosely defined where content
aggregation can take place either on the server or on the client side. The base standards for the mashup content aggregation are the XML interchanged as REST or Web
Services. Lightweight protocols such as RSS and Atom are commonly used for the
purpose of facilitating the content aggregation. The major difference between portals
and mashups is in the way content or services composition is administered. Portals
achieve composition through the use of application server as a mediator between a
client browser and services. Mashups, however, perform composition directly from
the end user's browser. Although the client-side architecture helps mitigate a performance problem by avoiding the use of the application server, it can introduce its
own problems in the design, use and maintenance of mashup applications where often
such application users find participating in mash-up process as time-consuming or
even a trouble. To address this problem, we require an environment that seamlessly
integrates devices and services into the physical world as well as to provide semantics
for mashing up. Mark Weiser, a researcher at Xerox PARC, called such environment
as "Calm Computing" [3,4,11]. Calm computing enables new ways of processing,
integrating and consuming information. In particular, it advocates peripheral
awareness of activity in a virtual world and ability to move easily from a service at
the periphery of our attention, to the center, and back according to the learning requests and needs. In this article, we present a general framework that enables the
development of calm personal learning environment using emerging technologies like
Enterprise Mashup, Widgets, Web-Harvesting, Garbage Collection and Web Intelligence. Figure 2 illustrates our general vision. More details on this vision can be de-
picted from the following sections.

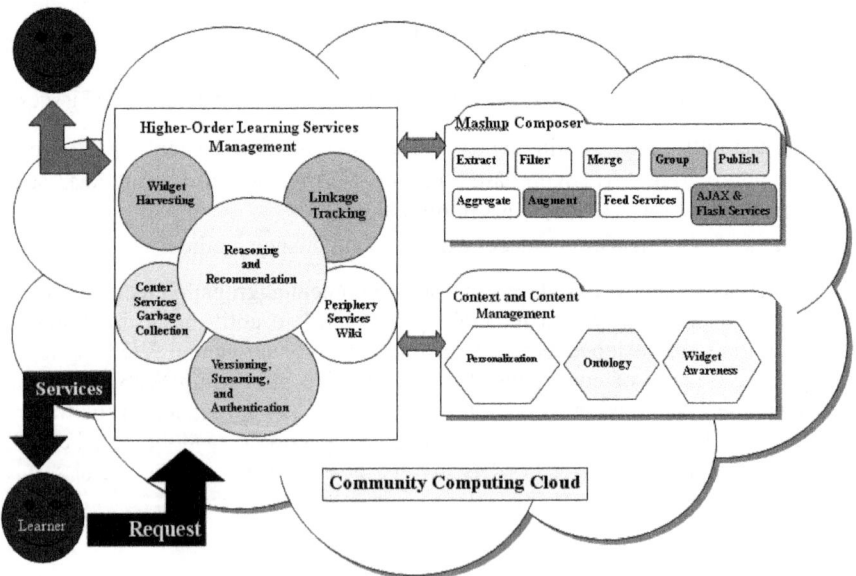

Fig. 2. Framework for Developing Innovative Personal Learning Environments

2 Towards Developing Personal Learning Environments

There are many historical attempts to develop a framework for developing personal learning environments (PLEs) including Learning portals, Web-Based Learning (WBL), Web-Based Instruction (WBI), Web Based Training (WBT), Internet-Based Training (IBT), Distributed Learning (DL), Advanced Distributed Learning (ADL), Distance Learning, Online Learning (OL), m-Learning, Remote Learning, Off-site Learning and a-Learning (anytime, anyplace, anywhere learning). However, a personal learning environment consists of a dynamic mix of many different types of resources and facilities, which should be aware of, and adapt to, the learner in his/her current context. This multiplicity of technologies including the recent waves of Web 2.0 and Web 3.0 demands sort of service-oriented approach. Figure 3 illustrates the different generations of personal learning environments.

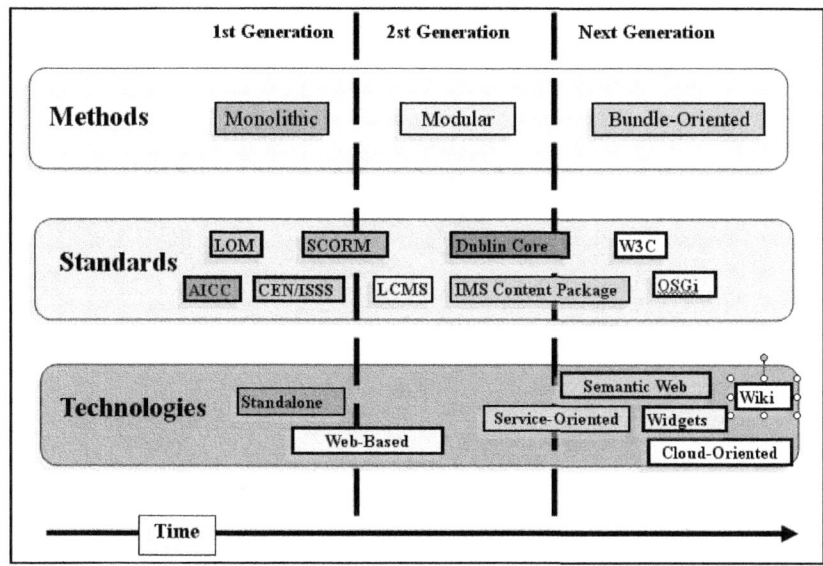

Fig. 3. Personal Learning Environments Generations

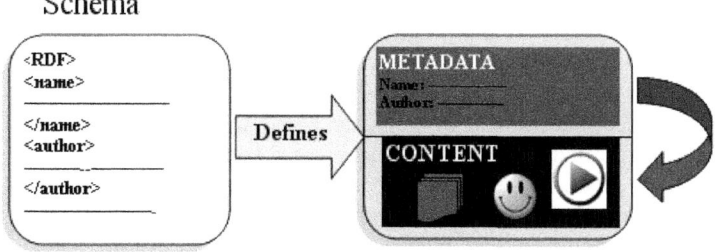

Fig. 4. The notion of Learning Object

Central to any type of personal learning environment is the notion of Learning Object [5]. Figure 4 illustrates the major components of typical learning objects.

The 1st generation of personal learning environments was based on standalone LCMS, where learning objects are deposited a central repository for possible future usage (Figure 5).

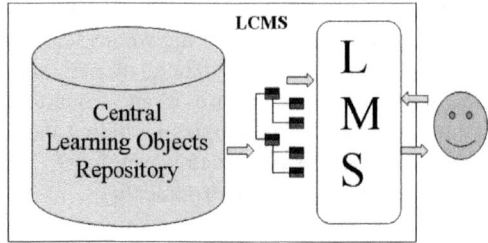

Fig. 5. Personal Learning Environment as Learning Content Management System (LCMS)

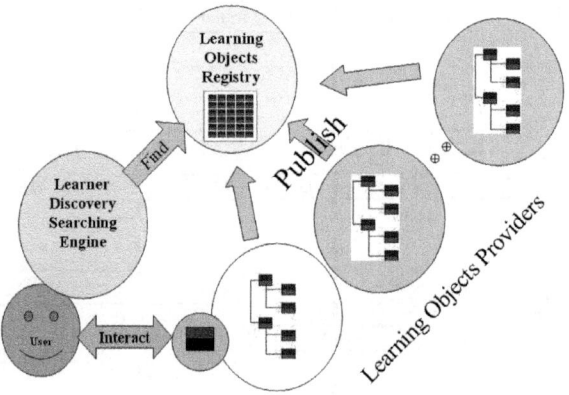

Fig. 6. The 2nd Generation Personal Learning Environment

The 2nd generation PLEs utilize web and service based framework to share learning objects on the web (Figure 6) but they do not promote collaboration and learning objects annotation and mashups. Such functionalities are part of the new technology trend which is generally termed as 'Community Computing' [6]. In fact, the idea of community computing is not totally new. By several projects such as PICO [7] and GAIA [8], community concept had been introduced. Yet despite these interests, a number of fundamental questions remained unanswered. In particular, the development model used is not well defined. In order to find an answer, we have researched on the development model and the development process to generate the community computing PLEs. As a progress, we find the Cloud infrastructure [9] as a satisfying model for developing community based PLEs. In this direction, learning objects can be shared based over the cloud users using what is known as bundles. In fact, bundles are sort of generic components that can be

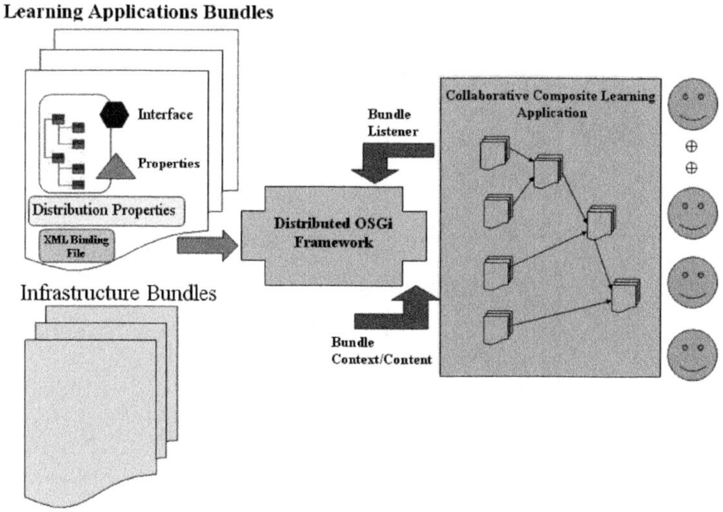

Learning Applications Bundles

Fig. 7. The Future Generation of Personal Learning Environments

identified by a web-based infrastructure (e.g. Distributed OSGi[5]) and be mashed up or composed with other bundles (Figure 7).

Based on infrastructures like the Distributed OSGi cloud, composite learning objects can be constructed using an Enterprise Mashup middleware which has the following components [10]:

- Services and information produced in a format that can be mashed, such as RSS/Atom, Web services, bundles or REST (representational state transfer)
- Visualization components such as portlets, widgets, and gadgets
- A tool to compose the mashup and wire components together
- A robust infrastructure to manage all the change and new combinations

Examples of Enterprise Mashups include JackBe[6], WebGlue[7], Oracle Fusion Middleware[8], WSO2 Middleware[9], Kapow Mashup Server[10], SnapLogic[11] and Apache XAP[12]. Generally, the architecture of an Enterprise Mashup consists of two components: *Mashup builder* and *Mashup Enabler*. The mashup builder produces the user interface of the resulting mashup through connecting several required widgets to create a composite application. The mashup enabler accessing the mashed-up unstructured data and makes the internal and external resources available based on REST, RSS or Atom. Both components may be called an *Enterprise Mashup Server*. Figure 8 illustrates the general structure of Enterprise Mashup Server.

---

[5] http://cxf.apache.org/distributed-osgi.html
[6] www.jackbe.com
[7] www.webglue.com
[8] www.oracle.com/middleware
[9] http://wso2.com/
[10] www.kapowtech.com/
[11] www.snaplogic.org
[12] http://incubator.apache.org/xap/

140   J. Fiaidhi

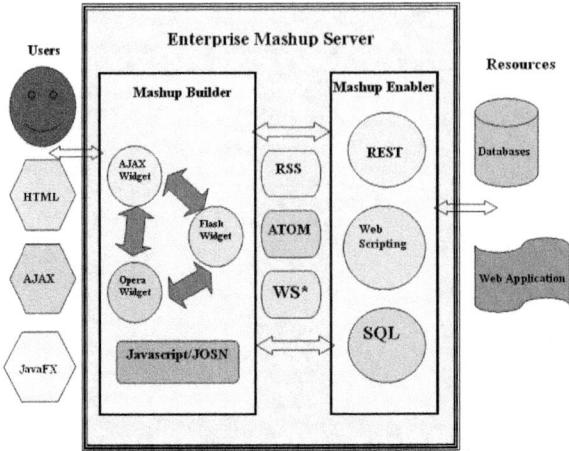

Fig. 8. The main components of Enterprise Mashup Server

The 2008 Horizon Report [1] calls the Enterprise mashup as the *Social Operating System* as it represent the base the organization of the network around people, rather than around content. However, the architecture of such social operating system becomes more complex as the degree of semantic awareness increases as well as with the increasing freedom of calm computing. To reduce such complexity, we propose a web or cloud widget approach, where the bundles can have more semantic capabilities when created and published as ready-to-use learning object components which can easily and cost-effectively be added to any learning applications. A web widget is a reusable, compact software bundle that can be embedded into a learning object or learning application to provide an added functionality. Most useful web widgets also combine on-line data resources with the learning site data to create mash-ups (e.g. Google Maps and Google AdSense web widgets). Web widgets can also be combined together and published as new components/bundles (e.g. with the Yahoo! Pipes service). Moreover, web widgets can have more semantics if they are hooked up with either metadata sources such as ontologies or the processed outputs of other

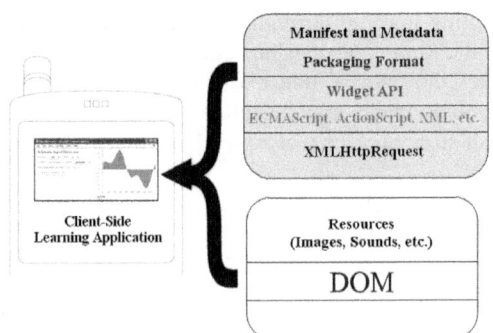

Fig. 9. Widget-Based Learning Object

components. Figure 9 illustrates our vision to the next generation PLEs learning objects which can coop with functionalities like mashups and harvesting required for future generation of learning systems.

3   Harvesting Learning Objects: The Calm Wiki Approach

The most important functionality in any calm computing learning application is the ability of harvesting relevant learning objects from the periphery repository and moves it to the learner active working area. For this purpose, PLEs require to have an underlying model of the knowledge described in its learning objects. Regular, or syntactic, learning objects have structured metadata text with some untyped hyperlinks. Semantic-based learning objects, on the other hand, provide the ability to identify information about the data within learning objects, and the relationships between learning objects, in ways that can be queried or exported like a database. Imagine a semantic-based learning system devoted to food. A learning object for an apple would contain, in addition to standard text information, some machine-readable semantic data. The most basic kind of data would be that an apple is a kind of fruit. The learning system would thus be able to automatically generate a list of fruits, simply by listing all learning objects that are tagged as being of type "fruit". Further semantic tags in the "apple" learning object could indicate other data about apples, including their possible colors and sizes, nutritional information and serving suggestions, and so on. These tags could be derived from the learning object metadata text but with some chance of error - accordingly they should be presented alongside that data to be easily corrected. If the learning system periphery exports all this data in RDF or a similar format, it can then be queried in a similar way to a database - so that an external learner could, for instance, request a list of all fruits that are red and can be baked in a pie. However, to implement new learning applications (e.g. food cataloguing system) with semantic capabilities requires a lot of functionality dealing specifically with ontologies and metadata. Currently, needed functionalities are typically created for each learning application individually, requiring a lot of work, time and specific skills. Being able to lower these implementation costs would be hugely beneficial. In developing any learning ontological system, finding and selecting the right concepts and instances is a central task of its own in ontological user interfaces. For end-user applications, any search usually begins by first finding the right concepts with which to do the actual ontological querying. For efficient semantic content indexing, accurate indexing entities need to be found with as little effort as possible. Also ontology developers need concept search when creating links between concepts, especially when developing distinct, yet heavily interlinked ontologies. For this purpose, finding and harvesting relevant learning object from the periphery requires sort of semantic wiki. Actually, wikis replace older knowledge management tools, semantic wikis try to serve similar functions: to allow users to make their internal knowledge more explicit and more formal, so that the information in a wiki can be searched in better ways than just with keywords, offering queries similar to structural databases. The amount of formalization and the way the semantic information is made explicit vary. Existing systems range from primarily content-oriented (like Semantic MediaWiki) where semantics are entered by creating annotated hyperlinks, via approaches mixing content and semantics in plain text, via content-oriented with a strong formal background (like KiWi), to systems where the formal knowledge is the primary interest (like Metaweb), where semantics are entered into explicit fields for that purpose. Also, semantic wiki systems differ in the level of ontology support they offer. While most systems can export their data as RDF, some even support various levels of ontology reasoning.

For the purpose of illustrating the difference between a plain keyword-based search and a semantic wiki search that uses an ontology, we compared our semantic wiki approach with the twitter widget searching that is based on pure keywords searching[13]. Figure 10 illustrates an example for searching for the keyword hardware using the twitter widget searching.

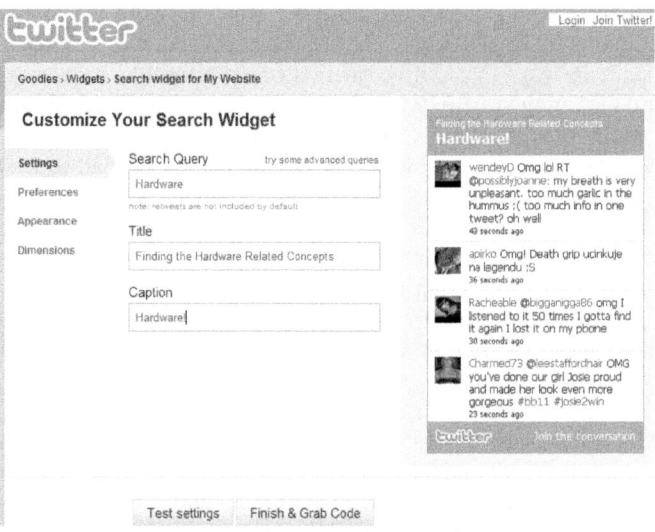

Fig. 10. The Twitter Widget Keyword Search Engine

However, we developed our own semantic wiki prototype is called "Twitter Image Search" where we can provide ontology for some selected words like hardware and cat (Figure 11).

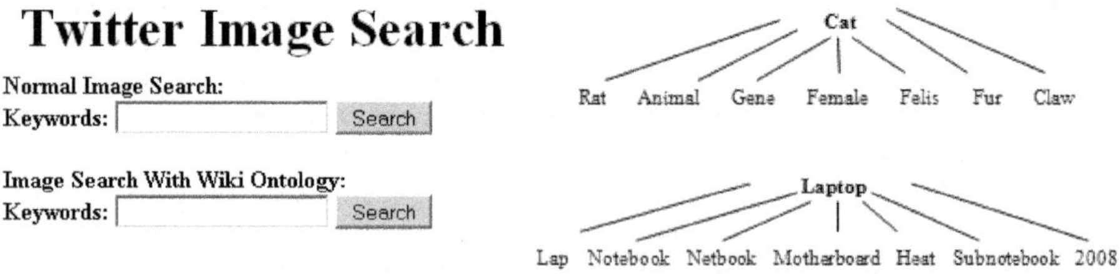

Twitter Image Search

Normal Image Search:
Keywords: [   ] Search

Image Search With Wiki Ontology:
Keywords: [   ] Search

Cat — Rat Animal Gene Female Felis Fur Claw

Laptop — Lap Notebook Netbook Motherboard Heat Subnotebook 2008

Fig. 11. The Twitter Image Search Engine (Keywords or Ontology)

---

[13] http://twitter.com/goodies/widget_search

Table 1. Comparing Keyword Search with Wiki Based Ontological Search

Normal Search

Keyword	Relevant	Irrelevant	Total	Percent	Results
computer	37	13	50	74	538
hardware	32	18	50	64	164
lake	15	35	50	30	435
tree	16	34	50	32	460
road	49	1	50	98	822
house	19	31	50	38	718
plane	2	48	50	4	199
boat	7	43	50	14	219

Ontology Search

Keyword	Relevant	Irrelevant	Total	Percent	Results
computer	12	38	50	24	1689
hardware	28	22	50	56	1085
lake	15	35	50	30	584
tree	16	34	50	32	974
road	49	1	50	98	1478
house	21	29	50	42	1536
plane	2	48	50	4	976
boat	30	20	50	60	601

Cleaned Query: hardware

Image Results:

Cleaned Query: hardware computer hardware metal technology tool cutlery

Images Using Wiki Ontology Results:

Fig. 12. (a) Keyword Search for Hardware. (b) Ontological Search for Hardware.

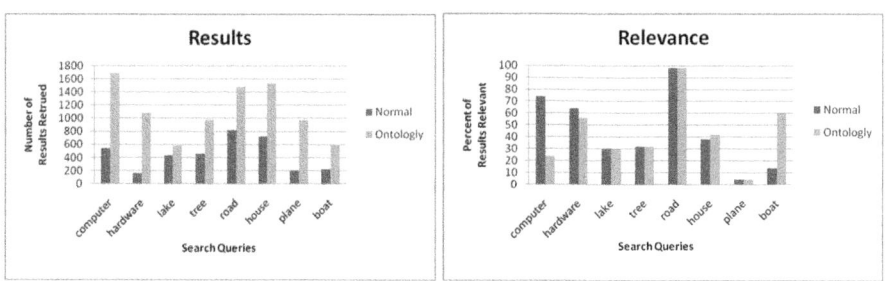

Fig. 13. Comparing Normal Keyword Search with Wiki-Based Ontological Search

Table 1 and Figures 12, 13 illustrate our findings. Certainly having an ontology-based Wiki enhances the search relevancy.

4 Learning Objects Garbage Collection: The Calm Approach

Garbage collection systems were first developed around 1960 and have undergone much research and refinement since then. The mechanism of garbage collection is fairly simple to describe although the implementation is more complicated. The garbage collector's goal is to form a set of reachable objects that constitute the "valid" objects in your application. When a collection is initiated, the collector initializes the set with all known root objects such as stack-allocated and global variables. The collector then recursively follows strong references from these objects to other objects, and adds these to the set. All objects that are not reachable through a chain of strong references to objects in the root set are designated as "garbage". At the end of the collection sequence, the garbage objects are finalized and immediately afterwards the memory they occupy is recovered (Figure 14).

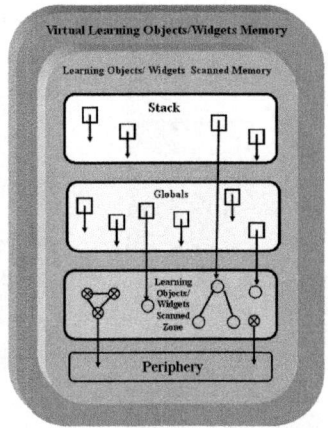

Fig. 14. The notion of Learning Objects Garbage Collection

There are several points of note regarding the type of learning objects/widgets garbage collector that can be used in any calm learning system:

- **The collector is conservative.** It never compact the heap by moving blocks of memory and updating pointers. Once allocated, an object always stays at its original memory location.
- **The collector is both request and demand driven.** The implementation makes requests at appropriate times. You can also programmatically request consideration of a garbage collection cycle, and if a memory threshold has been exceeded a collection is run automatically.
- **The collector runs on its own thread in the application.** At no time are all threads stopped for a collection cycle, and each thread is stopped for as short a

time as is possible. It is possible for threads requesting collector actions to block during a critical section on the collector thread's part.

- **The collector uses hybrid strategies (Open and Closed).** Most garbage collection systems are "closed"—that is, the language, compiler, and runtime collaborate to be able to identify the location of every pointer reference to a collectable block of memory. In contrast to closed collection systems, "open" systems allow pointers to garbage collected blocks to reside anywhere, and in particular where pointers reside in stack frames as local variables. Such garbage collectors are deemed "conservative." Their design point is often that since programmers can spread pointers to any and all kinds of memory, then all memory must be scanned to determine unreachable (garbage) blocks. This leads to frequent long collection times to minimize memory use. Memory collection is instead often delayed, leading to large memory use which, if it induces paging, can lead to very long pauses. As a result, conservative garbage collection schemes are not widely used. However, it is possible to strikes a balance between being "closed" and "open" by knowing exactly where pointers to scanned blocks are wherever it can, by easily tracking "external" references, and being "conservative" only where it must. By tracking the allocation age of blocks, the collector implements partial ("incremental") collections which scan an even smaller amount of the heap. This eliminates the need for the collector to have to scan all of memory seeking global references and provides a significant performance advantage over traditional conservative collectors.

5   Conclusions

This article describes our vision to the future generations of learning systems that are based on calm computing technologies. Central to this vision is the representation of learning objects as lightweight widgets where the learner can mash them up to compose new learning objects. Two major calm computing services are provided in our vision: The widgets harvesting from the preprimary repositories of widgets and the widget garbage collection from the learners virtual/central widget memory. The research described in this visionary article is far from complete as it currently works in progress. A comprehensive prototype is almost complete that utilizes a cloud computing infrastructure [9].

Acknowledgement. I would like to thank Tai-hoon Kim and Dominik Slezak for their comments and encouragements to present this article at the FGIT 2010 Conference. Also I would like to thanks NSERC for supporting my research. Finally, I would like to thank Daniel Servos for his work on Twitter Wiki prototype.

References

1. Horizon Report, The New Media Consortium and EDUCAUSE, ISBN 0-9765087-6-1 (2008), http://www.nmc.org/pdf/2008-Horizon-Report.pdf
2. Hinchcliffe, D.: A bumper crop of new mashup platforms, ZDNet Online Magazine (July 23, 2007), http://blogs.zdnet.com/Hinchcliffe/?p=111

3. Tugui, A.: Calm Technologies in a Multimedia World. ACM Ubiquity 5(4) (2004), http://www.acm.org/ubiquity/views/v5i4_tugui.html
4. Weiser, M.: The Computer for the 21st Century. Scientific American, 94–100 (September 1991), http://www.ubiq.com/hypertext/weiser/SciAmDraft3.html
5. Fiaidhi, J., Mohammed, S.: Design Issues Involved in Using Learning Objects for Teaching a Programming Language within a Collaborative eLearning Environment. International Journal of Instructional Technology and Distance Learning (USA) 1(3), 39–53 (2004)
6. Jung, Y., Lee, J., Kim, M.: Community Computing Model Supporting Community Situation Based Strict Cooperation and Conflict Resolution. In: Obermaisser, R., Nah, Y., Puschner, P., Rammig, F.J. (eds.) SEUS 2007. LNCS, vol. 4761, pp. 47–56. Springer, Heidelberg (2007)
7. Kumar, M., et al.: PICO: A Middleware framework for Pervasive Computing. In: Pervasive Computing 1268-1536, pp. 72–79 (2003)
8. Jennings, R.: Developing Multiagent Systems: The Gaia Methodology. ACM Transactions on Software Engineering and Methodology 12(3), 317–370 (2003)
9. Mohammed, S., Servos, D., Fiaidhi, J.: HCX: A Distributed OSGi Based Web Interaction System for Sharing Health Records in the Cloud. In: 2010 International Workshop on Intelligent Web Interaction (IWI 2010), Affiliated with Web Intelligence 2010 (WI 2010) International Conference, August 31 (2010)
10. Fiaidhi, J., Mohammed, S., Chamarette, L., Thomas, D.: Identifying Middlewares for Mashup Personal Learning Environments. Future Internet Journal 1(1) (2009)
11. Fiaidhi, J., Chou, W., Williams, J.: Mobile Computing in the Context of Calm Technology. IEEE IT-PRO, Editorial Article (May-June, 2010)

The Logistics Equipment Carbon Emission Monitoring System for a Green Logistics

Hyungrim Choi[1], Byoungkwon Park[2], Byungha Lee[1], Yongsung Park[2],
Changsup Lee[1], and Jeongsoo Ha[1]

[1] Seunghak campus Dong-A university, 840 hadna2dong,
sahgu, busan, Korea
[2] Bumin Campus Dong-A university, 1 bumindong 2ga,
segu, busan, Korea
{hrchoi,bpark,ys1126,cslee}@dau.ac.kr,
{leebh1443,charismaya}@naver.com

Abstract. Recently, due to the global enforcement of obligations to reduce green house gases and various environmental regulations, low carbon green growth strategies are required. Currently, in our country, environment friendly logistics activities are staying in the early stage compared to advanced countries because of our country's large energy consumption type industrial structures. As a measure to respond to the trend of the reinforcement of international environmental regulations in the sector of logistics, active green logistics systems should be established and to solve this problem, this study is intended to develop a monitoring system that can manage the carbon emission of logistics equipment(container truck, discharging equipment etc) in real time using a new technology named IP-RFID. The monitoring system developed in this study can actively manage the carbon emission of individual logistics equipment by attaching IP-Tags that can measure the carbon emission of individual logistics equipment in real time and transmit the information obtained from the measurement directly to users through IP communication. Since carbon emission can be managed by logistics equipment and drivers can check the carbon emission of equipment through this system, the carbon emission generated in the logistics sector may be reduced by using this system.

Keywords: Green Logistics, Monitoring system, Carbon Emmission, IP-RFID, i-tag.

1 Introduction

Globally, the average temperature on the earth has increased by 0.7℃ over the last 100 years and the average temperature is expected to increased by maximum 6.4℃ in the 21st century and thus global attention to and concern about climate changes are rising. These climate changes are working as a threatening factor on the survival of mankind with meteorological disasters or the destruction of ecosystems and resultant economic loss is increasing every year.

T.-h. Kim et al. (Eds.): UNESST 2010, CCIS 124, pp. 147–153, 2010.
© Springer-Verlag Berlin Heidelberg 2010

In the midst of the rising attention to global warming after the Kyoto Protocol, advanced countries and developing countries decided to allocate the amount of reduction of green house gas emission by country in order to reduce the emission of green house gases such as carbon dioxide and methane in particular among many factors that cause environmental pollution in order to prevent global warming. In the case of our country, total yearly green house gas emission was ranked around the tenth in the world and according to OBCE IEA data, carbon dioxide emission in Germany has decreased by 15.9% for 15 years from 1990 to 2005 while carbon dioxide emission in our country has increased by 97.6% for the same period and thus the increase rate was the second highest in the world next to China and it was expected that it would increase by maximum 38% by 2020. Although our country is not a country of obligatory reductions now, it is expected that our country will be imposed with the obligation to reduce the emission from 2013 and thus it is expected that carbon emission reductions will approach businesses in Korea as a new cost burden.[1][3][4][5]

Accordingly, the government became to declare the low carbon green growth vision and thereafter, various related government departments including the Ministry of Knowledge Economy(green IT industrial strategy, January 15, 2009), the Ministry of Public Administration and Safety(green information system plan, January 16, 2009) and the Korea Communications Commission(master plan for implementing green broadcasting and communication, April 8, 2009) have been developing environment friendly technologies and introducing environment friendly policies.

In the sector of logistics too, the air pollutants emitted from concentrated discharging equipment and trucks have been assessed to be at quite high levels and it is expected that of the entire CO2 emission in our country, the part attributable to the transport sector will increase from 20.3% in 2002 to 23.9% in 2020. This means the importance of environment friendly logistics activities in transport which is an important function of logistics and thus efforts to improve the state are necessary.

Therefore, this study is intended to discuss a monitoring system that can manage carbon emission by logistics equipment(container truck, discharging equipment etc) in real time to reduce green house gas emission by applying a new technology named IP-RFID.

2   Carbon Emission Calculation Methods

There are two carbon emission calculation methods including a direct method that directly measures the concentration and flux etc of carbon at the outlets of emission sources using measuring devices to calculate carbon emission based on the results and an indirect method that theoretically estimates emission considering the kinds and amounts of burnt fuels, their combustion efficiency and emission coefficients etc. Although the direct method has an advantage that accurate information on the final emission can be obtained as fuel burning processes are reflected, great deals of time and money are required for the installation and operation of necessary equipment and there are limitations in measuring. The indirect method has an advantage that calculations using this method are easy but has a disadvantage that the accuracy and reliability of data are low as the method calculates data through coefficients.

Table 1. Comparison between the carbon emission calculation methods

Calculation method	Advantage	Disadvantage
Direct	Accurate information on the final emission can be obtained	The installation and operation of necessary equipment require time and money
Indirect	Easy calculation	Low accuracy and reliability of data

Currently, most countries measure carbon emission with the indirect method and due to the inaccuracy of data presented above, some opinions are being raised that measures to accurately measure carbon emission are necessary.[2] This is because certificated emission reductions are currently transacted and have functions like those of cash. Therefore, in this study, a monitoring system that will enable accurate management of carbon emission will be presented.

3   IP-RFID Based Carbon Emission Monitoring System

3.1   Concept of IP-RFID

IP-RFID is a method that combines the advantages of RFID(Radio Frequency Identification) and USN(Ubiquitous Sensor Network) technologies and minimal IPv6 technology it is a technology intended to ensure wide expandability and mobility by loading IPs on tags in order to maximize the synergy effect of the combination of existing IP infra and USN & RFID infra and to directly manage and control the tags.

In the case of existing RFID Systems, user could not firsthand access to RFID Tags to obtain desired information. In addition, multiple users could not access to a single RFID Tag to register their information nor could enter the time to receive certain information and kinds of data to be received in order to receive the requested information at the time intervals to receive the information and there was no function to set threshold values for certain information so that users are notified when the information exceeds or falls shorts of the threshold values either.

When providing RFID services, IP-RFID uses the code information of existing RFID Tags as the IP address(or IP address and contents index) of the contents server that provides contents so that contents services can be provided quickly/easily and it can provide RFID Tags for IP address based RFID services that will enable fast responses to changes in the contents provided and methods for IP address based RFID services at RFID terminals or contents servers using the RFID Tags.

It was attempted to develop a system that can measure carbon emission utilizing these characteristics of IP-RFID that directly provides the information required by users.

3.2   System Concept Diagram

In this system, in order to manage in real time, the carbon emission of various types of logistics equipment that are used in the area of logistics, IP-Tags are attached to

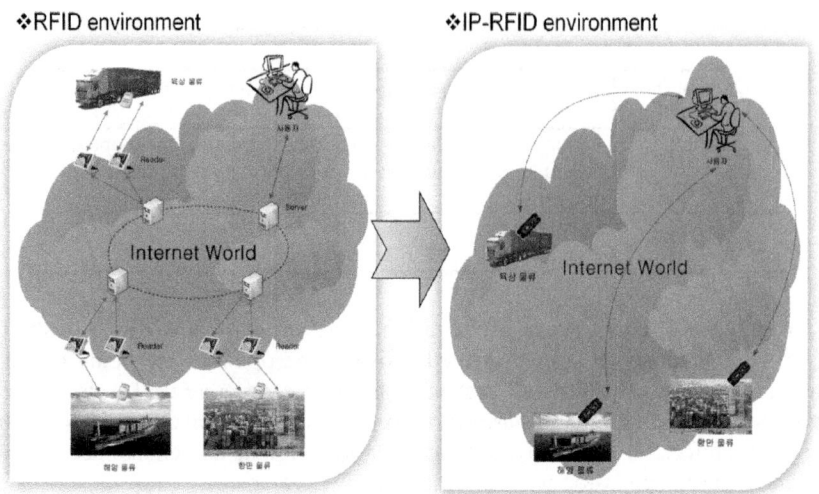

Fig. 1. Difference of RFID and IP-RFID environments

areas near the outlets of the equipment and the location information and carbon emission information of the logistics equipment are collected in real time through communication with the SPs(Smart Points) installed in the region to enable the management of carbon emitted in the area of logistics. A related conceptual diagram is shown in <Figure 2>.

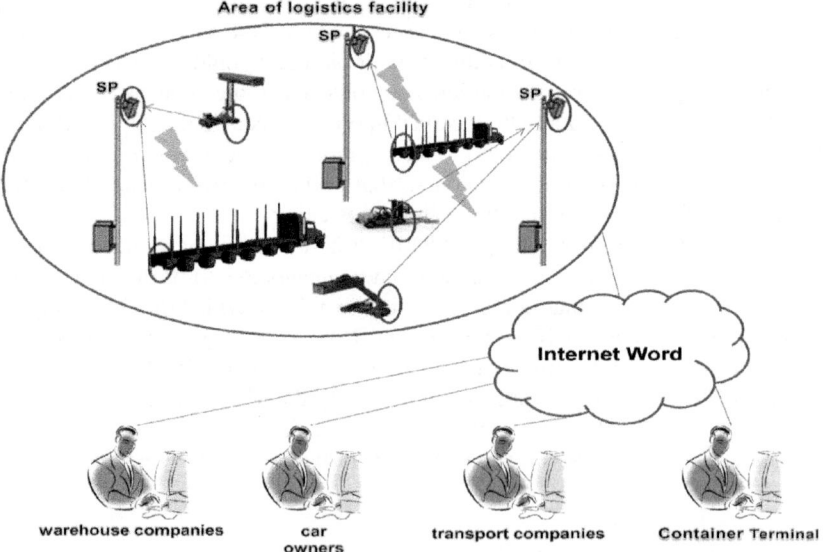

Fig. 2. System concept

3.3   User Interface

This system is characterized by the fact that user interfaces vary by party due to differences in the information to be utilized by different parties. First, container terminal operating companies have diverse types of logistics equipment and thus they should manage carbon emission by equipment. As shown in <Figure 4>, daily, weekly, monthly and quarterly pieces of emission information are managed depending of the types of equipment and through this, the carbon emission from each unit of logistics equipment occurring in the port is managed.

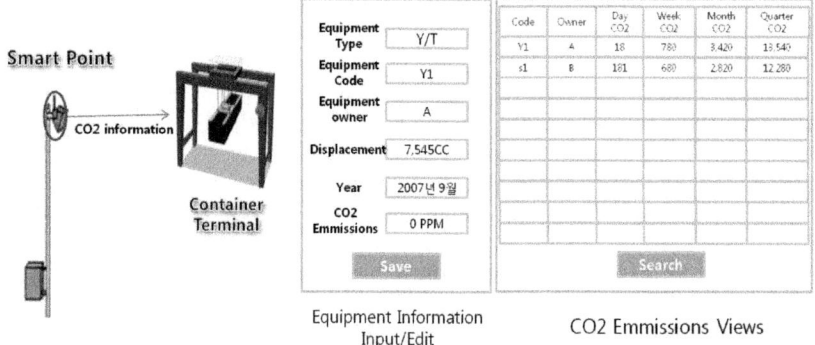

Fig. 3. Container Terminal User Interface

Secondly, in the case of transport companies, since they own and operate multiple cars, they should manage their total carbon emission through the management of the carbon emission of each car. These data can also be used when cars with similar mileages and specifications show different carbon emission values for follow-up actions such as car maintenance.

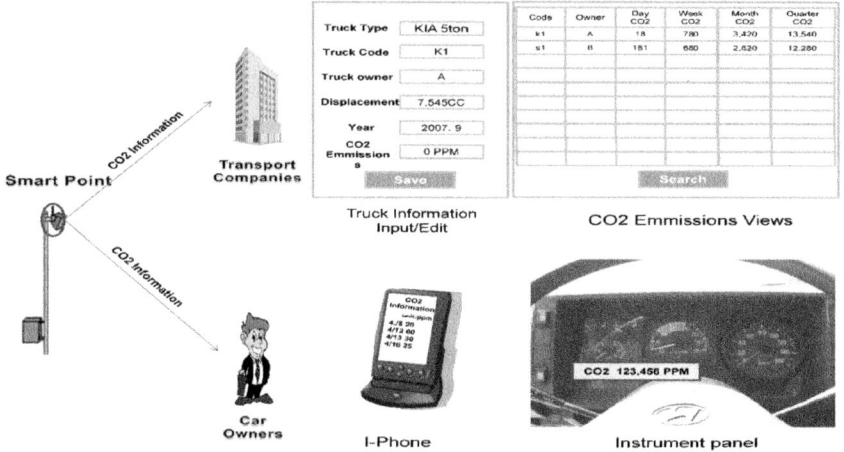

Fig. 4. Transport Company & Car Owner User Interface

Finally, car owners (drivers) that drive cars should be also provided with information because they perform activities related to carbon emission. As with total mileages that can be identified from instrument panels, carbon emission should be also identifiable and it is necessary to enable the drivers to identify information through mobile devices such as mobile phones when they wish to identify daily or monthly carbon emission.

4   Conclusion

In this study, a system that can measure and monitor the carbon occurring in the area of logistics was presented for the management of green house gases that are becoming an issue recently.

Existing methods indirectly manage carbon emission information through emission coefficients and they have problems in the accuracy and reliability of the carbon information resulting from the carbon emission coefficients that vary every time they are measured and other factors. As regulations on green house gases are being increasingly reinforced, these problems should be solved and to this end, carbon emission should be accurately managed through directly measuring methods.

In this respect, this study presented a system to provide information to parties in logistics through directly measuring method by attaching IP-Tags to the outlets of logistics equipment to sense carbon emission information and transmit it to parties in logistics through the SPs installed at many places in transport regions. Since different parties in logistics have different types of equipment to be managed and even the same equipment can emit different amounts of carbon depending on the situations of operation and management, the parties are enabled to immediately respond to changes through the monitored carbon emission information. They can screen out those units of equipment that emit large amounts of carbon in ordinary times to receive maintenance services and it can be expected that the information can help parties in logistics in their decision making for matters such as buying certified emission reductions if carbon has been emitted more than expected.

Acknowledgments

We inform that this study is a result of the Ministry of Land, Transport and Marine Affairs; Active IP-RFID Technology Development Project for Marine Logistics and thank for the support with the research fund.

References

1. GyeEui, S., ChulHwan, H.: A study on the Strategies for the Reduction of Port Pollution. Journal of Korea Port Economic Accociation 23(1), 95–113 (2007)
2. Junseok, C., Sanghyeok, K., Ilsoo, P., Younghoe, L., Seongnam, O., Jihyung, H.: An Estimation of Air Pollutants from Air Pollutants Emission Source. National institute of environmental research

3. Impact of the Policies to reduce GHG Emissions on the Korean Manufacturing Industries. Korea Institute for Industrial Economics&Trade (2008)
4. Junghyun, K.: USA Green Port Policy trends. Logistics and Policy 8, 47–62 (2008)
5. LA/LB Port Green Logistics Trends and Policy Implications. Maritime trends 1273, 1–10 (2008)

IP-RFID Based Container Monitoring System

Hyung-Rim Choi[1], Byung-Kwon Park[1], Yong-Sung Park[2],
Chang-Sup Lee[3], and Chang-Hyun Park[4]

[1] Professor of the Department of Management Information, College of Business
Administration, Dong-A University
{hrchoi,bpark}@dau.ac.kr
[2] Research Professor of the Department of Management Information, College of Business
Administration, Dong-A University
ys1126@dau.ac.kr
[3] Senior Researcher of the Media Device Research Center, Dong-A University
cslee@dau.ac.kr
[4] Master's Course, the Department of Management Information, College of Business
Administration, Dong-A University
archehyun@naver.com

Abstract. RFID technology in container management field is considered for increasing productivity and efficiency in logistics industry. But there are a lot of problems caused by inappropriate application of RFID technology in shipping logistics. Therefore, technology development based on IP is needed for accepting diverse technology applied before and offering better service to develop container management technology involved with RFID. In this study, realtime container monitoring system using IP-RFID is designed and implemented for supplementing weakness of information gathering using existing RFID and transferring data in real time to user.

Keywords: RFID, IP-RFID, Container, Monitoring System.

1 Introduction

The 2009 world port container traffic reached 586.93 million TEU involving an increase by 8.6% compared to the previous year and world port container traffic is continuously increasing every year (Drewry, 2008). Containers are a packing measure that is the most important and the most frequently used in port logistics. In addition, most of newly ports are constructed as dedicated container terminals. However, the development of methods or information systems for efficiently managing these containers is insufficient. Even when shipping companies or logistics related parties wish to the locations, states(full/ empty) or number of their containers, there is no way to efficiently support them. In addition, active management of container cargoes is insufficient. To check the states of container cargoes loaded in three to four layers, humans go up firsthand on ropes and when weather on the sea is bad, accidents with casualties occur sometimes (Yang Hyeon-Suk, 2007). Therefore, systems that can monitor the locations and states of containers are necessary.

T.-h. Kim et al. (Eds.): UNESST 2010, CCIS 124, pp. 154–163, 2010.
© Springer-Verlag Berlin Heidelberg 2010

Recently, diverse technologies such as RFID and e-seal are applied to containers and these technologies are to support efficient transport rather than to manage containers per se. The reason why RFID technology is applied to containers is to efficiently classify containers and grasp the flow of containers (Lim Seong-Woo, 2009, Choi Jong-Hee, 2007) and the reason why e-seal technology is applied to containers is to reinforce the security function of container logistics(Ryu Ok-Hyeon, 2007).

In this respect, this study is intended to present an information system for efficiently managing containers. In this study, IP-RFID technology was used for real time container management. IP-RFID technology refers to a new technology that incorporated IP technology into RFID technology to enable RFID tags to implement IP communication (Choi Hyung-Rim, 2010). Since IP-RFID tags (hereinafter IP tag) have their own IP addresses they can be globally tracked and the information stored in or created by the tags can be directly transmitted to diverse users. In the case of existing RFID systems, tags per se do not have IP addresses to be connected to Internet and the reader or middleware is connected to Internet and thus global tracking using tags is difficult. Therefore, in this study, a monitoring system that can manage container locations and states etc using IP-RFID technology that can perform global tracking was developed.

In chapter 2 of this study, the IP-RFID technology utilized to develop the container monitoring system is introduced, in chapter 3, the structure and functions of the container monitoring system are presented and in chapter 4, the results of tests of the system are presented.

2 IP-RFID Technology

IP-RFID is a method that combines the advantages of USN and RFID technologies and minimal IPv6 technology and it is a technology intended to ensure wide expandability and mobility by loading IPs on tags in order to maximize the synergy effect of the combination of existing IP infra and USN & RFID infra and to directly manage and control the tags(Choi Hyung-Rim, 2010).

Since existing RFID systems have been mainly used for limited use of transmitting simple recognition information stored in tags, their major objectives were minimizing their system resources and producing the systems at low costs. Therefore, it has been perceived that communication protocols that consume large amounts of system resources such as TCP/IP are not suitable. However, for a tag to serve the role as a new information provider, IP technology should be utilized. The effort to incorporate IP technology into USN technology in order to create new value can also be understood in this context. Based on existing IP infra, IP-RFID can provide wide expandability, ensure tag mobility and provide diverse services at desired places in linkage with Internet infra such as BcN(Broadband Convergence Network), IPv6(next generation Internet address system), Wibro and wireless LAN.

The IP-RFID developed in this study can firsthand manage tags in addition to utilizing existing IP infra and services, enable two-way communication between tags and users and apply RTLS (Real-Time Locating System) technology using the CSS (Chirp Spread Spectrum) method of IEEE 802154a.

156   H.-R. Choi et al.

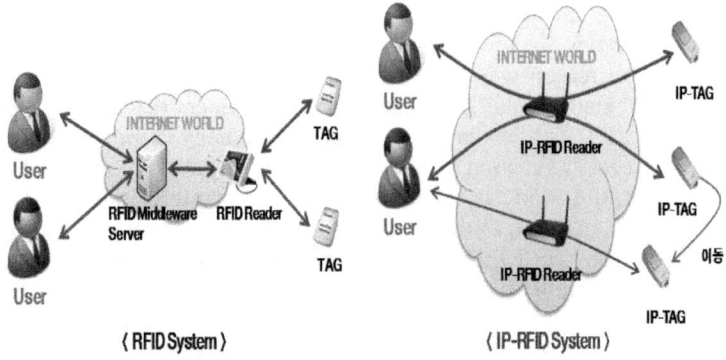

Fig. 1. RFID System and IP-RFID System

In existing RFID systems, tag information has gone through the reader to be stored in a certain information system altogether. Therefore, users could identify and utilize tag information only in the form provided by the certain information system. Furthermore, users could not store any information in tags or revise or delete the information because existing RFID systems are for one-way communication that can only provide the information stored in tags to users. In addition, unless a certain information system install readers throughout the world, no tag can be globally tracked.

However, in IP-RFID systems, tags have IP addresses and thus they can be tracked through Internet no matter where in the world they are and diverse kinds of information can be exchanged between the systems and users. In addition, users can directly receive any information they want from any tags they want. Furthermore, since Raw data can be collected, users can utilize information in any form they want in any application they want.

In IP-RFID systems, tags can serve the role of a new information related party to collect and provide diverse kinds of information and directly exchange the information with users.

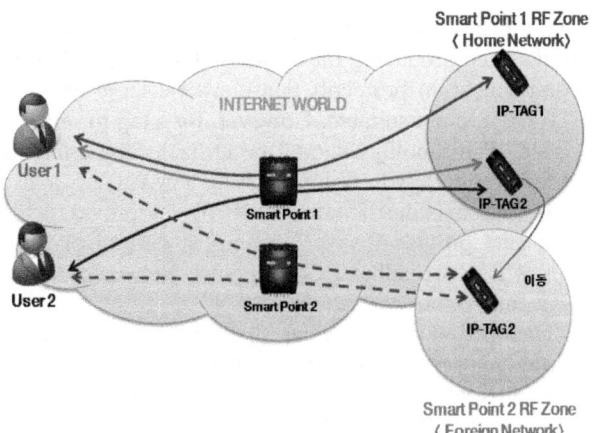

Fig. 2. Multi-Subscription Concept

To provide tag information to diverse users, IP-RFID systems utilize 'Multi-Subscriptions'. Multi-Subscriptions refer to multiple users' registrations of their information and desired data in IP tags in advance in order to be provided with their desired information from the IP tags. The IP tags can accurately deliver the necessary information to diverse users based on the registered information. Users can change online, their desired data and time of provision any time.

In this study, an information system was developed that can manage containers located anywhere in the world online utilizing these IP-RFID tags.

3   IP-RFID Based Container Monitoring System

3.1   System Structure and Services

The IP-RFID based container monitoring system installs IP tags in containers to provide state information such as container locations, whether cargoes are contained in the containers and temperatures/humidity/illuminance directly to diverse users in real time.

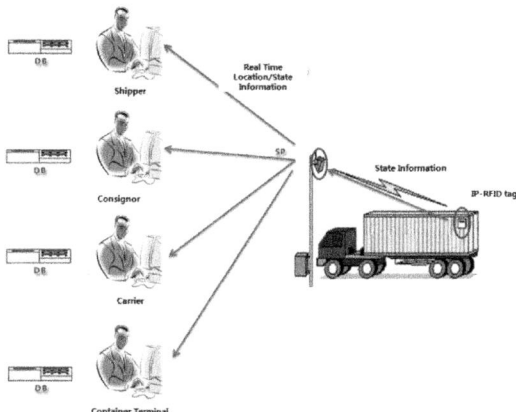

Fig. 3. System's Conceptual Diagram

The IP tags installed in this system are attached with temperatures/humidity/illuminance sensors and thus they can provide ambient temperature, humidity and illuminance information to users. The Smart Points used to transmit IP tag information to users are network devices that serve the same roles as those of the readers of RFID and the routers of IP communication. The IP tags provide information to users through S/P but can also transmit data to users through existing AP when necessary.

Once a container installed with an IP tag has gone into the RF area of S/P or the area of AP, the IP address of the IP tag and the specific Global ID will be combined to create an IPv6 address. Then, the user table will be inquired to provide subscribed users with information stored in the IP tag and sensed information. The information of the IP tag will be provided only to subscribed users.

Table 1. Details of major functions

Service type	Detail	Content
Provision of information in real time	Car identification	Services that can identify the cars where tags are attached utilizing unique information of Tags to manage individual cars separately
	Container identification	Services that can identify the containers where tags are attached utilizing unique information of Tags to monitor and manage to containers
Provision of state information in real time	Collection of state information through sensors	Services that can collect the state information of the containers or cars attached with tags in real time through sensors contained in the tags
	Transmission of monitored information	Services that provides tag information as information that can be monitored in real time through IP
Provision of statistical information	Creation of statistical information through the storage of Raw Data	Services to store the raw data transmitted from Tags in DB in order to utilize for statistical purposes (ex: yearly travel distances, the number of times of occurrence of dangers)

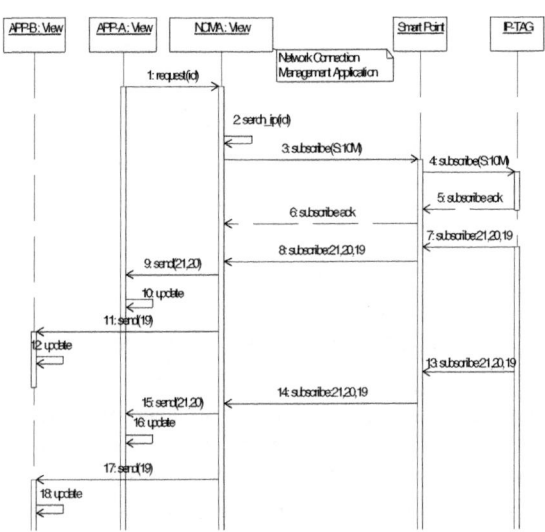

Fig. 4. Message exchanging between the IP tag and the application program

The services provided by this system are largely divided into three types including the provision of location information in real time, the provision of state information in real time and the creation of diverse statistics. Since all containers have their unique IP address values, their locations can be tracked no matter where they are in the world and through the sensors attached to the IP tags, temperature, humidity and illuminance information that is essential to container management can be monitored in real time. In addition, since users can firsthand collect Raw data through IP tags, they can create diverse statistical information using the raw data.

3.2 Design of Communication Protocols

A protocol for mutual communication between IP tags and application program was designed. Fig. 4 shows the messages exchanged between IP tags and applications in chronological order using a sequence diagram.

The user inquires IP tag information using a program that can search tags and manage connections and selects an IP-TAG for subscription. The user creates a subscription message based on [Table 4] and transmits it to the IP tag through Internet.

Table 2. Response Type, Separator and Parameter types

Response Type	Separator	Parameter	Description
Temperature		0x15	21도
Humidity		0x20	32%
Photometer	:	0x35	53lx
All		0x15 0x20 0x35	temperatures, humidity, illuminance

The subscription message indicates the data required by the user.

The subscribed IP tag transmits a subscribe ask message to the user and provides sensed data such as temperatures and humidity in designated periods. Each application program uses the data received in real time through Internet to store them in the database and renew the screen.

Table 3. The form of the message sent by the user to the IP-TAG

UDP Packet Message Format (User to IP-TAG, IP-TAG to User)		
(Command, Response) Type	Separate	Parameter
1 Byte	1 Byte	N Byte

3.3 Design of User Interfaces

In the RFID based container monitoring system, information systems for diverse purposes can be developed depending on how the user utilizes IP tag information. Even if the same IP tag information is provided, the functions of applied information

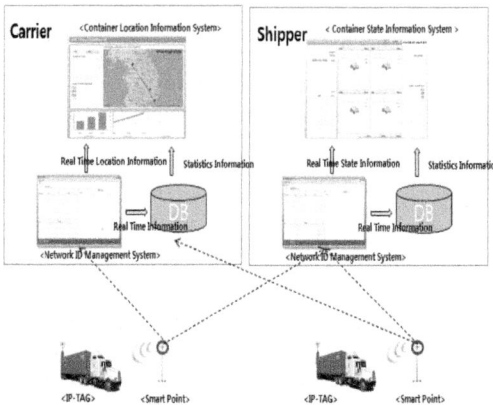

Fig. 5. Various Application of IP tag Information

systems will vary depending on for what purpose the information is utilized. In this study, interfaces of systems that can be developed from the standpoint of transport companies and shipping companies were designed. Transport company should require dynamically moving location information rather than static container locations and will require state information only in the case of special containers such as refrigerated containers. Shipping companies should require information on where their containers are, whether cargoes are contained and the state of the containers etc. That is, as shown in Fig. 5, even the data provided by the same IP tag can be diversely utilized depending on users' purposes.

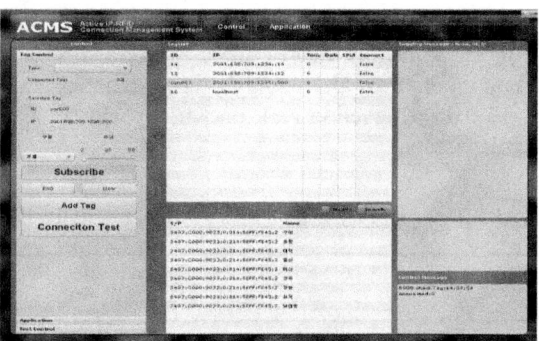

Fig. 6. Network Connection Management User Interface

shows an interface for managing networks with multiple tags(subscribed tags) that provide information in individual applied information systems. The user can check the list of the tags that provide information, can add or delete the tags and can check the state of connections of individual tags. In addition, the user can subscribe to individual tags or withdraw the subscriptions and identify the log information transmitted from the tags.

Fig. 7. State Information Management User Interface

shows the interface of the applied information systems that can be utilized by transport companies to identify dynamic locations of containers in real time. The locations of containers provided in real time are shown as a map.

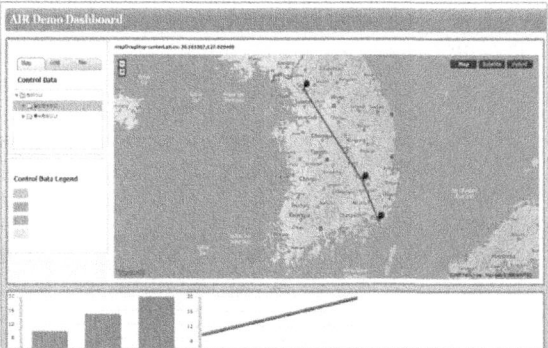

Fig. 8. Location Information Management User Interface

shows the interface of the applied information systems that can be utilized by shipping companies which provides container location and state information in real time. The state information provided by IP tags is provided in the form of a chart that can be easily understood by users. The information system includes a function to enable users to easily perceive any state information that is outside the normal value.

4   Implementation and Test

In this study, in order to test the feasibility and applicability of the IP-RFID based container monitoring system, a demo system was developed and tested. Major purposes of the test are to check if communication is properly implemented between IP tags and applications in IPv6 environments and check if the information created in the IP tags can

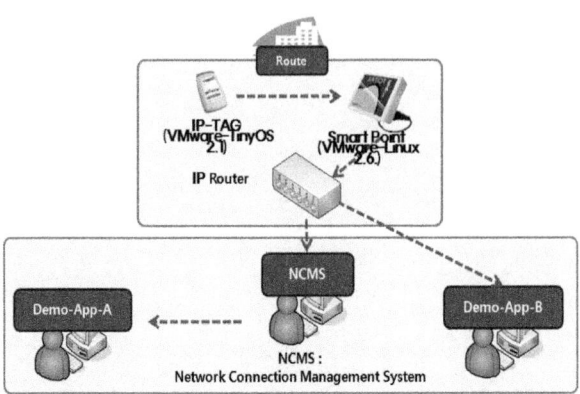

Fig. 9. Test Environment

be utilized in diverse applications. User interfaces were developed by Flex, communication modules were developed by JAVA and UDP packets were utilized.

In the test, IP tags were attached to cargoes on cars in the same way as done in cases where container cars are actually moving and S/Ps were installed at five locations to check if tag information would be transmitted to two applied information systems.

Fig. 10. Test Fulfillment

The two applied information systems are the 'application for transport companies' and the 'application for shipped companies' presented in chapter 3 and it was checked and tested if the information created in the tags was properly provided to the two applied information systems.

Based on the results of the implementation of the test, it could be identified every time a car loaded with IP tag cargoes passed an S/P, the information of the tags was provided to the two applications.

5 Conclusion

This study developed a system that can manage the locations and states etc of containers using a new technology named IP-RFID. Existing systems and studies had been focused on efficient transport of containers while this study presented a system intended to efficiently manage containers per se.

Since this system can transmit the information created in IP tags directly to diverse users, it will be able to provide new value to diverse container related parties in logistics such as shipping companies, transport companies and , container terminals. Since shipping companies can identify where their containers are, they can enhance the utility of containers and since transport companies and container terminals can identify the locations and states of containers in real time, they can enhance the efficiency and stability of their works.

In addition, this study discovered a new area of application where the new technology named IP-RFID can be applied. For the diverse applied information systems using IP-RFID technology to be utilized in the field, methods should be presented that will enable users to efficiently manage the data provided in real time by IP tags.

Acknowledgments

We inform that this study is a result of the Ministry of Land, Transport and Marine Affairs ; Active IP-RFID Technology Development Project for Marine Logistics and thank for the support with the research fund.

References

1. Drewry.: Annual Container Market Review and Forecast - 2008/09 (September 2008)
2. Ok-Hyeon, R., Jae-Gwang, L., Seong-Hol, N.: A Study on the Method to Improve Container Logistics Processes for Applying e-Seals in the RFID Method. OTSBA6 (2007)
3. Hyeon-Suk, Y., Heon-Jeong, I., Geon-Woo, K., Young-Gwal, K., Dong-Muk, K., Sung-Geun, L.: Development of a Refrigerated Container Remote Monitoring System for Ships in an RF Module Method. Korea Marine Engineering Society 31(4), 425–432 (2007)
4. Seong-Woo, L.: A Study on the Effect of RFID Introduction on the Reinforcement of the Competitiveness of Port Logistics Businesses. Kyungsung University (2009)
5. Jong-Hee, C., Soo-Yeop, K., Ho-Chun, L.: Measures to Introduce RFID technology for Advancing Port Logistics. Korea Maritime Institute (2007)
6. Hyung-Rim, C., Byung-Kwon, P., Hyun-Soo, K., Chang-Sup, L., Yong-Sung, P., Tae-Woo, K., Byung-Ha, L., Gi-Nam, C., Jung-Soo, H.: Development of IP-RFID-based Coastal Marine Traffic Control Systems. Journal of Korea Knowledge Information Technology Society 5(1) (2010.02)

Ways to Manage IP-RFID Based Navigation Aid Facilities

Hyung Rim Choi[1], Byoung Kwon Park[2], Min Je Cho[2],
Yong Sung Park[2], and Jeong Soo Ha[1]

[1] Seunghak campus Dong-A university, 840 hadna2dong,
sahgu, busan, Korea
[2] Bumin Campus Dong-A university, 1 bumindong 2ga,
segu, busan, Korea
{hrchoi,bpark,ys1126}@dau.ac.kr,
{mjcho78,charismaya}@gmail.com

Abstract. The aids to navigation that are separated by a secondary route of the ship to safety covers a large salvage ship safety and is an important role in accident prevention. Most of the equipment as high as the real-time safety and asset management needs, but the mechanisms behind this system is still lacking. Currently these are controlled by people directly, and there are some cases which is introduced for managing system. But it has an issue with lack of safety and compatibility, excessive operating expenses, volume, etc. In this study, management measure for course assistance facility is suggested that is applied IP-RFID technology integrated RFID technology and IP technology for solving these problems. Scenario is developed for efficient and rapid management with finding out problems of current course management, and then required service is suggested for integration management system which is applied IP-RFID technology.

Keywords: RFID, IP-RFID, i-Tag, Aids to Navigation.

1 Introduction

The majority of current domestic export/import traffic depends on maritime transportation. and the increase of freight space and traffic resulting from far bigger and faster vessels makes the maritime transport far more complex, with even greater loss of life and property and environmental damage caused by marine accident different from the past. Continuous efforts are being made to improve the management of navigation aid facilities which play the important role of preventing marine accidents and ensuring the safety of vessels, but the system is still in insufficient situation. Accordingly, this study tries to suggest the ways to efficiently manage navigation aid facilities by applying IP-RFID technology which grafts IP technology onto RFID, for which the management status and system of navigation aids were analyzed first of all. Further, in this study, scenarios and service for management of navigation aids are developed and the ways to apply and utilize this service are suggested.

T.-h. Kim et al. (Eds.): UNESST 2010, CCIS 124, pp. 164–172, 2010.
© Springer-Verlag Berlin Heidelberg 2010

2 Management Status of Navigation Aid Facilities

Harbor facilities can be defined as all facilities necessary to satisfy the harbor functions including anchorages, wharfs in the harbor and their accompanying structures and facilities, among which artificial facilities installed for safety of vessels and for increased efficiency of maritime transportation such as navigation aids are again distinguished as navigation aid facilities. Types of navigation aid facilities can be classified by location communication methods such as beacon, image, color, sound, and radio waves, which can be diversely used to communicate the location of the vessels even in nighttime and bad weather because it is necessary to always confirm the location of the vessels for safe navigation. Navigation aids can be classified as following table 1.

Table 1. Types and kinds of navigation aids

Type	Kind
Light Signal	Manned/Unmanned Lighthouse
	Light Beacon
	Leading Lights
	Searchlight
	Lantern
	Light Pole
	Light Buoy
Image Signal	Erect/Floating Buoy
Sound Wave Signal	Air/Electric/Motor Siren
Radio Wave Signal	Wireless Signal
	DGPS
	RACON
	LORAN-C
Special Signal	VTS
	Wave Signal Station

In Korea, the first navigation aid was installed by 'Ganghwado Treaty' in 1983, and total 94 units of navigation aids were identified in the survey of location and kinds of navigation aids in domestic coastal areas in 1901, and currently total 3,498 units are operated as of 2006 through continuous extension. Korea joined IALA in 1962, and domestic navigation aids are being managed on national level in accordance with 'navigation aids act', 'navigation aid facilities management guidelines', and 'standard for functions and specifications of navigation aids'.

The characteristics of such navigation aid facilities play an important role of assuring the safety of vessels and preventing marine accidents, basically having 2 requirements. First of all, these navigation aid facilities should be always fixed so that their locations can be identified, and they should be always available to check their situations for immediate inspection and use. Navigation aids should be internationally easy to identify by anyone, for which they should be always fixed at certain place and should be exactly operated. So, the navigator can either disregard them at normal times or immediately use them whenever necessary. The safety and reliability which are emphasized as above can make the navigator depend on navigation aid facilities by removing the risk factors of maritime safety.

But, due to the characteristics of installation and operation environment, it is difficult to have navigation aid facilities always fixed. There can be a situation that light buoys are lost due to the damage in fastening device which can maintain the location for reasons of vessel collision or high waves. Or there can be a case that light buoys don't properly function even if they maintain their places because the life of lighting device completed its span or was damaged. Recently, regular container shipping companies are pursuing the large-scaled economic effects with their super-large container ships, making loaded/unloaded traffic rapidly increase, so it is expected that the number of ports of call will be decreased to a few hub ports but feeder container shipping will be increased instead. Accordingly, as it is expected that maritime traffic will be rapidly increased with far more congestion, navigation aid facilities which don't function properly can cause fatal large-scale marine disasters.

Currently, the management, maintenance, and repair work of most navigation aid facilities are conducted by use of log lines, checking their overall functions and conducting management activities such as maintenance and repair. But, this method can not check the status in real time, and observing the location with naked eyes can make mistakes. Recently, locating system by use of GPS or DGPS receivers, or control and monitoring system by use of wire/wireless remote control devices are being introduced and applied, but they are not still widely used due to the problems of communication breakdown or operation cost, etc.

3   Definition and Characteristics of IP-RFID Technology

As all of network technologies are combined into IP(Internet Protocol) technology recently, RFID(Radio Frequency Identification) and USN(Ubiquitous Sensor Network) technologies are also being combined into IP communication. IP-RFID is a technology to directly manage and control the TAG which can assure wide extensibility and mobility by loading IP on TAG for maximization of synergy effects between existing IP infra and USN/RFID infra by grafting advantages of USN/RFID technologies onto minimum IPv6 technology.

Existing RFID system has some limits to development of application areas suitable for ubiquitous computing environment because it is one-way communication system which can provide the information stored in TAG only to specific system or limited number of users. On the contrary, IP-RFID system can play the role of new information source through the convergence of IP technology into TAG, where real time information can be obtained by directly connecting to TAG like visiting web-sites for specific information. Information stored in TAG or generated through sensors can be directly delivered to various users, and interactive communication between TAG and users is possible. Further, it is possible to develop various application areas suitable for ubiquitous computing environments.

Table 2. Comparison of IP-RFID and RFID Technology

Division	IP-RFID	RFID
Target of Information Provision	Directly to Users	Specific System or Limited Users
Communication	Interactive	One-Way
Development of Application Area	Various Areas	Limits

As a characteristic of IP-RFID, it is low-electricity Sensor Network Model the most suitable for WiFi Mesh which can extend existing IP World to RFID areas. Further, it can directly manage and control the node and realize RTLS(Real-Time Locating System) by use of CSS(Chirp Spread Spectrum) method in IEEE 802.15.4a.

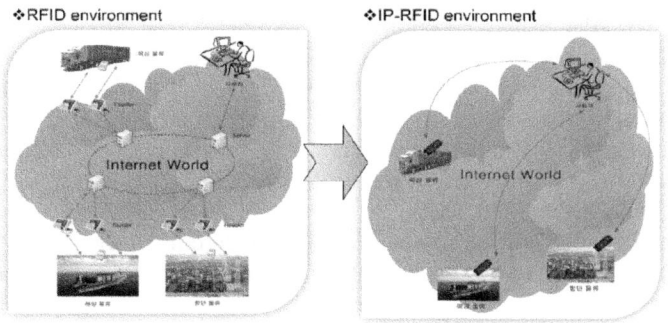

Fig. 1. Difference of RFID and IP-RFID environments

In existing RFID model, users must communicate through middle ware in order to request specific data to RFID TAG or to receive data from RFID TAG. So, middle ware should have all information about TAG, and particularly for communication between users and TAG, there should be separate Mapping Table which manages TAG. But, in IP-RFID model, various information can be utilized because TAG can directly provide information through Internet.

4   Service Development for Management of Navigation Aid Facilities

4.1   Requirements and Applied Scenarios

In order to extract requirements and scenarios for management of navigation aid facilities, analysis was conducted through literature research and expert interview, considering technical and environmental characteristics of IP-RFID. As previously described, navigation aid facilities need confirmation of location and real time operation status for the safety and operational efficiency.

Table 3. Requirements for Management of Navigation Aid Facilities

Division	Confirmation of Location	Confirmation of Status
Requirements	Confirmation of normal location and drifting location	Functional remote control of normal/abnormal operation

The result of interview with experts showed that the locations of marine buoys are identified by their administrators one by one with their naked eyes. Generally, navigation aid facilities are fixed to their locations by establishing sinker in ocean floor, but they can get out of their normal location and drift due to high waves or collision, which is difficult to identify with naked eyes. For confirmation of location through system, normal locations of buoys are being frequently or regularly watched by installing DGPS receiver on relevant signals, but this method were also incurring the relevant installation and operation costs.

Currently, relevant institutions are conducting maintenance and repair works by use of vessels, measuring overall functions. While they are sailing within the effective boundary of radio wave signals, they are measuring the location level of each system, receiving conditions of radio waves, and actual intensity and conditions of light signals, directly checking the storage battery, solar cells, light bulbs, and charge/discharge controllers. But, real-time condition checking and immediate discovery of the problems are not conducted. Accordingly, management scenarios were organized, considering two situations such as location management through identification and tracing of navigation aid facilities, and equipment management through remote control and collection of information on conditions.

First, exact location of navigation aid facilities was made to be easily confirmed through identification of each facility and by recognizing the facilities when they enter near IP-RFID network even if they get out of normal locations. At this time, the information needed by user can be directly provided and utilized thanks to the characteristics of IP-RFID, and the location of the missing equipments can be identified by use of RTLS technology.

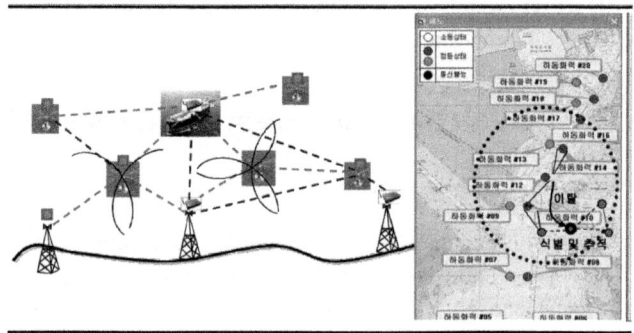

Fig. 2. Container Terminal User Interface

And in functional control, movement of installed navigation aid facilities is remote controlled, and particularly, functions of light-on and light-out, flickering cycle, and intensity of light are controlled. Further, condition information related to movement and function of the facilities is collected by use of sensors, and in case abnormal signs are discovered, their information is delivered to the administrator in real-time. The information on condition collected at this time is communication condition, lamp condition, battery condition, intensity of light, temperature, and the impact, etc. This applied scenario is operated with following procedures as in Fig. 3.

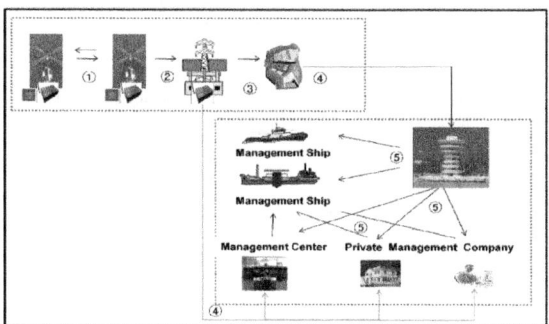

Fig. 3. Transport Company & Car Owner User Interface

① Exchange of condition information between IP-TAG installed in navigation signals and Smart Points.

② Control of navigation signals through control technology or RTSL technology or transmission of location information to ground receiving station.

③ Transmission from ground receiving station to control station.

④ Relevant transmitted information is provided to navigation signal general management center, management office, private navigation signal installer/commissioned management company

⑤ The problem of functional disorder or equipment is immediately informed to management ship to check and repair relevant navigation signal

4.2 Service Functions and Main Contents

For management of navigation aid facilities utilizing IP-RFID, scenarios and services were developed on the assumption that IP-RFID TAGS or SmartPoint which can receive information from them are installed on navigation aid facilities, through which network can be established in coastal areas with the characteristics of infra as shown in Fig. 4, and can be utilized in relevant scenarios and systems related to traffic control of coastal areas and management of fish farm facilities and fishing gears as well as management of navigation aid facilities. Fig. 4 shows that navigation aid facilities management system utilizing IP-RFID is operated through the control of general port facilities control center, which can produce and utilize additional various services.

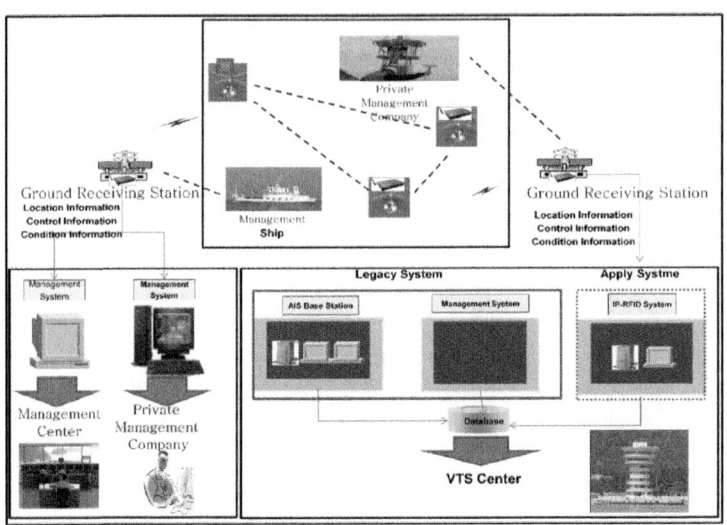

Fig. 4. Transport Company & Car Owner User Interface

Table 4 shows the data provided from IP-TAG, which was organized in order of number, kinds, location of navigation signals, kinds of sensors, and number of IP-TAG. The number and kind are for identification of navigation signals, and navigation signal number is imposed according to order of installation, and the number is also imposed to kind of navigation signals according to the form and type of the signals based on IALA standard. Location of navigation signals refers to fixed location where the navigation signal was first installed, shown in 8 digits of latitude/longitude coordinate. The kind of sensor refers to the information transmitted by the sensor for confirmation of any abnormal function or condition of navigation signals with 4 digits which transmits data according to each situation in case any abnormal condition is found. And finally, IP-TAG unique number is for identification of IP-TAG, which is imposed according to production order.

Table 4. Data provided by IP-RFID

Division	Digit	Expression	Remark
Navigation signal Number	4 Digits	AIR1 (#AIR 1 Signal)	-
Kind of navigation signals	2 Digits	Navigation Signal International Standard	-
Location of navigation signals	8 Digits	Latitude/longitude coordinate	-
Kind of sensor	4 Digits	Attach sensors for illumination intensity and impact	4 digits by each sensor
IP-TAG Unique Number	5 Digits	00001 (IP-TAG number 1)	Production order

IP-RFID based navigation aid facilities management system provides relevant data to navigation signal general management center and marine traffic control center. In addition, it also directly provides relevant data to navigation signal management center and private navigation signal installation company and commissioned management company which are main agents of management, making real-time management of navigation aid facilities possible.

Kinds of service are divided into total 2 kinds as described in Table 5 below, and can be classified into 5 detailed services.

Table 5. Detailed Contents of Each Major Service

Kind of Service	Details	Contents
Real-Time Information Service	Identification Service	A service where management by each navigation signal is possible by confirming on which navigation signal IP-TAG is attached utilizing unique information of IP-TAG
	Locating and Tracing Service	Location tracing by applying Smart Point or communication between facilities IP-TAG is installed or by applying RTLS technology
	Operation Status Notification Service	A service which directly provides information in real-time to relevant agents(general management center, installer, commissioned management company) by utilizing IP on IP-TAG
Remote Control Management	Functional Remote Control Service	A service which remote controls the functions of navigation signal equipments
	Abnormal function and problem notification service	A service which notifies the problems in operation of navigation signals, brightness of light beacon, collision with vessel or floating matters, and battery condition, etc identified through sensors attached on IP-TAG

5 Conclusion

As a way of real time management and efficient operation of navigation aid facilities, this study developed applied scenarios utilizing a new technology of IP-RFID and suggested relevant data and services.

By applying IP-RFID technology which is being developed, it is expected that time and cost can be saved for management/maintenance of navigation aid facilities which can be directly connected to large scale maritime accidents. Further, by being able to transmit the information to administrator and users in real time, reliability and safety of navigation signals can be improved, contributing to safety of the vessels and prevention of maritime accidents.

In this study, technical development is being conducted at the same time with development of applied scenarios and services, with system development and realization also in progress, and it is considered necessary to additionally carry out research on equipment installation and network organization for marine navigation aid facilities in the future.

Acknowledgments

We inform that this study is a result of the Ministry of Land, Transport and Marine Affairs; Active IP-RFID Technology Development Project for Marine Logistics and thank for the support with the research fund.

References

1. Kuk, S.-K.: A preliminary study on operation-effectiveness analysis of marine traffic safety facility. Journal of Korean Navigation and Port Research 31(10), 819–824 (2007)
2. Gug, S.-G., Kim, J.-H., Kim, M.-C., Suck, Y.-G.: A Study on the Construction of Ubiquitous Aids to Navigation. In: Proceding of 2005 The Korea Security Marin Environment & Safety Conference, pp. 59–64 (2005)
3. Kim, C.-J., Song, J.-U.: A Study on the Development of the Module for Remote-Controlling Aids to Navigation. Journal of Korean Navigation and Port Research 26(3), 269–274 (2002)
4. Brown, K., Schwenk, J., Bucciarelli, M.: Development and Application of an Aids to Navigation Service Force Mix Decision Support System, US Department of Transportation (1992)
5. Jeong, J.-H., Kim, J.-K., Kim, J.-U., Lee, H.-J., Kim, H.: Investigation of power supply systems for Aids to Navigation. In: Proceding of 2005 The Korean Institute of Illumination and Electrical Installation Conference, pp. 137–140 (2005)
6. Choi, H.R., Park, B.K., Kim, H.S., Park, Y.S., Lee, C.S.: IP-RFID Based Vessel Traffic Service System. Journal of Korean Knowledge Information Technology Society 5(1) (2010)
7. Kim, J.-C., Kim, C.-K., Jang, H.-S.: Psition of Light Buoy Using Method of Intersection. In: Proceding of 2004 Korean Society of Surveying, Geodesy, Photogrammetry and Cartography Conference, pp. 493–495 (2004)
8. Hall, John, S.: Radar aids to navigation. McGraw-Hill, New York (1947)
9. Gynther, J.W., Smith, M.W.: Radio Aids to Navigation Requirements: The 1988 Simulator Experiment, US Coast Guard Research and Development Center (1989)

Aquaculture Farm Facility Loss Management System

Hyung-Rim Choi[1], Byoung-Kwon Park[1], Yong-Sung Park[1], Chang-Sup Lee[2],
Ki-Nam Choi[1], Chang-Hyun Park[1], Yong-Hyun Jo[1], and Byung-Ha Lee[1]

[1] Dong-A University, Department of Management Information Systems,
Bumin-dong, Seo-gu, Busan, 602-760, Korea
[2] Dong-A University, Media Device Lab,
Hadan2-dong, Saha-gu, Busan, 604-714, Korea
{hrchoi,bpark,ys1126,cslee}@dau.ac.kr,
{dreizehn,archehyun,naspirin,leebh1443}@naver.com

Abstract. The loss of aquaculture farm facilities occurring from natural disasters of accidents can cause not only property damage but also marine environmental pollution and vessel safety accidents. When aquaculture farm facilities have been lost to sink down to the bottom of the water, those should be picked up through direct searches but it is difficult to find them because they cannot be visually identified and they are in the sea. In this study, a system that can efficiently manage aquaculture farm facility loss using a new technology IP-RFID will be presented. By attaching IP-Tags to aquaculture farm facilities, this technology enables the transmission of facility information and locations to diverse users in real time through the IPs and through this, the efficiency of aquaculture farm facility management and supervision can be improved and marine environmental pollution can be reduced.

Keywords: IP-RFID, Aquaculture farm loss, marine environmental pollution.

1   Introduction

With the elevation of the standard of living and the increase of demand for marine products, the perception of the finishing industry is switching from a catching industry to a raising industry and the importance of the aquaculture industry is increasing. Along with this, four major ills of farms including unlicensed farming, farming outside of fisheries, the use of mineral acids and acts of violating the rules that limit fishing are repeatedly occurring. Farming outside of fisheries among them and facility loss are causing marine pollution and threatening safe ship sailing and to solve these problems, the Ministry of Food, Agriculture, Forestry and Fisheries, the Korea Coast Guard and individual local governments are jointly performing guiding and controlling activities but they are experiencing many difficulties due to wide management areas and small numbers of personnel. In this respect, this study is intended to discuss aquaculture farm facility loss management systems for preventing and efficiently managing aquaculture farm facility loss.

T.-h. Kim et al. (Eds.): UNESST 2010, CCIS 124, pp. 173–179, 2010.
© Springer-Verlag Berlin Heidelberg 2010

2 Present State and Problems

It is estimated that approximately 400,000 tons of marine wastes are deposited in the coastal waters of our country and 150,000 tons of wastes are being dumped at sea every years. However, less than a half of them are being collected and thus they are being accumulated and neglected. If aquaculture farm facilities installed at sea are lost or sink due to natural disasters like typhoons or accidents, they will become marine wastes to cause marine pollution. Since it is difficult to identify the locations of lost aquaculture farm facilities, the locations should be identified firsthand through searches and sunken aquaculture farm facilities should be collected by mobilizing divers. Since methods require great deals of manpower and time for searches and collections and searching and collecting activities are done in the wide sea, it is impossible to remove the facilities dumped in wide areas and only some of them can be collected. In fact, the collecting activities done by local governments are not done in the entire waters but the waters are divided into certain zones to do the works in rotation every year. Since the facilities not collected but neglected will cause marine pollution and will threat safe ship sailing by being wound on ship screws or otherwise if the lost facilities flow into sea route areas, measures to solve these problems are necessary.

3 Farm Facility Loss Management System

3.1 Concept of IP-RFID

The IP-RFID is a method made by integrating the advantages of USN and RFID technologies with minimal IPv6 technology. This technology loads IPs on tags to maximize the synergy effects of the combination of existing IP infra and USN and RFID infra in order to ensure wide expandability and mobility and directly manage and control the tags.

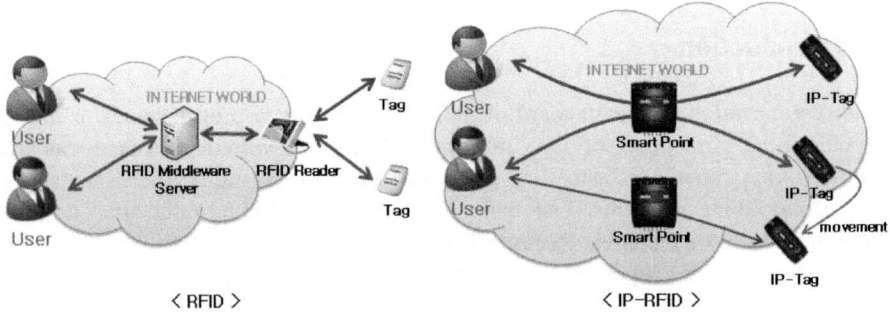

Fig. 1. Comparison between RFID and IP-RFID

3.2 Overview of the System

This system enables the management of general aquaculture farm facilities and lost aquaculture farm facilities that have been done firsthand by the naked eyes by local governments that are aquaculture farm facility management institutions to be implemented efficiently by collecting aquaculture farm facility registration information and location information in real time through communication between the IP-Tags installed in aquaculture farm facilities and the Smart Points installed in sea route assistance facilities and fishing guiding ships.

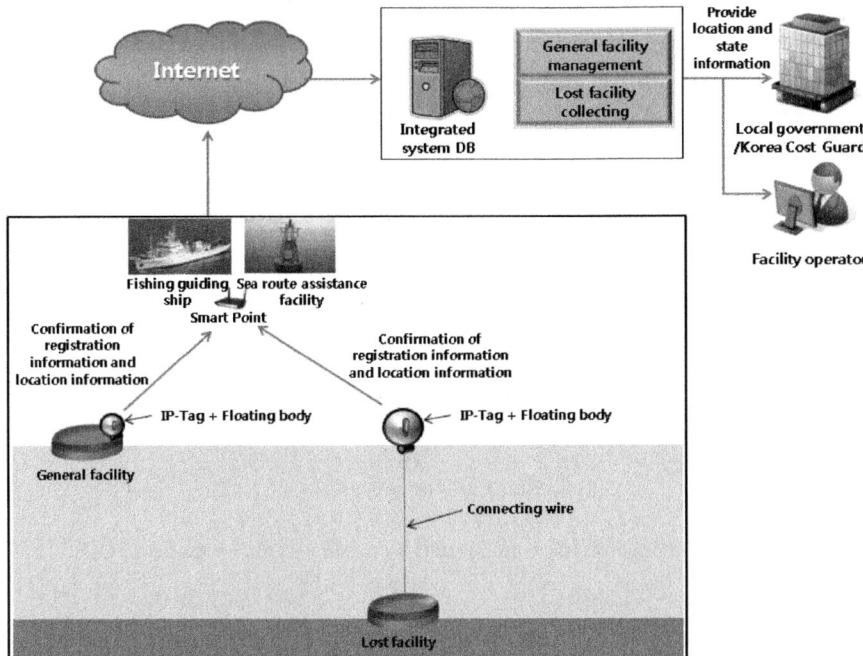

Fig. 2. Aquaculture farm facility loss management system configuration diagram

The components of this system consist of IP-Tags, Smart Points and sensors and the technologies required by this system include the communication technology to collect and transmit information from the IP-Tags attached to facilities, the RTLS technology for grasping the locations of the Tags and tracking the Tags and the sensing technology for detecting facility loss or sinking. Participants in the system can be divided into the local governments/the Korea Coast Guard that manage aquaculture farm facilities, implement guiding and controlling works and search/collect lost facilities and facility operators that produce marine products using the aquaculture farm facilities owned by them.

The IP-Tags that contain aquaculture farm facility registration information and location information are attached to aquaculture farm facilities and since IP-Tags cannot communicate in water, communication will be disabled if aquaculture farm facilities sink. Therefore, to maintain communication with the Smart Point always above the water, a structure as shown in the <Figure3> was designed. If the facility is lost and sinks, the floating body part of this device will be separated from the facility to float on the surface of the sea. In this case, the connecting wire wound on the roller on the bottom of the floating body will be unwound so that the connected state can be maintained while the floating body keeps floating on the surface of the sea. Through this way, the IP-Tag in the floating body can communicate with the Smart Point and can transmit information on the location of the lost facility.

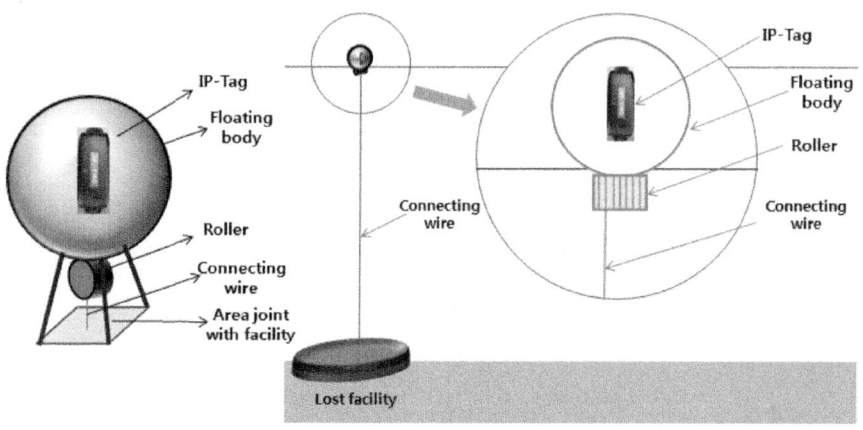

Fig. 3. IP-Tag structure

The operating procedure of this system consists of the steps as shown in the <Figure4>.

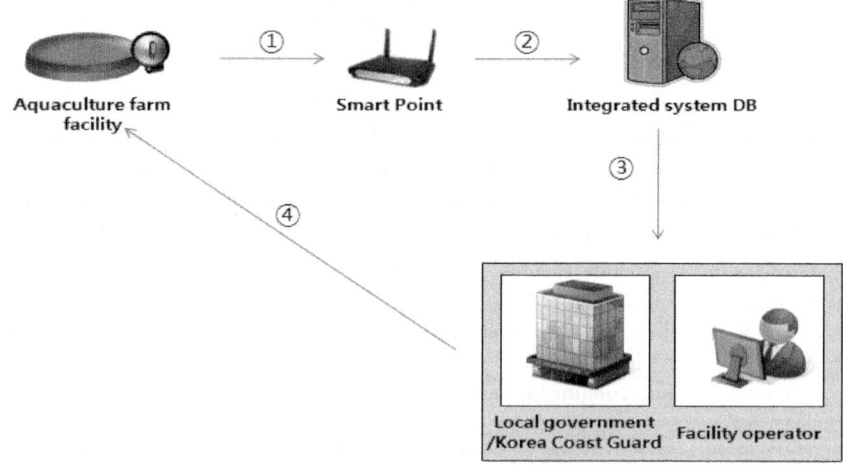

Fig. 4. Aquaculture farm facility loss management system's procedure

① Information from the IP-Tags installed in the aquaculture farm facility is perceived by the Smart Points installed in the sea route assistance facility and the fishing guiding ship

② The Smart Points collect the aquaculture farm facility's basic registration information and location information while transmitting the information to the integrated system DB at the same time

③ The collected information is provided to individual parties(local governments/the Korea Cost Guard, facility operators)

④ Based on the information grasped in real time, the lost or sunken facility is searched

3.3 Services to Be Provided

Through this system, aquaculture farm facility registration information and location information can be grasped in real time and services provided through this information are largely divided into general facility management services and lost

Table 1. Details of major services

Kind of service	Details	Content
General facility management service	Identifying facility (fishing gear) registration information	Individual facilities can be managed separately using the facility or fishing gear information stored in IP-Tags
	Providing facility (fishing gear) location and state information	Providing farm facility or fishing gear location information and state information utilizing the unique information of IP-Tags and RTLS technology
	Fishing activity location tracking	Grasping the locations of installed fishing nets with fishing gear location information obtained using the IP-Tags installed in fishing gears
	Illegal facility (fishing gear) controlling	Facilities can be checked to see whether they have been registered or whether they are installed and operated as registered using the facility or fishing gear registration information stored in IP-Tags
Lost facility collecting service	Transmitting facility (fishing gear) loss warning messages	Services to transmit facility or fishing gear loss warning messages immediately if any facility loss has occurred such as sinking into water
	Providing lost facility (fishing gear) location information	Even if facilities(fishing gears) are lost and sink into the water, their locations can be grasped through the unique information of the IP-TAGs that are connected to the floating body and floating on the surface of the sea and RTLS technology

facility collecting services. The general facility management services are enabling local governments to manage each facility using the facility information stored in the tag of each facility and the lost facility collecting services are collecting lost facilities through location tracking. If a aquaculture farm facility attached with an IP-Tag is lost while floating on the surface of the sea, the location of the lost facility can be grasped through the Smart Point. If the facility sinks and the IP-Tag connected to the floating body is separated from the facility, the IP-Tag will transmit loss warning messages at the moment and will float on the surface of the sea while being connected to the facility with the connecting wire so that the location of the lost facility can be grasped. In addition, these services can be applied to diverse fishing gears used on the sea in addition to aquaculture farm facilities and functions such as tracking the location of fishing activities that grasp the locations where nets have been installed, preventing the robbery of fishing gears and controlling illegal fishing gears can be also provided. The services provided through this system are summarized as per the <Table1> shown above.

Aquaculture farm facility information expressed in the system can be shown as per the following <Figure5>. User interfaces are configured differently depending of the parties. Common parts are registration information such as farm facilities' IP-Tag numbers, facility numbers and registered locations and state information such as current locations, water temperatures and air temperatures and differences are that local governments/the Korea Coast Guard can register, inquire and revise facility information for managing and controlling the facilities and facility operators can be provided with their facilities' registration information and state information.

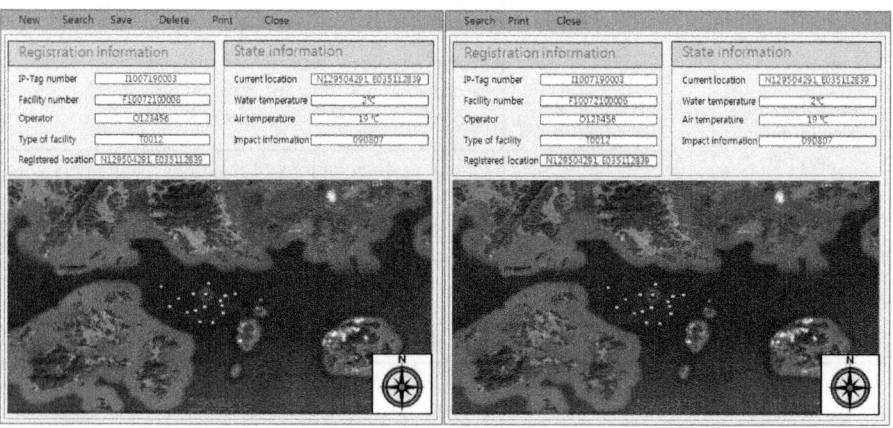

Fig. 5. User interface (local governments, the Korea Coast Guard / facility operators)

4 Conclusion

In this study, a management system was presented that can efficiently collect lost facilities and implement aquaculture farm management by attaching IP-Tags to aquaculture farm facilities. The aquaculture farm management systems using RFID technology and USN that have been studied previously are mainly purposed to efficiently support the work of fishermen who operate aquaculture farms but the aquaculture farm facility management system presented in this study is differentiated in that the system is purposed to support not only the work of fishermen who operate aquaculture farms but also the work of institutions that manage aquaculture farm facilities such as responding to aquaculture farm loss. In addition, through this system, aquaculture farm facility registration information and state information can be grasped in real time and thus environmental changes such as natural disasters or accidents can be immediately responded and lost aquaculture farm facilities can be quickly collected without unnecessary waste of time and manpower through grasping the locations of lost facilities. In addition, the effects to prevent the environmental pollution occurred due to lost facilities and enable safe ship sailing can be expected.

Acknowledgments

We inform that this study is a result of the Ministry of Land, Transport and Marine Affairs; Active IP-RFID Technology Development Project for Marine Logistics and thank for the support with the research fund.

References

1. Koo, B.-S., Hun, K., Hur, S.-H.: Study on the marine debris on the seabed in chinhae bay, korea. Journal of The Korea Society for Marine Environmental Engineering 3(4), 91–98 (2000)
2. Park, S.-S., Kang, H.-Y.: The quantity and characteristics of marine debris collected from the coastline in jeonnam. J. Korea Society of Waste Management 22(2), 203–212 (2005)
3. Choi, S.-P., Choi, H.-R., Park, B.-K., Park, Y.-S.: The business model for IP-RFID based small ship management. Korea Society of IT Services 2009(3), 211–215 (2009)
4. Lee, K.-H.: Current status and enhancement plans of porphyra cultivation industry in korea, Mokpo National Maritime University (2006)
5. Korea Maritime Institute: Study on potential investigation of fishing industry and way of development (2003)

The Proposal of the Model for Developing Dispatch System for Nationwide One-Day Integrative Planning

Hyun Soo Kim, Hyung Rim Choi,
Byung Kwon Park, Jae Un Jung, and Jin Wook Lee

Department of Management Information Systems,
Dong-A University, South Korea
{hskim,hrchoi,bpark}@dau.ac.kr,
{forshare,jw6416}@naver.com

Abstract. The problems of dispatch planning for container truck are classified as the pickup and delivery problems, which are highly complex issues that consider various constraints in the real world. However, in case of the current situation, it is developed by the control system so that it requires the automated planning system under the view of nationwide integrative planning. Therefore, the purpose of this study is to suggest model to develop the automated dispatch system through the constraint satisfaction problem and meta-heuristic technique-based algorithm. In the further study, the practical system is developed and evaluation is performed in aspect of various results. This study suggests model to undergo the study which promoted the complexity of the problems by considering the various constraints which were not considered in the early study. However, it is suggested that it is necessary to add the study which includes the real-time monitoring function for vehicles and cargos based on the information technology.

Keywords: Dispatch System, Container Transport, Constraint Satisfaction Problem, Decision Support System.

1 Introduction

Since the dispatch planning for the container cargos has been still controlled by manually for each district respectively, it could cause some adverse problems such as doubled route and inefficient vehicle assignments etc. Therefore, it requires system which could integrate the subdivided planning for each district as well as automate the dispatch planning which was controlled by manually. The dispatch planning problem of container vehicle has the characteristics of pickup and delivery problem with start-end time order constraints so that a number of study has been researched in order to resolve these problems. However, little study that considers capacity classifications, time window and decision support of user at the same time has been undergone.

Therefore, the purpose of this study is to propose model of the system which could support to plan for nationwide one-day integrative dispatch based on constraints from the site operations. In order to achieve the purpose, process and framework of dispatch system is suggested for solving problem. And solution structure based on

T.-h. Kim et al. (Eds.): UNESST 2010, CCIS 124, pp. 180–187, 2010.

CSP(Constraint Satisfaction Problem) and meta-heuristic technique is proposed to design algorithm in the future study. Besides, this study proposes the DSS(Decision Support System) model which enables the solution to be utilized under the views of practical business.

2 Literature Review

2.1 Types of Dispatch Planning Problems

The dispatch planning problems can be classified into VRP(Vehicle Routing Problem), VRPTW(VRP with Time Window), VSP(Vehicle Scheduling Problem) and VRSP(Vehicle Routing and Scheduling Problem) according to the various constraints.(Lee et al., 2004). In terms of these problems, Berger et al.(2003) researched the VRP which aimed to minimize the moving distance and Nazif et al.(2010) reported VRPTW problems which are to satisfy the transportation requests from the customers at the set time with the minimum costs. Also, Park(1997) introduced the VSP which is to minimize the total vehicle running and transportation delay time and Choi(2006) researched the VRSP which sets the optimized route for the container vehicles with the constraint of transportation time.

On the other hand, in this study, as the type of VRSP and VRPPD(VRP with Pickup & Delivery), the constraints such as multiple vehicle and container, time window with the different capacity of vehicle, and so on are considered.

2.2 Solution of Vehicle Scheduling Problems

In the existing study, the solution of dispatch planning problems had been approached with optimized model and heuristic model. Jang(2003) suggested the classification of these solutions<Figure 1>.

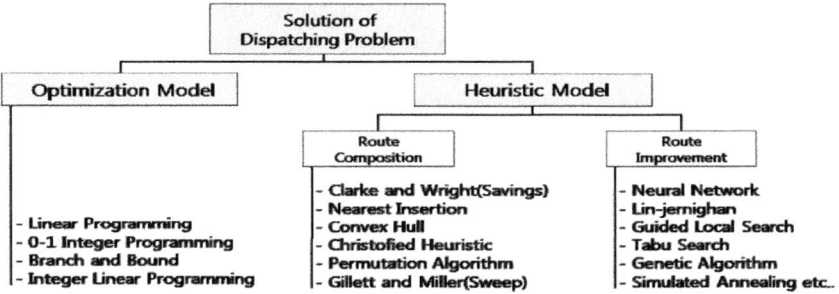

Fig. 1. Solution of Dispatching Problem in the existing study

On the other hand, in recent, some studies have been undergone in order to solve the dispatch planning problems with CSP technique. Kim et al.(2002) underwent the research to develop the vehicle scheduling system using the constraint programming and meta-heuristic system. Jeon et al.(2003) executed the research to establish the bus service scheduling along with the case-based reasoning and CSP technique simultaneously. Also, Gacias et al.(2009) suggested the architecture to support the decision making of vehicle route problem through the domain analysis and constraint programming, however, some constraints such as pre- and post-transportation constraint and vehicle capacity that should be considered under the container transportation constraints had been disregarded.

Differently from the general vehicle route problems, the vehicle dispatch planning problem of container vehicles can be regarded as the Multiple vehicle dial-a-ride type which transports the container with pre- and post-constraints of loading and unloading according to customers' requests through the multiple vehicles with capacity limitations. With regards to this, Maxwell and Muckstadt(1981) suggested vehicle movement model which minimizes the empty transfer under the transportation constraints and Yun et al.(1999) modelized the dispatch planning problems to minimize the empty vehicle movement and container movement time. However, both studies did not fully consider the time window. Therefore, it is considered that it is necessary to suggest the system which has the function of decision making that supports the flexible basic information management and rescheduling as well as considers the practical constraints which were disregarded in the existing studies.

Thus, in this study, based on the purpose to minimize the empty transfer distance, the method is suggested to realize the decision support function by reflecting the changed constraint of planning as well as reducing the time and costs through the CSP and meta-heuristic based algorithm.

3 Development of Dispatch Planning Support System

3.1 Definition

In this study, problems of vehicle scheduling to transport 1000TEU of container amounts which are dispersed at 18 transportation spots nationwidely to 400 vehicles are dealt with through the case of comprehensive transportation company in Korea. For this reason, in this chapter, considering the classification standards suggested by Giaglis et al.(2004), the purpose and constraints are suggested as followed.

- Objective function
  - Minimization of empty container transference distance
- Constraints
  - Transportation constraints: Multiple Pickup & Delivery, Multi Depot, Time Window, Consideration of dynamic events
  - Cargo constraints: Cargo capacity, Priority of cargo transportation, weight limitation, Consideration of dynamic events
  - Vehicle constraints: Multi vehicle, Vehicle capacity, Multi-rotation transportation, Priority of vehicle scheduling, Vehicle returning, Consideration of dynamic events

3.2 Solution of Problems

In order to standardization of the problems to be solved, the requirements from site operation such as the Kukbo corporation and SC global Busan branch is analyzed

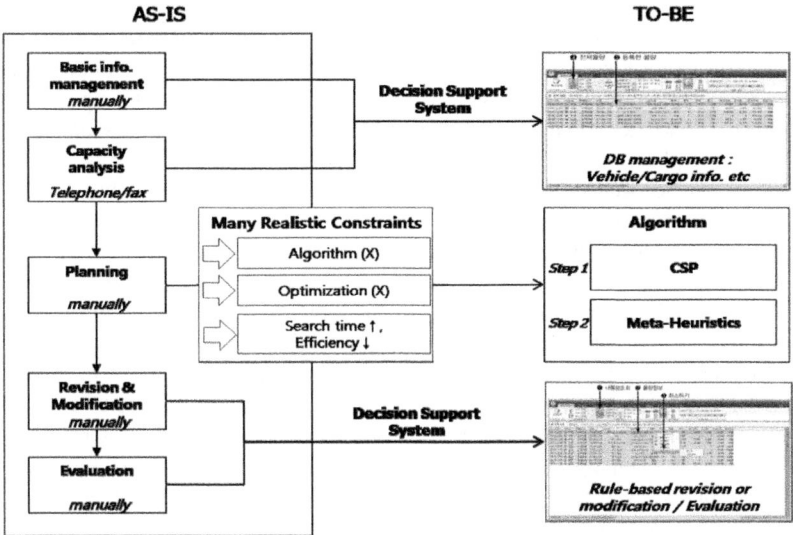

Fig. 2. Problem-solving process

through the interview. Based on these results, the problem with the solution is shown in the <Figure 2>.

3.3 Function and Structure of the System

This system is the decision supporting system which can amend and manage the basic information that can be changed during the planning process under the view of users and reflect the assessment for finally drawn solution. It is constructed with the system framework in the <Figure 3>.

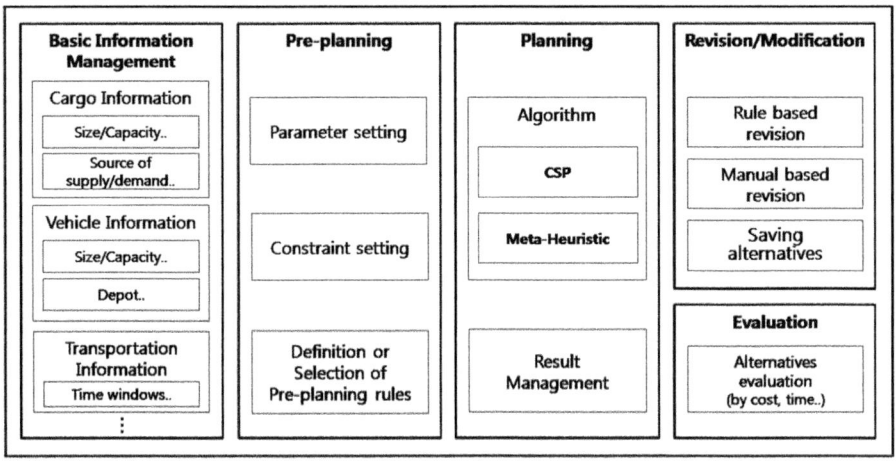

Fig. 3. Framework of dispatch support system

The framework of this system is composed by 5 kinds of modules. First, the basic information management module, as the module to manage cargo information and vehicle information that are necessary for dispatch planning, supports flexible planning and amendment/re-planning process. The pre-planning setting module supports the pre-constraint and parameter that should be considered to be reflexed to the planning. On the other hand, the planning module based on CSP and meta-heuristic technique reduces the errors that can be occurred during the handworks, enhances the quality levels of the planning and supports planning result management. The planning amendment and re-planning modules supports scheduling process based on the rule and manual in order to reflect the dynamic events caused after the planning to the early planning. The assessment module supports the drawing of the most preferable proposal by comparing and examining the variously established planning results.

On the other hand, the CSP technique in the above expresses the problems to be solved as constraint and finds the solution, which is relatively recently introduced for the dispatch planning problems compared to other solutions. With regards to this, Kim et al.(2002) suggest dispatch planning solution using constraint programming technique as ILOG Dispatcher solution structure. However, in this study, since it is necessary that the rule-based decision making function to support systematic basic information management and re-planning and amendment should be additionally considered, the solution structure which is mentioned in the above is described as followed in the <Figure 4>.

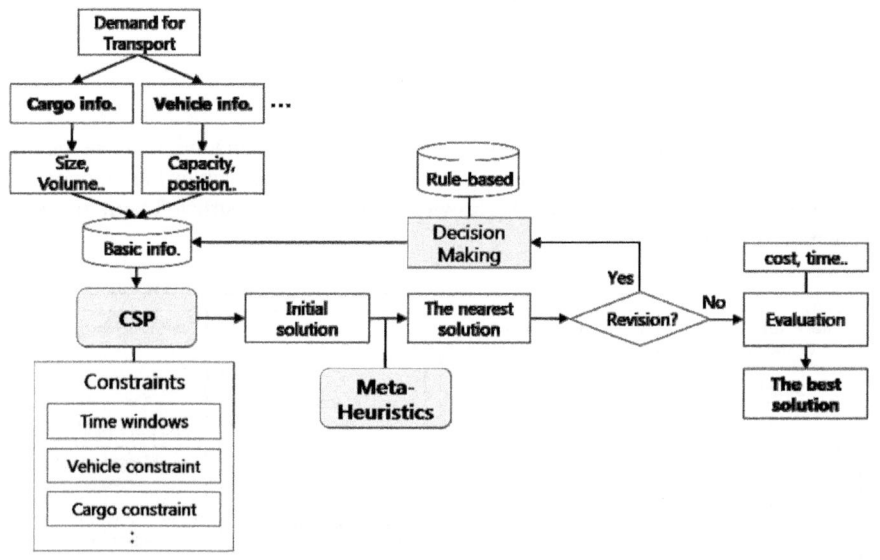

Fig. 4. Solution structure of this problem

3.4 Implementation

▪ Data base

The DB structure of this system can be described as the <Table 1>. However, since the <Table 1> is the example of DB structure for dispatch planning by Kim(2002).

Table 1. Structure of Database(example)

Table	Field	Description
Vehicle	car_kubun	Classification of Vehicle
	car-no	Vehicle number
	driver_name	Name of driver
	driver_phone	Cellphone number of driver
	load_status	Constraint of load
	car_size	Vehicle size(20feet/40feet)
Cargo	start_addr	Address of pickup position
	start_time	Pickup time
	end_addr	Address of delivery position
	end_time	Delivery time
	cont_size	size of cargo(20feet/40feet)
	cont_wgt	weight of cargo
Shipper	c_code	Client code
	c_kubun	Classification of client
	tel	Telephone
	crg	The person in charge
	addr	Address
:	:	:

Source : Kim(2002)

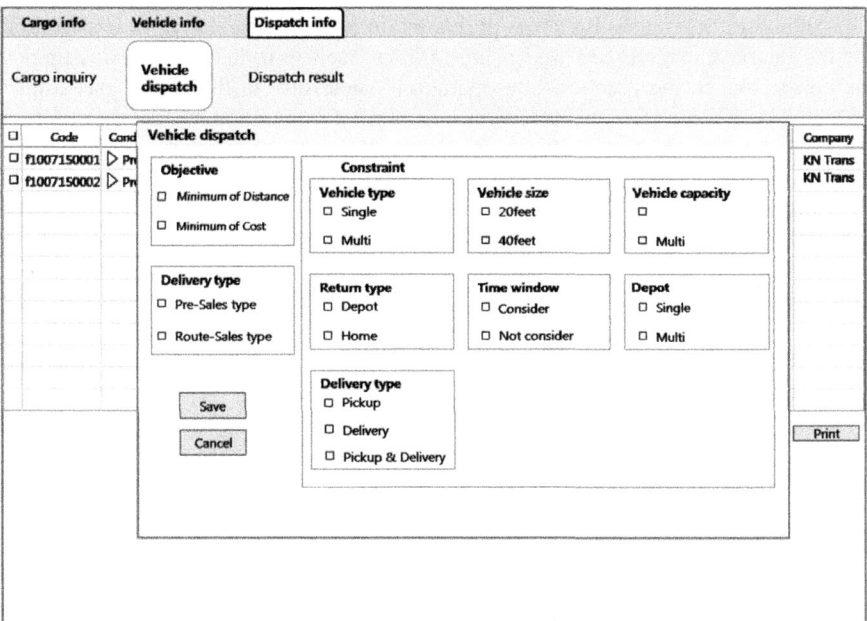

Fig. 5. Interface of this system(example)

▪ Interface

Considering the basic data in the above and planning constraints, the interface can be constructed as the <Figure 5>. This interface is utilized for more systematic display while realization of the system in the future. The example of interface in this system is as below.

In this chapter, based on the proposed direction of system development, it is planned to develop the real system in the further study. This system requires Window 2003 server with MS-SQL 2000 DB based on J2SE language and undergoes the drawing solution process through CSP technique and meta-heuristic technique along with pre-fixed constraint and data.

3.5 Assessment Plan

As the result of further study, it analyzes the function of algorithm in order to assess the developed system. For this reason, the differences between the required time for the planning by adding the meta heuristic technique to CSP technique and the required time for the scheduling with CSP technique is compared. In addition, the degree of solution that is improved by adding meta heuristic technique to existing CSP technique is compared with ultimately saved number of vehicles and rate of empty vehicles during the planning process by each solution.

4   Conclusion

The problems of container dispatch planning that transport the cargos nationwidely are very complicated problems which should consider the practical and various constraints. In order to solve these problems, in the existing study, various solutions for the heuristic technique-based solution have been introduced, however, there are the constraints in the practical site operation. Therefore, in this study, based on the collected data from the various constraints and site operation which have not been considered in the existing study, the method is suggested for the development of the nationwide one-day integrative dispatch planning support system. Also, the system structure is provided that requires CSP and meta-heuristic technique, and organize 5 kinds of modules that construct the systems for this reason. This study promoted the practical utility by considering the constraints such as vehicle and capacity, amounts load regulations etc and the priority of transportation in the site operation. In the further study, the realization and development of dispatch planning system that supports users' decision making based on the solution and system structure proposed in this study and compare the various planning results to assess the system. Nevertheless, it is suggested that it is necessary to undergo the study which includes IT-based real-time vehicle and cargo monitoring function such as RFID and GPS etc in order to support more appropriate and rapid decision making than this system.

Acknowledgments. This work was supported by the Grant of the Korean Ministry of Education, Science and Technology (The Regional Core Research Program/Institute of Logistics Information Technology).

References

1. Berger, J., Barkaoui, M.: A new hybrid genetic algorithm for the capacitated vehicle routing problem. Journal of the Operational Research Society 54, 1254–1262 (2003)
2. Fisher, M.L.: Optimal solution of vehicle routing problems using minimum k-trees. Operations Research 42(4), 626–642 (1994)
3. Giaglis, G.M., Minis, I., Tatarakis, A., Zeimpekis, V.: Minimizing logistics risk through real-time vehicle routing and mobile technologies: Research to date and future trends. International Journal of Physical Distribution and Logistics Management 34(9), 749–764 (2004)
4. Ho, S.C., Haugland, D.: A tabu search heuristic for the vehicle routing problem with time windows and split deliveries. Computers and Operations Research 31(12), 1947–1969 (2004)
5. Jeon, S.H., Kim, M.K.: The Design of a Vehicle Fleet Scheduling System using CBR and CSP. Journal of the Korean Institute of Plant Engineering 8(3), 37–48 (2003)
6. Lee, M.H., Yi, S.H.: A Design of Vehicle Delivery Planning System for the Improvement Logistics Plant Services. Journal of the Korean Institute of Plant Engineering 9(3), 49–59 (2004)
7. Maxwell, W.L., Muckstadt, J.A.: Design of Automated Guided Vehicle Systems. IIE Transactions 14(2), 114–124 (1981)
8. Min, H., Jayaraman, V., Srivastava, R.: Combined location-routing problems: a synthesis and future research directions. European Journal of Operational Research 108, 1–15 (1998)
9. Nazif, H., Lee, L.S.: Optimized Crossover Genetic Algorithm for Vehicle Routing Problem with Time Windows. American Journal of Applied Sciences 7(1), 95–101 (2010)
10. Park, Y.B.: Multiobjective Vehicle Scheduling Problem with Time and Area-Dependent Travel Speeds: Scheduling Algorithm and Expert System. Journal of the Korean Institute of Industrial Engineers 23(4), 621–633 (1997)
11. Savelsbergh, M.W.P.: The general pickup and delivery problem. Transportation Science 29(1), 17–29 (1995)
12. Yang, J., Jaillet, P., Mahmassami, H.S.: Real-Time Multivehicle Truckload Pickup and Delivery Problems. Transportation Science 38(2), 135–148 (2004)
13. Yun, W.Y., Ahn, C.G., Choi, Y.S.: A Truck Dispatching Problem in the Inland Container Transportation with Empty Container. Journal of the Korean Operations Research and Management Science Society 24(4), 63–80 (1999)
14. Gacias, B., Cegarra, J., Lopez, P.: An interdisciplinary method for a generic vehicle routing problem decision support system. In: International Conference on Industrial Engineering and Systems Management, Montreal (2009)
15. Kim, Y.H., Jang, Y.S., Ryu, H.J.: A Study on Developing Vehicle Scheduling System using Constraint Programming and Metaheuristics. In: Proceedings of Korean Institute of Industrial Engineers and Korean Operations Research and Management Science Society Spring Conference, pp. 979–986. KAIST, DaeJeon (2002)
16. Choi, H.J.: Vehicle Routing Planning in Static Freight Container Transportation Environment Using Simulated Annealing. Unpublished master's thesis, Korea National Defence University, Seoul (2006)
17. Jang, D.W.: Tabu Search Based Vehicle Routing Planning for Freight Container Transportation. Unpublished master's thesis, Pukyong National University, Busan (2003)
18. Kim, B.H.: A Study ERP System for Integration Transport Information Brokering. Unpublished master's thesis, Paichai University, Daejeon (2002)

Microscopic Approach to Evaluating Technological Convergence Using Patent Citation Analysis

Kihoon Sung[1], Taehan Kim[2], and Hee-Kyung Kong[2,*]

[1] Department of Information and Communications Technology Management, University of Science and Technology, 113 Gwahangno, Yuseong-gu, Daejeon, Republic of Korea
skh64261@etri.re.kr
[2] Technology Strategy Research Division, Eletronics and Telecommunications Research Institute, 138 Gajeong-ro, Yuseong-gu, Daejeon, Republic of Korea
{taehan,konghk}@etri.re.kr

Abstract. Technological convergence has been an important source of technological innovation in industries. We take a microscopic approach to the question for measuring and evaluating the level of technological convergence using patent citation analysis. We develop a convergence indicator that shows the relative convergence degree of a patent. This indicator is based on the backward and forward patent citations that could assess the extent of the level of convergence or originality. In this paper, we test the method that could evaluate the relative level of convergence in individual patents.

Keywords: Technological Convergence, Convergence Indicator, Patent Citation Analysis.

1 Introduction

Technological innovation is widely considered as one of the most important indicators for understanding the industry trend. In recent years, the main paradigm of technological innovation has been represented by the term 'convergence.' Technological convergence is a phenomenon of collective technological innovation [1], occurring in the course of resolving technical problems faced by various industries. Technological convergence is considered an essential phenomenon in the march of progress in scientific, technology and industry fields. As a phenomenon which is an integral part of the process of technological innovation, technological convergence is indeed a necessary step for developing cutting-edge technologies. This is one reason why it is perceived in many countries around the world as a strategically-important process, which can tremendously contribute to the creation of high added value. The US National Science Foundation, stating that the ultimate goal of technological convergence is to enhance human capabilities, proposed a technological convergence framework, with nanotechnology, biotechnology, information technology and cognitive science as its main pillars [2]. In Europe, partly out of the concern that American-style technological convergence may overly emphasize the development of artificial technologies, a roadmap for convergence has

---

* Corresponding author.

T.-h. Kim et al. (Eds.): UNESST 2010, CCIS 124, pp. 188–194, 2010.
© Springer-Verlag Berlin Heidelberg 2010

been issued, resting on a broader definition of convergence and focused on human-oriented technologies. Convergence, according to this roadmap, is a larger phenomenon touching fields like sociology, anthropology, philosophy and geography, as well as nanotechnology, biotechnology, information technology and cognitive science [3].

In academic researches, where technological convergence is also a hot topic, the phenomenon is studied primarily to discern related trends, either through analysis of patterns of convergence or attempts at identifying promising fields of convergence. Most of these studies investigate the phenomenon of technological convergence from a macroscopic perspective, examining convergence between industries from a statistical approach based on patent analysis [4, 5, 6, 7]. Macroscopic studies, although they provide useful indicators for assessing the level of convergence between two different technology fields, are not without some major flaws. On the one hand, a macroscopic analysis requires numerous operational definitions when selecting patents or processing patent classes, and on the other hand, due to its top-down approach, this method is limited in terms of ability to assess the level of convergence according to a practical definition of convergence. Even though it is a fine method for understanding the trend characteristics of technological convergence or characteristics of convergence in specific fields, a macroscopic approach does not allow for a direct assessment of the level of convergence between individual technologies, and is, for this reason, unable to explain the practical process of technological innovation. To remedy this limitation in the existing literature, in this study, we conduct a microscopic investigation of technological convergence through patent citation analysis, from a bottom-up approach.

2 Literature Review: Research on Technological Convergence

Technological convergence has begun in the Industrial Revolution in England. Rosenberg confirmed the emergence of technological convergence through analysis of the history of technological innovation in British machine tools [1]. The phenomenon of technological convergence, first discovered by Rosenberg, reached further conceptual refinements, when Kodama used the alternative term, 'technology fusion.' Kodama classified technological innovation in two categories, breakthrough and fusion, describing 'technology fusion' as a phenomenon in which the convergence between two distinct technologies gives birth to new functions absent in existing technologies [8]. In many studies, the term 'convergence' is used interchangeably with 'fusion,' and technological convergence, similar to technology fusion as an innovation process, ultimately includes the latter in its scope. Therefore, in this study, we considered that these terms, taken in their broad sense, designate an identical type of innovation and decided to use the term 'convergence,' having a more inclusive meaning.

In recent years, statistical analysis has become the preferred method among many researchers for studying technological convergence. In order to ensure objectivity and validity, an analysis of technological convergence must use publicly-available statistical data. Patents, given their leading role in technology development, are data that are particularly suited for understanding technological convergence, and their statistical use is broad and varied. Jung-Tae Hwang investigated the multi-technology capabilities of Korea and Taiwan by analyzing patterns in creative research activities from the perspective of technological convergence, using patent bibliometrics [4]. Clive-Steven, meanwhile, developed a patent indicator for converged monitoring of the nutraceuticals and functional foods (NFF) and information and communication technology (ICT) fields [5]. Kong-rae Lee researched on the pattern and process of technological convergence in the intelligent robot field through the analyses of the level of patent concentration and patent citations [6]. Hyun Joung No, in his study of technological convergence, measured the degree of fusion in cross-disciplinary technologies to classify the trajectory patterns [7].

3 Method

Based on the results of the above-described studies, we conducted, in this study, an analysis of technological convergence from a microscopic perspective. As was revealed through the literature review in the preceding section, a considerable number of studies on technological convergence were conducted from a macroscopic approach, through patent analysis, to measure the level of convergence between technology fields or between industry fields. The results of these macroscopic studies, as they were conducted under subjective and qualitative assumptions formulated by researchers, are limited in terms of usability. Further, the classification of patents within a specific technology field often consists of statistically-determined categories, and convenience is a major criterion. In studies based on such a classification system, a researcher is forced to rely on his or her subjective judgment to assess the level of convergence. For example, when defining technological convergence in the ICT field, researchers define a certain patent class as belonging to the ICT field, and the rest of patent classes as non-ICT patents. The results of a study involving such a classification process are bound to be exposed to criticism about taxonomic limitations. All of these problems are issues stemming from the top-down approach to the analysis. In this study, to overcome these issues, we devised a new analytical method consisting in determining the level of convergence of individual patents.

From a microscopic perspective, the level of convergence in a given technology field may be considered equal to the average level of convergence among patents belonging to this field. This means that the level of convergence in a given technology field can be determined based on the level of convergence of individual technologies in the same field. Meanwhile, evaluating the absolute level of convergence in a patent requires assessing the actual value of the patented technology and the value of the existing technologies that were converged to create the new technology. As doing this is impossible, based on basic patent data, in this study, we propose a new method allowing for the measurement of convergence from a relative perspective.

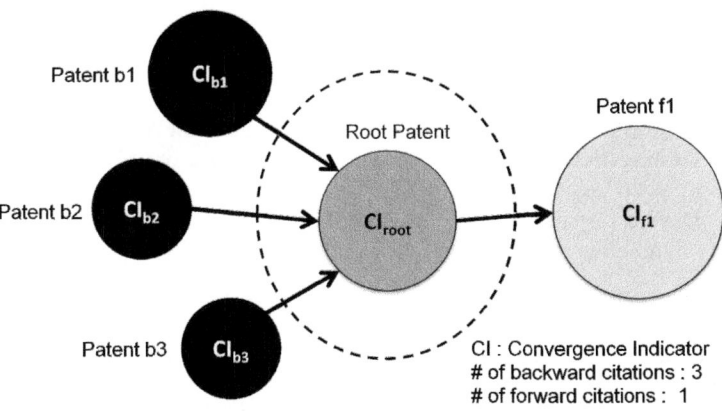

Fig. 1. The concept for measuring the level of technological convergence using relative convergence indicator, *CI*

The process of technological convergence in a patent citation network is shown in Fig. 1. An elementary technology (patent b1), having a certain function, is combined with another elementary technologies (patent b2, b3) to create a converged technology (root patent) with a new function. Based on this process of technological convergence, one can derive a relative convergence indicator as in the following:

$$CI = \frac{N_b}{N_f + 1} \cdot \frac{\sum CI_{b.patents}}{N_b} = \frac{\sum CI_{b.patents}}{N_f + 1} \tag{1}$$

If $N_b = 0$, then $CI = 1$

CI is the convergence indicator for a patent. N_b is the numbers of backward citation patents and N_f is the numbers of forward citation patents. CI is calculated by multiplying the ratio of the number of backward citation patents to the number of forward citation patents by the average of convergence indicators of backward citation patents. The ratio of backward/forward citation indicates that; having cited many patents means it has higher value as a converged technology, and having been cited by many patents means it has higher value as a source technology. This ratio for determination of the relative level of convergence in individual patented technologies takes into consideration both backward and forward citations, as both influences the relative level of convergence. '1' is added to N_f in the denominator because a patent adds a new function by virtue of its creation. When the number of forward citations for a patent is 0, the level of convergence of this patent is the sum of the convergence indicators for its backward citation patents. If the patent cites no other patents, the level of convergence is set to 1, the base value. This means that if the convergence indicator for a patent is greater than 1, there is convergence between this patent and others, and if it is smaller than 1, the patent is widely used as an original technology.

In Section 4 of this study, we will test the validity of the methods described above by applying them to an empirical analysis of the citation network and the level of convergence of patents.

4 Empirical Analysis

For an empirical analysis of convergence, we used citation information obtained from the US patent information database and derived convergence level. Two patents were selected for testing the methodology proposed in this study: 'Remote Broadcast Recording' (patent registration # US7130623B2, 2006); and 'Personal Video Recording Device' (patent registration #US7778520B1, 2010). The citation information on these two patents is as follows:

Table 1. Patent citation information

Patent	Timeline	# of forward citations	# of backward citations		
			Depth 1	Depth 2	Depth 3
Remote Broadcast Recording	No limitation	4	10	95	742
	Up to 10 years before	4	8	21	42
Personal Video Recording Device	No limitation	0	8	60	536
	Up to 10 years before	0	6	21	29

Table 2 provides citation information on a root patent by timeline. In this study, for comparison purposes, we calculated the level of convergence in the two patents for both timelines; namely, the unlimited timeline and the limited one up to ten years before the patent registration.

Table 2. Convergence Indicators by Timeline and Backward citation depth

Patent	Timeline	Convergence Indicator	Avg. CI in backward citations	
			Depth 1	Depth 2
Remote Broadcast Recording	No limitation	0.15	0.08	0.17
	Before 10 years	0.64	0.40	0.62
Personal Video Recording Device	No limitation	18.93	2.37	0.914
	Before 10 years	4.91	0.82	0.86

The results are provided in Table 2 above. In the case of 'Remote Broadcast Recording,' the CI under an unlimited timeline was fairly low at 0.15, whereas the corresponding figure under a limited timeline was much higher at 0.64. This result is explained by the fact that there are a large number of patents cited by the patent in question, that are receiving many forward citations. In other words, many of the existing patents cited by this patent had become generalized to a high extent by the time it was registered. Meanwhile, the fact that the CI of this patent is higher in value when the timeline is restricted means that the level of convergence is higher, when the evaluation only considers more recent patents, excluding older ones that are quite widely known. As for 'Personal Video Recording Device,' the CI had quite a high value of 18.93 when there was no timeline restriction, and a lower value of 4.91 when the timeline was restricted. The CI value is lower under a restricted timeline due to the fact that a significant number of existing patents cited by this patent have lost much of their value and are no longer cited as much. This shows that when patents with little or no remaining value are excluded from cited patents considered, the convergence level of a patent can be lower.

As for the average CI of the two patents by backward citation depth, when there is no significant difference in the value of CI, it means that a patent and the patents cited by it are not much different in terms of level of convergence. If the value of CI increases, this indicates that the level of convergence increased at the point in time where the CI is higher. While there was little difference in the value of CI for the 'Remote Broadcast Recording' patent, a sharp increase in the value of CI was noted for the 'Personal Video Recording Device' patent. A sharp increase in CI means that the patent is rather new and is not yet cited much by others at the current point in time, and that it cites patents that show a high level of convergence.

5 Conclusion

In this paper, we aimed at testing our concept for measuring the level of technological convergence in individual patents by calculating a convergence indicator based on the results of a patent citation analysis. The methodology proposed in this study is not adapted to a macroscopic analysis of technological convergence, but rather to a microscopic one based on the citation analysis of individual patents. This method, allowing for the evaluation of the relative level of convergence in individual patents, has the merit of minimizing the amount of operational definitions required. We plan to apply this method, in future researches, to the evaluation of convergence level in different patent subclasses within a given technology field so as to assess convergence trends. We also plan to expand this method by developing a method for analyzing technological convergence based on the co-classification of patents, so as to more accurately measure levels of technological convergence.

References

1. Rosenberg, N.: Technological Change in the Machine Tool Industry, 1840-1910. Journal of Economic History 23(4), 414–446 (1963)
2. Roco, M.C.: Converging Technologies for Improving Human Performance: Nanotechnology, Bio-technology, Information Technology and Cognitive Science. In: Bainbridge, W.S. (ed.) NSF Report (2002)
3. Nordmann, A.: Converging Technologies-Shaping the Future of European Society. Converging Technologies for the European Knowledge Society (2004)
4. Hwang, J.T., Kim, B.K.: Analysis on the Multi-technology Capabilities of Korea and Taiwan Using Patent Bibliometrics. Asian Journal of Technology Innovation 14(2), 183–199 (2006)

5. Curran, C.S., Leker, J.: Patent indicators for monitoring convergence - examples from NFF and ICT. Technological Forecasting & Social Change, Corrected Proof, (available online August 8, 2010) (in press)
6. Lee, K.R.: Patterns and Processes of Contemporary Technology Fusion: the Case of Intelligent Robots. Asian Journal of Technology Innovation 15(2), 45–65 (2007)
7. No, H.J., Park, Y.T.: Trajectory Patterns of Technology Fusion: Trend Analysis and Taxonomical Grouping in Nanobiotechnology. Technological Forecasting & Social Change 77, 63–75 (2010)
8. Kodama, F.: Analyzing Japanese High Technologies: the Techno Paradigm Shift. Pinter Publish, London (1991)

A Qualitative Meta-analysis
on Convergence around ICT Sector

Yong-Gook Bae[1] and Hee-Kyung Kong[2,*]

[1] MBA, Dept. of Management Science, KAIST, 335 Gwahak-ro
Yuseong-gu, Daejeon, 305-714 Republic of Korea
`yong-gook@kaist.ac.kr`
[2] Technology Strategy Research Division, ETRI, 138 Gajeong-ro
Yuseong-gu, Daejeon, 305-700 Republic of Korea
Tel.: 82-42-860-1736; Fax: 82-42-860-6504
`konghk@etri.re.kr`

Abstract. Convergence is a term which often used to explain the change of current society, but the meaning of the convergence differs according to the context. This paper defines convergence based on other research and analyzes 40 articles about convergence in the ICT area. Each paper was gathered from journals and databases in August of 2010 and was analyzed through a qualitative meta-analysis method based on the PEST concept. The result of the meta-analysis can be used to understand the current trends in convergence in ICT environments and to develop a future convergence strategy.

Keywords: Convergence, Information, Communications, Meta-Analysis, Trends, PEST.

1 Introduction

In the information and communications area, there have been several paradigm shifts as new technologies have been developed. These changes have become familiar to not only scholars or engineers but also to the public. However, few can discuss convergence clearly because the uses of convergence differ according to the context. Therefore, defining and understanding convergence requires realization of current social and technical trends as well as business models which rapidly change with every day. This paper defines convergence based on related literature and discusses convergence based on a meta-analysis of recent literature in the information and communications sector. This approach can assist with an understanding of the current trends in convergence and develop a future strategy in the area of information and communications.

2 Convergence and Study Selection

Although the term convergence is used widely and has become one of the most important trends in current society, the term is used with different meanings in

---

* Corresponding author.

T.-h. Kim et al. (Eds.): UNESST 2010, CCIS 124, pp. 195–205, 2010.

different contexts. Therefore, it is necessary to define convergence clearly before research can be done in this area. Wikipedia defines convergence as "the approach toward a definite value, a definite point, a common view or opinion, or toward a fixed or equilibrium state" [2]. It explains convergence via a dictionary definition and lists different meanings in different areas. Deloitte (2005) characterizes convergence as combining two or more previously discrete lines of business to create something new – a new product or service, a new alliance, a new value chain structure, or a new economic model – that generates greater value for a business and its customers [3], whereas Tang (2006) distinguishes it as a process of qualitative change that connects two or more existing, previously distinct markets [4, 5]. Deloitte also classified convergence into the three levels of platform, organization, and products and services, and Tang categorized it into three types – industrial, service, and technology convergence. Deloitte and Tang saw convergence in light of business regardless of the applicable area. Although these definitions were drawn based on the trends in the information and communication technology area, they are too broad to utilize in a specific area. The OECD (2004) defines convergence as the process by which communications networks and services, previously considered separate, are being transformed such that: (1) different network platforms carry a similar range of voice, audiovisual and data transmission services (2) different consumer appliances receive a similar range of services and (3) new services are being created [6]. This paper defines convergence in the information and communication sector as a process of combining information and communication technology with one or more types of technology, service or product out of the ICT sector to create new value.

Table 1. Paradigm shift [1]

Legacy Paradigm	changes into	New Paradigm
Static market		Dynamic Market
Divergence		Convergence
Circuit-switched		Packet-switched
Local		Global
Low-speed		High-speed
Switch-on		Always-on
Fixed		Mobile + Fixed
Single medium		Multi-media
Distinct		Bundled

This paper utilizes qualitative meta-analysis to grasp convergence. It is customary to collect literature from top journals to do, but, in addition to journals, this research makes use of two large databases: SCOPUS [7] and NDSL [8]. Three keywords were used for the topic search: convergence and ICT and IT. Although some regions use fusion rather than convergence, the search results at the initial stage were scant; therefore, fusion was ignored and convergence was focused on in a meta-search. Initially, the searched papers were refined again based on their title and abstracts. For instance, NDSL papers published before 2005 were omitted. Finally, all remaining papers were reviewed in detail and 40 papers were selected at last and analyzed.

The structure of this paper is as follows: Chapters 1 and 2 introduce convergence and explain the details of this paper. Chapter 3 argues the results of meta-analysis from selected 40 studies, and chapter 4 then draws implications from the findings in chapter 3, discusses the limitations of this research, and suggests subsequent researchable topics.

3 Results of the Meta-analysis and Discussion

3.1 Sources and Publication Period

As mentioned in chapter 2, 40 studies were selected for the meta-analysis. Table 2 shows the number of papers according to the database and the source journals and the databases of the selected research.

Table 2. Sources for Meta-Analysis

Database	Journal	Number
	Communications & Convergence Review	8
Emerald	Emerald Journal	7
	Management Decision	1
	Journal of Management Development	1
NDSL	Public Relations Review	1
	IEEE Transactions on Consumer Electronics	1
	IEEE Transactions on Signal Processing	1
	Wireless Personal Communications	5
	Automation in Construction	1
	Nuclear Instruments & Methods in Physic Research	1
	The Howard Journal of Communications	1
	International Journal of Wireless Information Networks	1
	Telematics and Informatics	1
	The International Information & Library Review	1
	SIAM Journal on Applied Mathematics	1
	Journal of Korean Home Management Association	1
	Journal of the Korean Society of IT Services	1
	Journal of Broadcast Engineering	1
SCOPUS	The 4th International Workshop on SDL and MSC, SAM 2004	1
	IFIP International Federation for Information Processing	1
	Automation in Construction	1
	Telecommunications Policy	1
	Future Generation Computer Systems	1
Total		40

Figure 1 shows the publication period of the selected papers by year. Through the refining process, numerous papers published before 2005 were excluded, but four papers from the Emerald journal remained. The number of papers is relatively small from 2007 to 2008 compared to 2005, 2006 and 2009. Most of the papers in 2003 and 2004 were rejected during the refining process, and many studies were selected from August of 2010; therefore, the numbers of papers in 2010 and the number before 2005 are small. As mentioned in chapter 2, during 2004-2006, there were many studies on convergence, including the definition by the OECD (2004). The number held steady for two years after that period, and then the lull finished with rapid changes in business models and technologies, such as smart phone and TVs, application stores, the future internet/network and other such areas.

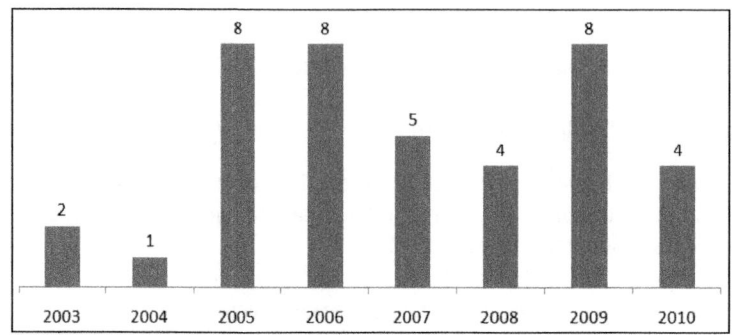

Fig. 1. Numbers of Studies by Years

3.2 Focused Areas

This paper uses a PEST analysis to understand the current issues in convergence. The selected 40 papers came from diverse journals and different areas. Thus, it is necessary to understand their focus and topic. PEST refers to political, economic, social and technological. Occasionally this is referred to as PESTLE with the addition of legal and environment, but in this research legal and regulation issues are included in politics, and social issues includes environments. In addition, business/industrial issues are categorizes as economical issues. Studies were also categorized into quantitative and qualitative research, and case studies were counted separately. Table 3 shows the result.

Table 3. Focused Area of the Studies based on PEST

PEST	Qualitative	Quantitative	Total	Case Study
Political	6	-	6	1
Economical	8	2	10	3
Social	6	2	8	1
Technological	10	6	16	-
Total	30	10	40	5

The number of technological studies is the highest among all areas, and economics and social studies follow. Most of the studies were done qualitatively, and there are several case studies in each category except for technological studies.

3.3 Topics in Detail

Politics. In the political area, there were six studies, including one case study. Shin (2009) researched regulatory issues around mobile DMB (digital media broadcasting) and suggested multi-sector regulations [9]. Henten et al. (2003), Wu et al. (2004) and Yoo (2009) studied regulatory issues focusing on the telecommunication sector [10, 11, 12]. Yoo (2009) discussed the convergence between telecommunications and broadcasting, and Henten et al. (2003) and Wu et al. (2004) focused on regulation of communication technologies. Garcia-Murillo (2005) analyzed the regulatory convergence of the UK, India, Malaysia and South Africa and showed the similarities and differences between the countries [13]. Menon (2005) discussed Indian regulatory and institutional contexts regarding convergence in telecommunications [14].

All of these studies researched regulatory issues in various ways, but all of them are also qualitative research, including the case study, in the four countries. This is quite natural because these are regulatory studies. Although these studies focused on slightly different sectors, the scholars suggested a new concept for regulation and regulatory agencies. As convergence emerges, legacy regulations had become a barrier to advanced technology and business models. As Garcia-Murillo (2005) showed, the regulations have been changing to adopt convergence, but there remain a number of limitations. Regulatory issues in convergence represent an important area of further study.

Economics. Unlike political research, the selected studies showed different approaches in the business area. Wei (2008) carried out a survey of 208 users to show different motivations predict diverse uses of mobile phones [15]. His research recognized that people use mobile phones for instrumental purposes and for entertainment. In addition, the study showed differences according to the device and the age of the user.

Degkwitz (2006) showed an overview of the convergence of services via the case of the ICMC/IKMZ of Cottbus University in Germany [16]. The ICMC/IKMZ was founded in 2004 to provide the converged service of a library, a multimedia center, a computer center and an administrative data processing center. Founding it, the organization and its service needed to be highly developed. This paper showed the details, limitations and implications of the work for other organizations.

Palmberg and Martikainen (2006) and Kumaraswamy et al. (2006) discussed R&D. Kumaraswamy et al. (2006) studied two cases of the development of Information and Knowledge Management systems and showed the importance and the roles of technological convergence [17, 18]. Palmberg and Martikainen (2006) analyzed patentable technologies of Finnish telecom firms statistically and showed that the Finnish telecom industry had diversified from its technological base while the impact of R&D alliances grew.

Kim et al (2010), Kwon and Lee (2010), and Godoe and Hansen (2009) discussed convergence issues pertaining to mobile technology [19, 20, 21]. Kim et al (2010) discussed UCC (User-Created Content) in this area. Their paper showed that mobile video UCC could have superior value compared to existing mobile services and it discussed the implications on various groups, including users, MNOs, content/software providers and terminal vendors. Kwon and Lee (2010) discussed the hegemonic struggle between mobile network operators and banks in Korean mobile banking. In another way, Godoe and Hansen (2009) insisted that there are some technological regimes in m-commerce and that a strategy of convergence based on symbiosis and co-operation could result in a rapid diffusion process of m-commerce.

Rangone and Turconi (2003) discussed the television business, which is rapidly changing with the development of technology [22]. The paper showed related technology and new business models including a new service and value chain. Lee et al. (2010) focused on context-aware computing and developed a new conceptual framework for designing business models [23]. Chang (2009) also discussed industrial digital convergence theoretically in detail [24].

The papers selected in the economics area studied business applications of convergence between information and communications technologies along with the legacy value chain. As Kwon and Lee (2010) and Godoe and Hansen (2009) showed, convergence does not promise success in business. However, convergence can create a new value chain and deliver higher value to industrial players as well as end-users.

Society. Papers categorized in the social area consider how society reacts to convergence. These studies discussed philosophy, culture, individual reactions and differing sizes of communities in the face of convergence.

Christians (2009) discusses convergence based not on technology and business, but on philosophy [25]. The paper discusses the emerging issues of the invasion of privacy and government surveillance and shows how these issues should be addressed. Bradley (2006) analyzed social changes related to the use of information and communications technologies [26]. The paper studied workforces, organization design and structure, psychological communications, and work content. It also suggests a theoretical model which describes the relationship between ICT, globalization, the life environment, the life role and the effects of humans. Bradley tried to explain social changes through a developed model.

Mehra and Papajohn (2007) analyzed Internet use patterns of international teaching assistants quantitatively and found communication-convergence in their use of the Internet as a global network as well as a local network – the authors termed this a "Glocal" network [27]. Barry (2005) studied another topic at a university in Egypt in a case study [28]. Through the case study, he found that computer skills and the English language can affect public relations education. This research showed another example of the effect and importance of convergence. A study of the business model and value chain of video UCC was done in the economical area, and another study was conducted in the social area.

Kim and Park (2008) researched customer behavior in the face of changes in the communication environment [29]. They analyzed secondary data from Internet service companies and found that a web-based customer acts as a "Prosumer," although there were some differences according to age, gender and other factors. Na (2009) also discussed the changes in audiences caused by convergence [30]. This paper insists that the audiences, or the customers, of media were passive receivers but changed into active participants. The audiences are also active appliers as well as dynamic creators. Both Kim and Park (2008) and Na (2009) argued that customer behavior changes as technologies develop and converge.

Mitra (2009) reviewed the literature about flagship projects and the implementing process of ICTs in government and found dependencies of the public sector on private sector in ICT projects [31]. Megwa (2007) showed the role of ICTs in a community radio station in South Africa [32]. He used face-to-face interviews, document analysis, observation, and community conversation. His study proved the importance of radio stations in South Africa and showed how ICTs can contribute to radio stations and to the rural community.

Technology. Each paper in the technological area discusses different technologies. It is difficult to understand the details of many of these papers, though this is not the purpose of this paper. Unlike other areas, the studies will be categorized in terms of the topic and convergence area.

All of the papers in technological area focused on the development of a new system or model, apart from one paper. Lee et al. (2010) studied broadband diffusion and bandwidth capacity in OECD countries empirically [33]. Other studies investigated topics that were more technological.

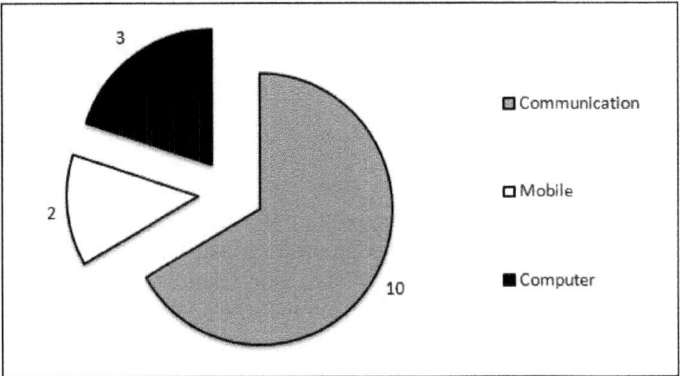

Fig. 2. Numbers of Papers according to the Technological Area

As Figure 2 shows, more than half of the studies focused on communication technology. Communication technology includes wired and mobile networks as well as related services and technologies, such as transmission. Two papers among 10 studied convergence between communication and broadcasting [34, 35]. They suggested system improvements in a multimedia framework of BcN and home-based networks. Another paper introduced a new service model based on convergence between communication and navigation [36]. In addition, two papers focused on mobile networks, developing a service development framework [37] and discussing a paradigm shift in processor development [38]. Nielsen and Jacobsen (2005) suggested new system, service, and strategy of an All-IP environment [39], while Madsen (2006) studied a unified global physical infrastructure [40]. In addition, Aguiar et al. (2009) discussed an operational conceptual model for a global communication infrastructure [41]. Ferreira et al. (2006) and Dahl et al. (2007) focused on more detailed technologies [42, 43]. Ferreira et al. (2006) discussed convergence between mobile and wireless communications conceptually and Dahl et al. (2007) studied convergence in TDD MIMO communication. Bræk and Floch (2005) brought up modeling issues in ICT system modeling [44] and Buyya et al. (2009) studied cloud computing in detail [45]. Vinogradov (2007), Jha (2007), and La and Ranjan (2007) discussed technologies focused on computing hardware and software [46, 47, 48].

The 15 aforementioned papers can be categorized as studies that focused on hardware, software, a concept/model, a platform and combinations of these, as shown in Figure 3.

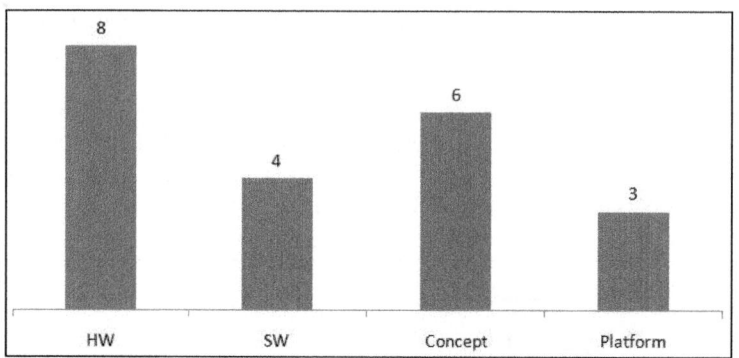

Fig. 3. Numbers of Papers according to the Category. Some studies are repeatedly counted in different categories.

Most of the papers studied hardware and platforms, or infrastructure. It is notable that most studies of convergence were focused on hardware convergence. It is also quite interesting that more than half of the papers studied a concept or model of convergence. This shows that convergence in the ICT sector has many possibilities in the near future.

4   Conclusion

This paper defines convergence around the ICT sector and reviews recent literatures on convergence around the ICT sector using a meta-analysis based on the concept of PEST (Politics, Economics, Society and Technology). Forty papers were chosen by a developed process and the selected papers were analyzed qualitatively. The results of the meta-analysis showed that convergence is discussed in various areas and in various ways. Although there are many differences in different research fields, there are a number of broad trends in the study of convergence, including regulation in political areas, developing new business models in economics, social changes, and developing new hardware technologies in communication technologies. These studies also show the potentiality of convergence in different sectors.

It is not possible to conclude that the selected studies represent all of the research on convergence. Although it is challenging to analyze the literature on convergence statistically, a quantitative meta-analysis of the large number of studies can be helpful to those to attempt to understand the trends and the issues associated with convergence more precisely.

In addition, this paper centers on political, economical, social and technical research. Another meta-analysis, focusing on other areas, may show results that add depth and augment the findings here.

References

1. Zhano, H.: Digital Convergence: Challenges and Opportunities. In: IT Ministerial Conference, ITU (2007),
   http://www.itu.int/net/ITU-SG/speeches-deputy/2007/apr19.ppt
2. Wikipedia, http://en.wikipedia.org/wiki/convergence
3. Deloitte: The Trillion Dollar Challenge: Principles for Profitable Convergence. Deloitte & Touche LLP, London (2005)
4. Tang, D.: Convergence: a Necessary Process for Transformation. Huawei Technologies Communicate (25), 5–10 (2006)
5. Sokolova, K.: What do you Understand by the Concept of Technological Convergence and What are its Key Trends. The ITU Young Minds, ITU (2007)
6. OECD: The Implications of Convergence for Regulation of Electronic Communications. DSTI/ICCP/TISP(2003)5/Final. Head of Publication Service, OECD, Paris (2004)
7. SCOPUS, http://www.scopus.com
8. NDSL, http://www.ndsl.kr
9. Shin, D.H.: Technology Convergence and Regulatory Challenge: a Case from Korean Digital Media Broadcasting. Emerald Journal 7(3), 47–58 (2005)
10. Henten, A., Samarajiva, R., Melody, W.: Designing next Generation Telecom Regulation: ICT Convergence or Multi-sector Utility? Emerald Journal 5(1), 26–33 (2003)
11. Wu, I., McElvane, R., Dey, A., Duwadi, K.: The Impact of Competition and Technology on Telecommunications Regulation: Call for Further Research on Regulatory Procedures and the Convergence of Wireless, Wireline, and Cable. Emerald Journal 6(4), 225–233 (2004)
12. Yoo, C.S.: The Convergence of Broadcasting and Telephony: Legal and Regulatory Implications. Convergence & Communications Review 1(1), 44–55 (2009)
13. Garcia-Murillo, M.: Regulatory Responses to Convergence: Experiences from four Countries. Emerald Journal 7(1), 20–40 (2005)
14. Menon, S.: The Role of Diverse Institutional Agendas in the Importation of Convergence Policy into the Indian Communications Sector. Emerald Journal 7(4), 30–46 (2005)
15. Wei, R.: Motivations for using the Mobile Phone for Mass Communications and Entertainment. Telematics and Informatics 25, 36–46 (2008)
16. Degkwitz, A.: Convergence in Germany: the Information, Communication and Media Center (ICMC/IKMZ) of Cottbus University. Emerald Journal 24(3), 430–439 (2006)
17. Palmberg, C., Martikainen, O.: Diversification in Response to ICT Convergence – Indigenous Capabilities versus R&D Alliances of the Finnish Telecom Industry. Emerald Journal 8(4), 67–84 (2006)
18. Kumaraswamy, M.M., Palaneeswaran, E., Rahman, M.M., Ugwu, O.O., Ng, S.T.: Synergising R&D initiatives for e-enhancing management support systems. Automation in Constructions 15, 681–692 (2006)
19. Kim, S.C., Na, E.K., Ryu, M.H.: Convergence between Mobile and UCC Media: the Potential of Mobile Video UCC Service. Communication & Convergence Review 2(1), 26–35 (2010)
20. Kwon, Y.S., Lee, H.K.: Evolution of Mobile Banking in Korea: Who gets Hegemony and Why. Communication & Convergence Review 2(1), 13–25 (2010)
21. Godoe, H., Hansen, T.B.: Technological Regimes in m-Commerce: Convergence as a Barrier to Diffusion and Entrepreneurship? Telecommunications Policy 33(1/2), 19–28 (2009)

22. Rangone, A., Truconi, A.: The Television (r)evolution within the Multimedia Convergence: a Strategic Reference Framework. Management Decision 41(1), 48–71 (2003)
23. Lee, Y.H., Shim, H.D., Park, N.I.: A New Convergence Business Model Framework for Context-aware Computing Service Market. Communications & Convergence Review 2(1), 1–12 (2010)
24. Chang, S.K.: Industrial Dynamics of Digital Convergence: Theory, Evidence and Prospects. Communications & Convergence Review 1(1), 56–81 (2009)
25. Christians, C.G.: Philosophical Issues in Media Convergence. Communications & Convergence Review 1(1), 1–14 (2009)
26. Bradley, G.: Social Informatics – from Theory to Actions for the good ICT Society. IFIP International Federation for Information Processing 223, 383–394 (2006)
27. Merha, B., Papajohn, D.: "Glocal" Patterns of Communication-Information Convergences in Internet Use: Cross-cultural Behavior of International Teaching Assistants in a Culturally Alien Information Environment. The International Information & Library Review 39(1), 12–30 (2007)
28. Barry, W.I.A.: Teaching Public Relations in the Information Age: a Case Study at an Egyptian University. Public Relations Review 31(3), 355–361 (2005)
29. Kim, Y.J., Park, S.Y.: Multimedia UCC Services as a Web 2. 0 and Consumer Participation. Journal of Korean Home Management Association. 26(1), 95–105 (2008)
30. Na, E.Y.: Upgrade of the Position of Audience caused by the Convergence of Broadcasting and Communication. Communications & Convergence Review 1(1), 107–130 (2009)
31. Mitra, A.: Convergence in ICT Use Expectations between the Public and Private Sectors: An Imperative or an Indicator of Efficiency? Journal of Management Development 28(6), 550–554 (2009)
32. Megwa, E.R.: Bridging the Digital Divide: Community Radio's Potential for Extending Information and Communication Technology Benefits to Poor Rural Communities in South Africa. The Howard Journal of Communications 18(4), 335–352 (2007)
33. Lee, S.W., Lee, S.M.: An Empirical Study of Broadband Diffusion and Bandwidth Capacity in OECD Countries. Communications & Convergence Review 2(1), 36–49 (2010)
34. Ji, K.H., Moon, N.M., Kim, J.G.: Study of Event Reporting Service for Digital Contents on the Convergence Network of Broadcasting and Communication. Journal of Broadcast Engineering 10(2), 190–201 (2005)
35. Park, W.K., Kim, D.Y.: Convergence of Broadcasting and Communication in Home Network using an EPON-based Home Gateway and Overlay. IEEE Transactions on Consumer Electronics 51(2), 485–493 (2005)
36. Ruggieri, M.: Next Generation of Wired and Wireless Networks: The NavCom Integration. Wireless Personal Communications 38(1), 79–88 (2006)
37. Kim, S.H., Shin, G.C., Je, D.G., Kang, S.Y., Bae, J.S., Kim, J.H., Park, S.K., Ryu, S.W.: Key Technological Issues and Service Development Framework for Provisioning of Next Generation Mobile Convergence Services in Ubiquitous Information Society. Journal of the Korea Society of IT Services 7(3), 215–237 (2008)
38. Jha, U.S.: Convergence of Communication, Infotainment, and Multimedia Applications Require Paradigm Shift in Processor Development and Reuse Pattern. Wireless Personal Communications 37(3/4), 305–315 (2006)
39. Nielsen, T.T., Jacobsen, R.H.: Opportunities for IP in Communications Beyond 3G. Wireless Personal Communications 33(3/4), 243–259 (2005)

40. Madsen, O.B.: Towards a Unified Global ICT Infrastructure. Wireless Personal Communications 37(3/4), 213–220 (2006)
41. Aguiar, R.L., Einsiedler, H.J., Moreno, J.I.: An Operational Conceptual Model for Global Communication Infrastructures. Wireless Personal Communications 49(3), 335–351 (2009)
42. Ferreira, L., Serrador, A., Correia, L.M.: Concepts of Simultaneous Use in Mobile and Wireless Communications. Wireless Personal Communications 37(3/4), 317–328 (2006)
43. Dahl, T., Pereira, S.S., Christophersen, N., Gesbert, D.: Intrinsic Subspace Convergence in TDD MIMO Communication. IEEE Transactions on Signal Processing: a Publication of the IEEE Signal Processing Society 55(6), 2676–2687 (2007)
44. Bræk, R., Floch, J.: ICT Convergence: Modeling Issues. In: Amyot, D., Williams, A.W. (eds.) SAM 2004. LNCS, vol. 3319, pp. 237–256. Springer, Heidelberg (2005)
45. Buyya, R., Yeo, C.S., Venugopal, S., Broberg, J., Brandic, I.: Cloud Computing and Emerging IT Platforms: Vision, Hype, and Reality for Delivering Computing as the 5th Utility. Future Generation Computer Systems 25, 599–616 (2009)
46. Vinogradov, V.I.: Advanced High-Performance Computer System Architectures. Nuclear Instruments & Methods in Physics Research 571(1/2), 429–432 (2007)
47. Jha, U.S.: Object Oriented HW Functions Accelerate Communication, Computing, and Multimedia Convergence. International Journal of Wireless Information Networks 14(4), 281–288 (2007)
48. La, R.J., Ranjan, P.: Convergence of Dual Algorithm with Arbitrary Communication Delays. SIAM Journal on Applied Mathematics 68(5), 1247–1267 (2008)

A Patent Analysis on Realistic Media
for R&D Projects

Sung-Hyun Hwang and Seung-Jun Yeon[*]

Electonics Telecommunication Research institute,
138 Gajeongno Yuseong-gu, Daejeon, korea
Hyun052@etri.re.kr, sjyeon@etri.re.kr

Abstract. In this paper, we use patent statistics as the recent status of R&D in international patents. The number of patents was used to compare different countries' share in the overall number of technology patents. Using the degree of patent citations, the influence and technological prowess of patents were examined. Also, implications were drawn from an analysis of patent contents for realistic media.

Keywords: Realistic Media, Immersive Media, Patent Analysis, R&D projects selection.

1 Introduction

The rapid development of digital and network transmission technologies has led to the appearance of new, diverse multimedia services. In the 2000's, the boundary between broadcasting and communication fields has broken down, and broadcasting and tele-communication convergence services, reflecting their respective strengths, are currently being provided. With the appearance of such new media, keen attention is being paid to an improvement of the quality of multimedia that can stimulate the user's five senses to allow him/her to feel a sense of immersion. Realistic media constitute a new concept of media that can enhance the quality of information on the five senses, similar to a realistic feeling. In developed nations, fierce competition is already being made to develop realistic media technologies and secure the relevant patent rights. Notably, acquisition of international patents is the key to R&D efforts.

In order to acquire international patent rights, a systematic survey of previous relevant patents is essential. Information on those patents makes it possible to eliminate duplicate R&D investments, and formulate key technology strategies, through selection and concentration. Patent information is essential for understanding new technologies, and is widely used in analyzing technological levels and in determining the direction of innovation [1].

---

[*] Corresponding author. Technology Strategy Research Division, ETRI, 138 Gajeong-ro, Yuseong-gu, Daejeon, 305-700 Republic of Korea (Tel.: 82-42-860-6437; Fax: 82-42-860-6504.

T.-h. Kim et al. (Eds.): UNESST 2010, CCIS 124, pp. 206–213, 2010.
© Springer-Verlag Berlin Heidelberg 2010

Most studies on patents have thus far centered on their importance as econometric indices to show a firm's R&D strength or each country's governmental patent policy. Few studies have concentrated their attention on strategic viewpoints. This lack of strategic viewpoint may arise from the conventional notion that a patent application is only an ex post facto process following inventions in R&D. Now, analysis of the target patents necessary for a particular product development is needed. Researchers can then start their actual R&D activity. In this way, they are able to acquire effective patents and form an adequate functioning portfolio. Moreover, in their examination of a series of technologies to be developed, the selection of research themes is made so that they effectively complement others already in the comprehensive group of patents [2].

Thus, an analysis of patents was conducted in order to select realistic media R&D projects. Micro Patent's Aureka program was used to analyze the relevant databases. Keywords were searched to extract the relevant data. The examination period spanned from 2001 to June 2009. To obtain quality data, patent data from intellectual property offices of the US, the EU, and Japan, along with WIPO (World Intellectual Property Organization) data, were examined.

2   Theoretical Foundations

Patent statistics have been used as a reliable measure of the output of inventive activities [3]-[6], innovative activities [7], technological changes [8], technological strengths [9], accumulated capabilities [10], and specialization [11] in many industries, and thus are widely accepted. Patent statistics are publicly available, remain up-to-date, and provide very specific and detailed information for tracing inventive activities over time [12]. Furthermore, patent statistics are the only formally and publicly verified output measure of inventive activities. For these reasons, researchers have begun to favor patent statistics and use them exclusively as measures of innovation and inventive activities [7], [13]-[15].

A patent index is an excellent technology analysis tool that enables us to understand various characteristics of new technologies from both a macroscopic and microscopic perspective. Patent indices are widely used to determine innovation factors and factors driving economic growth, trace the extent of diffusion of a technology between technology fields, countries, regions and companies, and to measure technology development accomplishments, the structure of an industry enabled by a given technology and its level of development [16].

Since Schmookler first interpreted patent statistics from an economics perspective in the late 1950s, many organizations including NBER and Yale University are using patent analysis. Patent indices are considered today the best indices available for measuring innovation.

Patent information is used in research primarily for two purposes: one is to understand the correlation between R&D and patent production, as exemplified by the work of Hall and Grilliches [17], and the other is to derive R&D strategies, examples of which include works by the US DOC and Japan's METI. Patent information analysis is used particularly frequently for developing R&D strategies in government-sponsored studies.

In 1994, the OECD issued its Patent Manual, as part of the group of manuals (Frascati Family) devoted to the quantitative assessment of science and technology activities. Since then, the OECD has published various analytical guidelines for the statistical analysis of patents. More recently, the OECD developed a patent analysis index, based on data from patents registered with organizations like the EC (European Community), EPO (European Patent Office), JPO (Japan Patent Office), NSF (National Science Foundation), USPTO (United States Patents and Trademark Office) and the WIPO (World Intellectual Property Organization), which is being used in projects for promoting industrial growth and scientific and technological progress.

The US NBER (National Bureau of Economic Research) conducts the statistical analysis of patents using macroeconomic indices. Patent analysis services are provided, meanwhile, by CHI and other private-sector organizations, using their own patent indices, based on US patent citation information.

As for Japan's METI (Ministry of Economy, Trade and Industry), it has published guidelines on its intellectual property strategy index [18].

In Korea, the STEPI (Science and Technology Policy Institute) evaluates the level of technology development in the IT and BT fields, using the patent index developed by the US company, CHI, publishing also policy reports on policy implications of the state of technology thus measured [19].

In this paper, we use patent statistics as the recent status of R&D in international patents. Also, the number of patents was used to examine the development trends of particular technologies and to compare different countries' shares in such technologies. Using the degree of citations of patents, the influence patents and technological prowess were examined. Also, implications were drawn from an analysis of patent contents of realistic media.

3 Results and Implications

Certain keywords were searched in the titles and abstracts of patents and were used in order to create a database for patent analysis. On the basis of an examination of existing literature on realistic media, the keywords, i.e., those that could represent realistic media the best, were set as "realistic and media", "immersive and media", "single and media and multi and device", "SMMD", and "five and sense and media". The search found 1,157 patents, of which 16 duplicate patents were excluded, leaving 1,141 patents to be analyzed.

3.1 Quantitative Analysis and Implications

First, to review the overview of patent registration for realistic media, the data were analyzed yearly. The yearly analysis is shown in Table 1.

Table 1. Yearly registration of patents for realistic media

Year	JPO	EPO	WIP	USPT	Total
2001	-	5	29	11	45
2002	1	2	44	63	110
2003	-	7	38	80	125
2004	-	14	17	82	113
2005	-	7	40	109	156
2006	1	11	42	105	159
2007	1	4	56	110	171
2008	1	8	42	100	151
2009	1	5	23	82	111
Total	5	63	331	742	1,141

As shown in Table 1, as time went on, the registration of realistic media patents increased. The patent database was built as of June, 2009, and thus the total number of patents for the whole of 2009 is estimated at over 220. By patent office, as shown in Table 2, a greater number of patents were applied for and registered with patent offices, including WIPO in foreign countries such as the US, rather than in the countries to which those patents belonged. This is true of most patent analyses, proving that the US is forecasted to be the largest market for realistic media patents, and offering implications for patent applications.

Table 2. Yearly patent registration for realistic media

Year	KR	JP	etc.	EU	US	Total
2001	3	2	-	4	36	45
2002	-	3	5	3	99	110
2003	-	6	5	8	106	125
2004	1	6	16	7	83	113
2005	1	6	18	14	117	156
2006	7	14	8	16	114	159
2007	9	5	13	9	135	171
2008	4	7	4	12	124	151
2009	5	2	6	6	92	111
Total	30	51	75	79	906	1,141

The largest patent holders include Microsoft (47 patents), Silverbrook (22 patents), IBM (17 patents), and Samsung Electronics (17 patents); universities filed applications for and registered only 12 patents. Large IT companies are leading the R&D efforts. This suggests that realistic media, technologically, are more like application and commercialization technologies rather than fundamental technologies, and this point should be taken into account when selecting target R&D projects.

3.2 Qualitative Analysis and Implications

Numerous attempts have been made over the years to make use of patent information for the assessment of the competitiveness of a given technology field and for
the development of national R&D policies. The US DOC (Department Of
Commerce), for example, analyzes the competitiveness of five technology fields
using five patent indices (PA, AI, TCT, CII, TS) and applies the results in planning science and technology policies [20]. Some of the most notable of the many
varieties of patent indices are listed in Table 3 below.

Table 3. Types of Patent Indices

Patent Index	Type	Definition	Calculation	Use
Activity Index (AI)	Measurement of innovation activities	Patent activities in a specific technology field	AI = (Total patents of a patentee in a specific technology field / Total patents in the same technology field)/(Total patents granted to a patentee /Total patents)	Companies, governments
Patent Family Size (PFS)	Measurement of market potential	Number of family patents	PFS = Average number of international families of a patentee / Average number of total international families	Companies
Ratio of Dependency (RD)	Measurement of technology protection	Degree of technology protection in a country	RD = Number of patents registered by a foreign national in a given technology field/ Number of patents registered by a citizen in the same technology field	Governments
Cites Per Patent (CPP)	Technological competitiveness/ market potential indicator	Average number of times a given patent was cited by subsequent patents	CP P= Number of citations received /Number of patents	Companies, governments
Patent Impact Index (PII)	Measurement of technological competitiveness	Quality of a patent	= The ratio of citations received by a patentee in a specific technology field / Total ratio of citations received = CPPa (Number of citations received in a specific technology field / Number of patents in the same technology field)/CPPt (Total number of citations received /Total number of patents)	Companies, governments
Technology Strength (TS)	Measurement of technological competitiveness	Technological competitiveness indicator	TS = Number of patents * Patent impact index (PII)	Companies, governments

The Activity Index (AI) is an indicator measuring the concentration of a specific technology in a company's patents or total registered patents. When the value of the index is greater than 1, this means that a company's patent activity in a given technology field is above the average. Technologies or companies whose AI exceeds 3 are referred to as "highly-specialized technologies" or "highly-specialized companies." The specialization indicator does not compare a company with others, but measures, instead, whether a given company is specialized in a specific field, and is expressed most often as a LQ (location Quotient). Patent family size (PFS) is an indicator of market share competitiveness.

Each patent registered for a given invention is called a family patent, and given the fact that patents are filed in a third-party country only when there is a commercial interest in this country or a relationship of technology competition with it, the greater the number of family patents, the greater the market potential of a patented invention is deemed. The ratio of dependency (RD) is an indicator of the extent of technology protection in a given country, based on the ratio of patents registered by its nationals and foreign nationals. Cites per patent (CPP) is a mean value of citations received by a given patent from other patents registered subsequently.

The greater the value of CPP, the greater the number of essential or fundamental patents. In other words, a rights holder of a patent which is frequently cited has a competitive advantage over others. The patent impact index (PII) measures past technology activities from a specific point in time and is an indicator of the quality of technology possessed by a given patent owner. When the PII has a value of 1, this indicates that the citation frequency is average, and when it is at 2, the citation frequency is above average. Technology strength (TS) is an indicator of technological capacity; the greater the value of TS, the stronger a country's technological capacity.

In this study, we only included CPP, PII and TS in the scope of consideration. The goal of this study being to analyze technological competitiveness in realistic media and derive implications for future R&D directions, we only considered those patent indices that are suited for measuring technological competitiveness in this field.

The results showed that US patents had the highest CPP, PII and TS, and Korean patents the lowest. Korean patents' scores in CPP and PII were less than half those of US patents, and in TS, a mere 2% of the latter.

The quality of the realistic media patents of various nations was examined using CPP, PII, and TS indices, the results of which are shown in Table 4. The analysis indicates that the US patents boast the highest CPP, PII, and TS, suggesting a great dependence upon the US for realistic media technologies.

Table 4. Qualitative analysis of realistic media patents

Country	CPP	PII	TS
KR	0.93	0.46	13.80
etc.	1.05	0.52	38.94
JP	1.82	0.90	45.84
EU	1.43	0.70	55.69
US	2.21	1.09	986.73

3.3   Content Analysis and Implications

A theme map[1] for content analysis, which adopts the data-mining technique, shows that Create Interactive, Optical Light, Image Display, and Wireless Transmitting are located at high altitudes on the contour lines, and of the five senses, the development of technologies focused on the visual sense and those using video games is prominent. This suggests that when selecting new realistic media technologies for development, it is desirable to select non-visual technologies, and that the initial realistic media technology markets are forecasted to be activated in game markets.

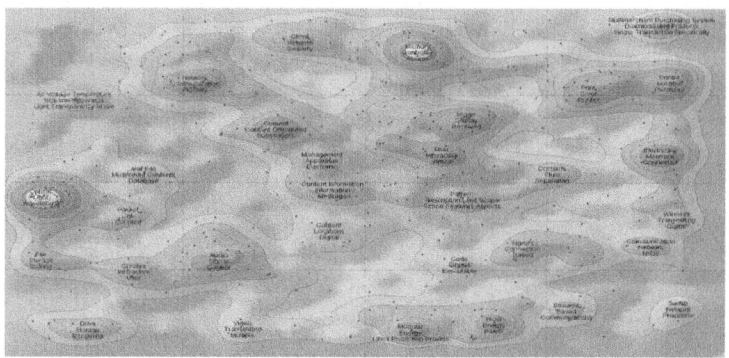

Fig. 1. Theme Map of Realistic media

4   Conclusion

In this paper, we use patent statistics as the recent status of R&D in international patents. Some results and implications were drawn from an analysis of the quantity, quality, and contents of realistic media patents. The results and implications presented in this paper will perhaps provide some ideas and directions for selecting R&D projects. This paper serves as a good starting point from which to clarify certain implications.

References

[1] Archibugi, D.: Patenting as an Indicator of Technological Innovation: A Review. Science and Public Policy 19(6), 357–368 (1992)
[2] Tsuji, Y.S.: Organizational behavior in the R&D process based on patent analysis: Strategic R&D management in a Japanese electronics firm. Technovation 22, 417–425 (2002)
[3] Grupp, H.: Science, technology, and the competitiveness of EU. Camb. J. Econ. 19(1), 209–223 (1995)
[4] Chakrabarti, A.K.: Competition in high technology: analysis of patents of US, Japan, UK, West Germany, and Canada. IEEE Trans. Eng. Manage. 38(1), 78–84 (1991)

---

[1] A theme map shows contour lines connecting frequently appearing words, where those words located at high altitudes indicate the fields in which technology development is active. The map also shows the relevant markets.

[5] Griliches, Z.: Patent statistics as economic indicators: a survey. J. Econ. Lit. 28, 1661–1707 (1990)

[6] Kodama, F.: Analyzing Japanese High Technologies. Pinter, London (1991)

[7] Acs, Z.J., Audretsch, D.B.: Patents as a measure of innovative activity. Kyklos 42(2), 171–180 (1989)

[8] Basberg, B.L.: Patents and measurement of technological change: a survey of literature. Res. Policy 16(2), 131–141 (1987)

[9] Narin, F., Noma, E., Perry, R.: Patents as indicators of corporate technological strength. Res. Policy 16(2), 143–155 (1987)

[10] Etemad, H., Lee, Y.: The inherent complexities of revealed technological advantage as an index of cumulative technological specialization. In: Proceedings of the Administrative Sciences Association of Canada, IB Division, pp. 22–37 (1999)

[11] Archibugi, D., Pianta, M.: The Technological Specialization of Advanced Countries. The Kluwer Academic Publishers, Dordrecht (1992)

[12] Ma, Z., Lee, Y., Chen, C.P.: Booming or emerging? China's technological capability and international collaboration in patent activities. Technological Forecasting and Social Change 76, 787–796 (2009)

[13] Etemad, H., Seguin-Dulude, L.: Patenting patterns in 25 large multinational enterprises. Technovation 7, 1–15 (1987)

[14] Sirili, G.: Patents and inventors: an empirical study. In: Freeman, C. (ed.) Output Measurement in Science and Technology, pp. 157–172. North Holland, Amsterdam (1987)

[15] Tong, X., Frame, J.D.: Measuring national technological performance with patent claims data. Res. Policy 23, 133–141 (1994)

[16] Shin, H.-S.: Design of Consolidated Patent Index for Effective Utilization of Patent Information. Korea Management Science Review 24(2) (2007)

[17] Grilliches, Z.: Patent statics as economic indicator. Journal of Economic Literature 18(4) (1990)

[18] Ministry of Economy, Trade and Industry, http://www.meti.go.jp

[19] http://www.chiresearch.com

[20] DOC, New Inventors (1998)

Indexing Distributed and Heterogeneous Resources

Michał Chromiak[1], Krzysztof Stencel[2], and Kazimierz Subieta[3,4]

[1] Institute of Computer Science, Maria Curie-Skłodowska University, Lublin, Poland
mchromiak@umcs.pl
[2] Institute of Informatics, University of Warsaw, Warsaw, Poland
stencel@mimuw.edu.pl
[3] Polish-Japanese Institute of Information Technology, Warsaw, Poland
subieta@pjwstk.edu.pl
[4] Institute of Computer Science Polish Academy of Sciences, Warsaw, Poland

Abstract. Indexing virtually integrated distributed, heterogeneous and defragmented resources is a serious challenge that so far was not even considered in the database literature. However, it is difficult to imagine that very large integrated resources (millions or billions of objects) can be processed without indexes. This paper presents the pioneering approach to solve the problem. Our idea is based on SBQL object-oriented virtual updatable views that are implemented in the ODRA system. SBQL views have full algorithmic power concerning mapping of stored objects into virtual ones and full algorithmic power in mapping updates addressing virtual objects into updates of stored objects. An important concept that allows to achieve that is called virtual identifier. Virtual identifiers can be used as non-key values in indexes. Because an integrator of Distributed, heterogeneous and defragmented resources can be implemented as an SBQL view, it is possible to use its virtual identifiers to create any indexes addressing such resources. The paper presents the motivation for the research, explains the idea of SBQL views and presents the idea of such an index.

Keywords: object-oriented, database, query language, ODRA, SBQL, distributed database, heterogeneous database, query optimization, index, updatable view.

1 Introduction

Integrating distributed data and service resources is an ultimate goal of many current technologies, including distributed and federated databases, brokers based on the CORBA standard [1], Sun's RMI, P2P technologies, grid technologies, Web Services [2], Sun's JINI [3], virtual repositories [4], metacomputing federations [5, 6] and perhaps others. The distribution of resources has desirable features such as autonomic maintenance and administration of local data and services, unlimited scalability due to many servers, avoiding global failures, supporting security and privacy, etc. On the other hand, there is a need for global processing of distributed resources that treats them as a centralized repository with resource location and implementation transparency. Distributed resources are often developed independently (with no central management) thus with the high probability they are heterogeneous, that is, incompatible concerning, in particular, local database schemas, naming of resource entities, coding of values and access methods. There are methods to deal with heterogeneity, in

T.-h. Kim et al. (Eds.): UNESST 2010, CCIS 124, pp. 214–223, 2010.
© Springer-Verlag Berlin Heidelberg 2010

particular, federated databases, brokers based on the CORBA standard and virtual repositories.

If a global defragmented collection is very large (millions or billions of records) it would be practically impossible to process it sequentially record-by-record. Hence some optimized query language is required. For instance, some optimization methods such as query rewriting and indexes are described respectively in [10, 11] and in [12]. To some extent, these methods can also be applied to distributed heterogeneous databases with the fragmentation transparency, but their scope is limited. Distribution, heterogeneity and defragmentation concerning object-oriented databases imply very challenging optimization problems which are practically not considered so far in the database literature.

The rest of the paper is organized as follows. Section 2 presents the motivation of global indexing. Section 3 presents ODRA virtual repository which is an existing implementation of SBQL and the updatable views. This implementation, including its indexes, will be a start point for our further research. Section 4 presents, in more detail, the idea of SBQL updatable views that are crucial for our idea towards global indexing architecture. Moreover we include here a simple exemplification of our idea. Section 5 presents the concept and the architecture supporting indexing distributed and heterogeneous resources. Section 6 presents our conclusion and future work.

2 Motivations of Global Indexing

In this paper we present our approach to indexing distributed and heterogeneous collections with the fragmentation transparency.

Classical centralized indexes have many physical forms (B-trees, hash tables, etc.) but from the conceptual point of view they can be understood as two-column tables, where the first column contains key values (e.g. strings being surnames of employees) and the second column contains non-key values, usually references to database entities (objects). In object-oriented databases a non-key value is an object identifier (OID). It is implicitly assumed in all existing systems that knowing an OID allows for practically immediate access to the corresponding object. Note that this idea works also for updating: if a non-key value is an OID then it can be used as an l-value in assignment statements, as an argument in delete statements, etc. How the situation with indexes is changed when one would attempt to develop such a feature for distributed, heterogeneous and defragmented object databases? First radical change concerns the non-key column from the described above index conceptual model. Objects delivered to global applications are virtual, given by specifications of wrappers and mediators. Physically they do not exist, hence there are no OIDs. Any form of materializing virtual objects is unacceptable, because it would compromise autonomy and scalability. Moreover, local servers have own methods assuring fast access (e.g. local indexes) that should be utilized by global applications. These methods can be different for different servers.

The problem looks as terribly challenging. However, lack of a solution of this problem causes that the idea of distributed, heterogeneous and defragmented databases is unrealistic for global applications addressing millions or billions of objects.

Summing up, we are facing the following knot of problems:

- What kind of entities are to be stored as non-key values in a global index to heterogeneous, distributed and defragmented resources?
- How these entities are to be processed by queries?
- How procedural parts (methods) implemented on the side of local servers can be utilized through the index?
- How such an index is to be defined and populated by proper data?
- How materialization of objects on the side of the global server can be avoided?
- Can such an index be used to support updating operations acting on local databases?

We show that it is possible to develop a very general solution that answers positively to all the above questions. To understand our idea of indexing distributed and heterogeneous resources it is essential to realize how our updateable views work. The major concept we call *virtual identifier*. A virtual identifier is a triple *<flag, viewId, seed>*, where *flag* distinguishes virtual identifiers from ordinary object identifiers, *viewId* is an identifier of a compiled view definition and *seed* is some value (usually named object identifier) that allows to uniquely distinguish a virtual object. A collection of seeds is returned when a view is called; then they are turned into the collection of virtual identifiers. Virtual identifiers behave very similarly to ordinary identifiers concerning query operators. However, when an updating (or dereferencing) operation is attempting to process a virtual identifier *<flag, viewId, seed>*, due to the *flag* it is recognized that the action concerns a virtual rather than stored object. In this case a proper overloading function from the view definition identified by the *viewId* is chosen. Then the function is called with the *seed* as a parameter.

The idea of indexing distributed and heterogeneous resources assumes the use of virtual identifiers as non-key values of the indexes. In this case a virtual identifier must be extended with a symbolic identifier (e.g. IP address) of a local server. The key value of the index can be chosen according to current indexing needs, as in centralized indexes. Physical organization of such indexes does not differ from physical organization of ordinary indexes. Although the idea looks a bit sophisticated for persons not familiar with SBQL, it is indeed very simple, powerful and universal. We illustrate it on comprehensive examples (but for full understanding we recommend reading various sources on the SBQL web site [9]).

3 ODRA Virtual Repository

ODRA has been developed within two big European projects eGov Bus [18] and VIDE [19]. It is also the basis of several other projects, in particular devoted to workflows. ODRA is a combination of object-oriented database management system with an own query and programming language (SBQL), virtual updateable views, stored procedures, stored classes and methods and with many interoperability modules that can be used in different configurations, depending on needs of a particular application. In Fig.1 we present some architectural variant for a virtual repository that can be developed for distributed applications.

An integration view on an ODRA server allows for the virtual integration and defragmentation of data and services supplied by distributed sources, supporting data and function abstractions. If the integration view is stateless then it may be copied to many servers. In this way the availability of resources and scalability of applications can be much increased.

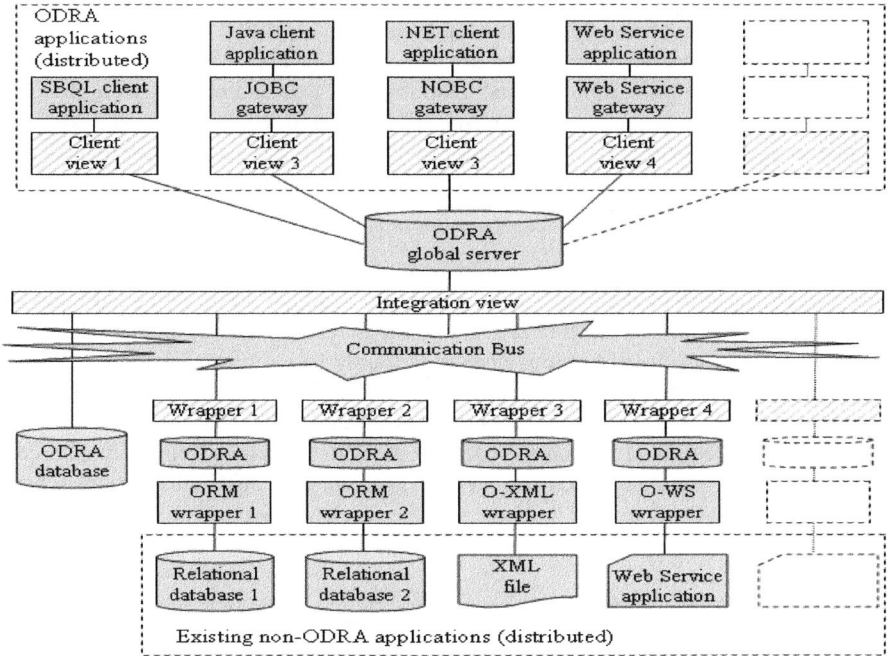

Fig. 1. Reference architecture of an ODRA virtual repository

4   Integrating Heterogeneous Resources – Example

As already mentioned in section 3 ODRA based virtual repository architecture allows for the virtual integration. SBQL database updatable views are the main programmer's facility for implementing virtual repositories, as shown in Fig.1. They present the most distinguishable feature of ODRA. The most important property of views is transparency, which means that the user formulating a query needs not to distinguish between stored and virtual data. Transparency is easy to achieve for read-only views. In such a case a view is a function (returning a collection) that is known from a lot of programming languages, including SBQL. Actually, SQL views are programming functions with a single *return* statement parameterized by a query.

4.1   Seeds of Virtual Objects

SBQL view does not return complete virtual objects as the result of a view invocation. This feature is motivated both by the new concept of views and by performance.

Invocation of an SBQL view returns only *seeds* of virtual objects. A seed is a small piece of a virtual object that uniquely identifies it. The nature of seeds is not constrained, it can be a reference to an object, a value, a structure, etc. The rest of a virtual object is delivered according to the need of an application. For instance, if a virtual object has a virtual attribute *address*, but an application does not use it, then *address* is not delivered. Seeds are also the conceptual basis for updating virtual objects: they parameterise updating operations that are specified by the view designer.

The first part of a view definition is a declaration of virtual objects. It states their name, type and cardinality after the keyword *virtual*. The second part of the view definition body has the form of a functional procedure named *seed*. A *seed* procedure returns a bag of seeds. Seeds are then (implicitly) passed as parameters of procedures that overload operations on virtual objects. Usually, seeds have to be named. This name is used in overloading procedures and within sub-views.

4.2 View Example

For exemplification of the idea, we are describing a simple integrated auctioning system. Concerning this introductory article it is focused on main integration and indexing goals and therefore the example is constrained only to basic level. Omitting the production environment complexity will help here to clearly introduce the target solution.

Description of the distributed resources is based on two parties, each involving separate database scheme and data model origin. Both database schemes are containing the same set of integrated data however represented with different database scheme. The aspect of diversity in both database schemes is clearly depict in Fig. 2 and Fig 3.

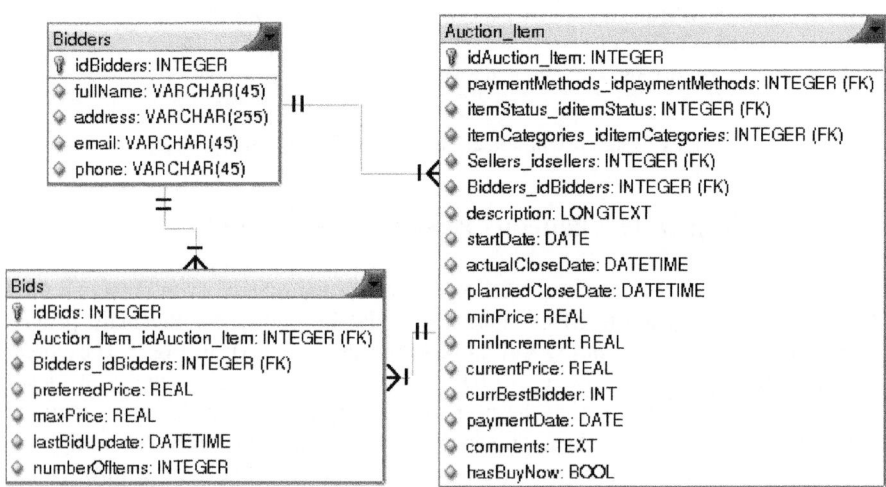

Fig. 2. First integrated auction site

Each of the sites participating in auctioning system needs to start an ODRA instance to introduce its contributory view. Thanks to a wrapper infrastructure present in virtual repository enabling access to generic data scheme became intuitive.

Wrappers, present at each site instance, enables creation of contributory views (here basing on schemes depict in Fig.2 and Fig3).

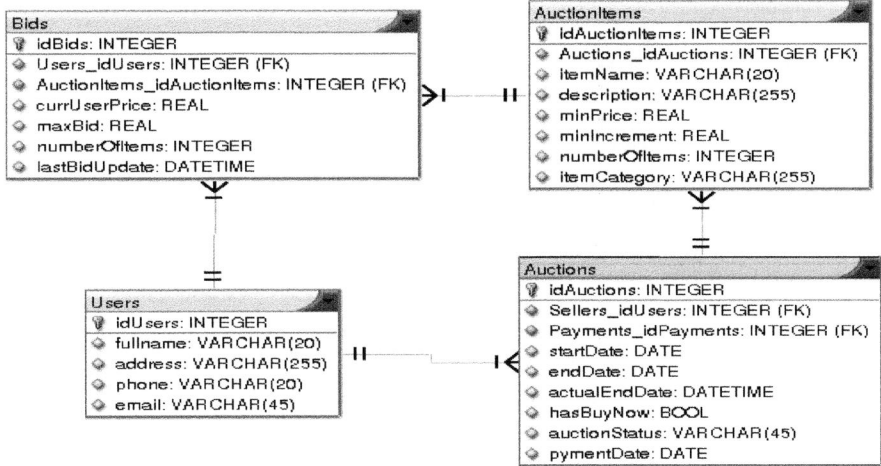

Fig. 3. Second integrated auction site

Auction site 1:

```
view contribAuctionUserSite1_Def {
   virtual AuctionUSerSite1 : record {
        subject:     string;    seller:      string;
        minPrice:    real;      minIncrement:real:
        winPrice:    real;      startDate:   date;
        endDate:     date;      endStatus: string;
        buyNow:      bool;      currency:  string;      language:  string;
   }[0..*];
      seed: record {AI: ref Auction_Item; currency : string;
                               language : string}[0..*]{
      return (Auction_Item as  AI,  "USD" as  currency,   "ENG(US)"
                      as language);
   }
 on_retrieve  {
   return AI.(description      as subject,
           (Users where idUsers =    A.Sellers_idUsers)
    .deref(fullname)+deref(email)) as seller,
               minPrice         as minPrice,
               minIncrement     as minIncrement,
               winPrice         as winPrice,
               startDate        as startDate,
               endDate          as endDate,
               comments         as endStatus,
               hasBuyNow        as buyNow
               );
 }}
```

Auction site 2:

```
view contribAuctionUSerSite2_Def {
   virtual contribAuctionUserSite2 : record {
      subject:   string;   seller:      string;
      minPrice:  real;     minIncrement:real:
      winPrice:  real;     startDate:   date;
      endDate:   date;     endStatus:   string;
      buyNow:    bool;     currency:    string;      language:  string;
   }[0..*];
   seed: record {A: ref Auctions; currency : string;
                 language: string}[0..*]{
            return (Auctions as A, "PLN" as currency,
                                   "PL" as language);
      }

  on_retrieve   {
    return A.(ref (AuctionItems where
               Auctions_idAuctions = idAuctions).itemName
                            as subject,
             (Sellers where idSellers =
                  Sellers_idSellers).deref(name)+deref(email))
                            as seller,
             ref (AuctionItems where A.idAuctions =
                            Auctions_idAuctions).minPrice
                            as minPrice,
             ref (AuctionItems where A.idAuctions =
                  Auctions_idAuctions).minIncrement
                            as minIncrement,
             winPrice              as winPrice,
             startDate             as startDate,
             endDate               as endDate,
             auctionStatus         as endStatus,
             hasBuyNow             as buyNow
        );
  }
}
```

   Construction of each of the contributory views is relevant to the present local scheme but as a result produces an output that must conform the contributory scheme. In our example the contributory scheme has been determined in a way introduced in *virtual* part of each of the views. However, one needs to remember that this contributory scheme can be determined in a completely different form (e.g. having only subject and winprice fields) determined by virtual repository admin depending on current integration needs. At this stage, having the contributory views ready to be integrated, the ODRA admin can define the integration view collecting the data gathered from the virtual repository underlying, integrated resources. Here we assume that the data is present in UK English and currency is the Euro (€).

```
view auctionIntegrator {
        virtual contribAuctionSite2 : record {
        subject:    string;    seller:      string;
        minPrice:   real;      minIncrement:real:
        winPrice:   real;      startDate:   date;
        endDate:    date;      endStatus: string;       buyNow:    bool;
        currency:   string; // expressed in euro currency
        language:   string;// in uk English
        }[0..*];
        seed: record { a: Auctions }[0..*] {
        return {connect(Site1).contribAuctionUserSite1
              union
              connect(Site2).contribAuctionUserSite2 as a; }
        }

        view subjectDef {
                virtual subject: string;
                seed : record {s: string;} {
                        return a.subject as s;
                    }
                on_retrieve { return
                Translator.translate (a.language, "ENG(UK)", s);
                }
        }
//...
        view winPriceDef {
                virtual winPrice: real;
                seed : record {wp: real;} {
                        return a. winPrice as wp;
                }
                on_retrieve { return
                CurrencyConverter.convert(a.currency, "EUR", wp);
                }
        }
//...
}
```

The function *connect* with site as a parameter belongs to the communication protocol and returns a reference to the site, which is treated by SBQL as a reference to a large object containing all database objects. The connection protocol may include more such functions, for instance, pinging a site, calculating the transmission time, finding an alternative route, processing exceptions, etc. Seeds returned by the function *seed* are references to remote objects named *a* in the above example. The name is local to the view definition, it is not seen outside it. Virtual objects are identified by name *auctionIntegrator*; their original names *contribAuctionUserSite1* and *contribAuctionUserSite2* are not seen. In ODRA a remote reference consists of an internal unique identifier of a remote site and an internal identifier of an object from this site, unique for it. Alternatively, we can assume that a seed is a pair:

```
record{s: site_reference, e: object_reference}
```

where s and e are names chosen by the view programmer.

Moreover what needs to be noticed is the fact of the currency calculator and a translation used as integration scheme criteria. Each site is expected to have data represented in its local scheme language and currency. Integration of such data is possible thanks to wrappers representing the local schemes in an unambiguous way. However, the data itself would still be present in local format of currency and described in terms of the local language. Our endeavor to integrate the heterogeneity will be pushed forward not only to the level of the data schemes but we move one step further i.e. manipulating the data content itself. Our idea involves the Web Services and data scheme modification. In this particular case this would mean, two additional fields, representing local currency and language, to be included into the contributory and integration views. Their values are set at the stage of forming the contributory view. Those values are later utilized as an input for two Web Services objectsi.e. *Translator* and *CurrencyConverter* both vested with dedicated methods. Each method operates on the value provided by the appropriate field of the contributory view (i.e. *currency* and *language*), the target integration criteria determined by a string field (e.g. *ENG(UK)*) and the adequate seed. Those Web Service objects are placed in *on_retrieve* procedure and therefore produces the actual result when user application retrieves the processed field.

4.3 Indexing the Integrated Resources – Example

At this stage having the resources of auction information integrated from those two sources we can easily process with the indexing of this data. For instance let us assume that the goal is to index the auction items by their names, here the `subjects` field of the integrating perspective. The ODRA administrator in such case would create the index with the following construct:

```
create index  IndexAuctionItem for auctionIntegrator using subject;
```

Then while a query would request for auctions involving particular item i.e. a book worth more than 50 Euro and has 'buy now' option the use of index and integration perspective is depict in following query:

```
IndexAuctionItem ( "book") where winPrice > 50 and buyNow;
```

5 Conclusion and Future Work

We have shown that apparently terrible challenge of defining indexes addressing distributed, heterogeneous and defragmented resources has a reasonable and hopefully efficient solution on the ground of SBQL virtual updatable views. Seeds of virtual objects, wrapped within virtual identifiers, unify the problem of such indexes with the problem of ordinary indexes. However, we are at the beginning of the research. A lot of development and experimentation should be performed to turn the idea into the feasible and practical technology.

Note that there is a problem concerning refreshing a global index in response to updating local databases. This feature is solved and implemented in ODRA for centralized applications, but for a global index addressing virtual resources there is no solution that does not violate the autonomy of local servers. Such a feature requires informing the global server on changes that happened on local servers. This topic will be the subject of our next research.

References

1. OMG: Catalog of OMG CORBA®/IIOP® Specifications (2010),
   http://www.omg.org/technology/documents/corba_spec_catalog.htm
2. Wikipedia: List of Web service specifications (2010),
   http://en.wikipedia.org/wiki/List_of_Web_service_specifications
3. Jini architecture specification, Version 2.1 (March 2009),
   http://www.jini.org/wiki/Jini_Architecture_Specification
4. Kuliberda, K., Adamus, R., Wislicki, J., Kaczmarski, K., Kowalski, T.M., Subieta, K.: A Generic Proposal for a Transparent Integration of Distributed Data by an Autonomous Layer in a Virtual Repository. Multiagent and Grid Systems, an International Journal (MAGS) 3(4), 393–410 (2007)
5. Sobolewski, M.W.: SORCER: Computing and Metacomputing Intergrid. In: Proc. 10th International Conference on Enterprise Information Systems, Barcelona, Spain (2008)
6. Sobolewski, M.W.: Federated Collaborations with Exertions. In: Proc. of 17th IEEE Intl. Workshops on Enabling Technologies: Infrastructures for Collaborative Enterprises, pp. 127–132. IEEE Computer Society, Los Alamitos (2008) ISBN 978-0-7695-3315-5
7. Özsu, M.T., Valduriez, P.: Principles of Distributed Database Systems, 2nd edn. Prentice-Hall, Englewood Cliffs (1999)
8. ODRA (Object Database for Rapid Application development): Description and programmer manual (2010),
   http://www.sbql.pl/various/ODRA/ODRA_manual.html
9. Stack-Based Architecture (SBA) and Stack-Based Query Language, SBQL (2010),
   http://www.sbql.pl/
10. Kozankiewicz, H.: Updateable Object Views. Ph.D Thesis, Institute of Computer Science Polish Academy of Sciences, Warsaw (2005), http://www.sbql.pl/phds/
11. Kozankiewicz, H., Stencel, K., Subieta, K.: Implementation of Federated Databases Through Updatable Views. In: Sloot, P.M.A., Hoekstra, A.G., Priol, T., Reinefeld, A., Bubak, M. (eds.) EGC 2005. LNCS, vol. 3470, pp. 610–619. Springer, Heidelberg (2005)
12. Kozankiewicz, H., Stencel, K., Subieta, K.: Integration of Heterogeneous Resources through Updatable Views. In: Proc. 13th IEEE Intl. Workshops on Enabling Technologies (WETICE 2004), Modena, Italy, pp. 309–314. IEEE Computer Society, Los Alamitos (2004)
13. Adamus, R., Kaczmarski, K., Stencel, K., Subieta, K.: SBQL Object Views - Unlimited Mapping and Updatability. In: Proceedings of the First International Conference on Object Databases, ICOODB 2008, Berlin, March 13-14, pp. 119–140 (2008) ISBN 078-7399-412-9
14. e-Gov Bus - Advanced e-Government Information Service Bus (European Commission 6-th Framework Programme, IST-26727) (2009),
   http://www.egov-bus.org/web/guest/home
15. VIDE - VIsualize all moDel drivEn programming (European Commission 6-th Framework Programme, IST 033606 STP) (2009), http://www.vide-ist.eu/
16. Cybula, P., Subieta, K.: Query Optimization through Cached Queries for Object-Oriented Query Language SBQL. In: Proceedings of the 36th Conference on Current Trends in Theory and Practice of Computer Science. LNCS, vol. 5901 (2009)

Association Rule Based Situation Awareness in Web-Based Environmental Monitoring Systems

Meng Zhang[1], Byeong Ho Kang[1], and Quan Bai[2]

[1] School of Computing and Information Systems,
University of Tasmania, Hobart, Australia
{mzhang3,Byeong.Kang}@utas.edu.au
[2] Tasmanian ICT Centre, CSIRO,
Hobart, Tasmania, Australia
Quan.Bai@csiro.au

Abstract. The Tasmanian ICT of CSIRO developed a Sensor Web test-bed system for the Australian water domain. This system provides an open platform to access and integrate near real time water information from distributed sensor networks. Traditional hydrological models can be adopted to analyze the data on the Sensor Web system. However, the requirements on high data quality and high level domain knowledge may greatly limit the application of these models. To overcome some these limitations, this paper proposes a data mining approach to analyze patterns and relationships among different hydrological events. This approach provides a flexible way to make use of data on the Hydrological Sensor Web.

Keywords: Sensor Web, data mining, association rules, knowledge discovery, data presentation.

1 Introduction

The Sensor Web is a distributed information system that connects sensors, observation archives, processing systems and simulation models using open web service interfaces and standard information models [14]. As shown in Fig. 1, the Sensor Web is targeting at providing an open platform for users in different domains and organizations to share their data, information and knowledge. It can enable the integration of web-enabled sensors and sensor systems for a global scale collaborative sensing.

The Tasmanian ICT Centre, as part of CSIRO Water for Healthy Country Flagship project, has developed a Sensor Web system called the South Esk Hydrological Sensor Web[1] (SEHSW) [15]. It collects sensor data from five water agencies, and real-timely monitors the South Esk catchment, which covers an area of approximately 3350 square kilometers in north-east of Tasmania. SEHSW makes the South Esk catchment a sensor-rich environment with an opportunity to study the hydrology phenomenon in a catchment and test-bed to study the development of Sensor Web systems. Fig. 2 shows sensor distribution on the SEHSW.

---

[1] http://www.csiro.au/sensorweb/au.csiro.OgcThinClient/OgcThinClient.html

T.-h. Kim et al. (Eds.): UNESST 2010, CCIS 124, pp. 224–232, 2010.
© Springer-Verlag Berlin Heidelberg 2010

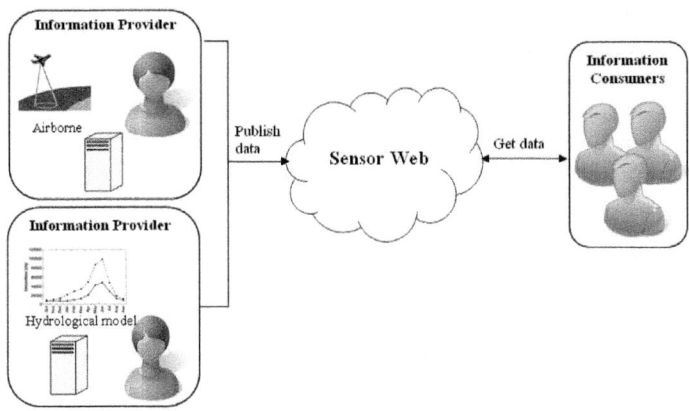

Fig. 1. Conceptual Architecture of Sensor Web

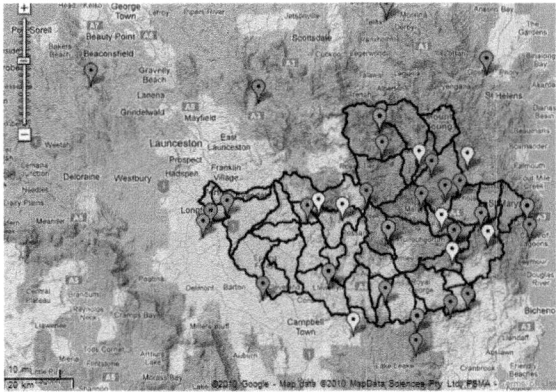

Fig. 2. Sensor distribution on the South Esk Hydrological Sensor Web

With the deployment of the SEHSW, huge amount of real time data are collected from the physical environment and shared on an open platform. Meanwhile the value of data needs to be exploited by some data analysis and knowledge discovery approaches. In the water domain, hydrological data are normally manipulated and interpreted by traditional hydrological models. These models are very powerful in stream forecasting, water quality monitoring, etc. However, most hydrological models have some limitations which can block their applications:

- Most of hydrological models ask for high level domain knowledge to generate the structure and analyze data.
- Most of hydrological models require high quality data. Due to the particularity of water related data, the real water data ask for the integrity and veracity. The data also need to manipulate accuracy during the process.
- Most of hydrological models have the specific region.

Compared with hydrological models, data mining provides a more flexible way to achieve knowledge discovery [10]. It can analyze hidden patterns and relationships among data from a data-driven perspective. Namely, it can be operated based on available data. In this paper, we propose the use of association rule based approach to analyze hydrological data. The proposed approach can interpret data on the SEHSW to useful information without high domain expertise.

2   Methodology

The process flow of the approach is illustrated in Fig. 3. In the approach, hydrological data are transformed into a proper format and sent to the association rule analysis component. Then a number of association rules will be generated from the rule analysis component. These rules will be pruned and stored in a rule base. Finally, the stored rules can be presented based on users' queries.

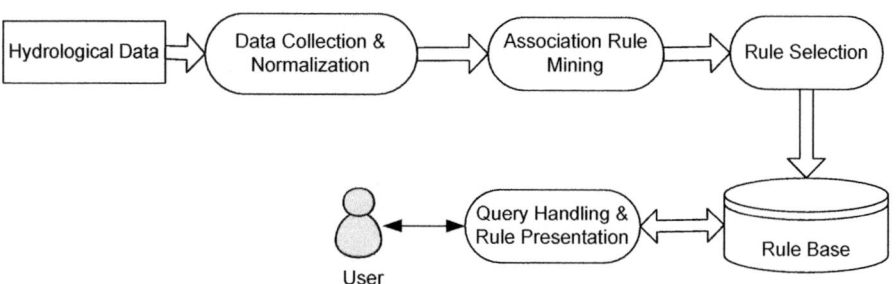

Fig. 3. The process flow of mining hydrological sensor data

2.1   Association Rules Method Description

Association rule mining is an application which leads to the discovery of associations and correlations among different items in related data sets [1]. A classic example is the market-basket problem [3]. In transactional data-sets of supermarkets, rules like {bear}→{diapers} means that most of customers buy bears, meanwhile, they may buy diapers as well. Such rules will then suggest the supermarket managers to put bear and diapers together which may improve their profits. From this example, it can be seen that association rules provide a useful mechanism for discovering relationships among the underlying data.

In this research, we define a rule is defined as a form A = {L=> R}, where A is an association rule, L and R are two disjointed item sets of event E (L ∩ R = ϕ). L is called the antecedent of A; and R is called the consequent of A. There are two important constraints for selecting useful rules, i.e., the minimum thresholds on support and confidence [8]. Support is the ratio of the number of transactions that include all items the antecedent (see Equation 1). Confidence is the probability of finding the consequence in transactions under the condition that these transactions also contain the antecedent (see Equation 2).

$$S(L, R) = P(L) \tag{1}$$

$$C(L, R) = P(L \mid R) \tag{2}$$

There are a number of learning algorithms which can find association rules based predefined support and confidence thresholds. In this research, the Apriori algorithm [1] was adopted build up rules.

2.2 Data Collection and Normalization

We are expecting to discovery spatio-temporal patterns in different hydrological events. In this research, we particularly focus on analyzing the relationships between rainfall events and other phenomena, e.g., humidity, air-temperature, etc.

To achieve the purpose, firstly, we record the maximum or minimum values of rainfall events from the sensor web, and extract them into a new database. In addition, to simplify the implementation, we also assign an index to each location and phenomenon type. Table 1 describes index values for different location and phenomenon types. In this table, location 1 represents the locations that a corresponding phenomenon may happen (e.g. Humidity). Location 2 represents the locations of rainfall events.

Table 1. The description of location and phenomenon

Location 1	Index (J)	Phenomenon	Index(K)	Location 2	Index (L)
Ben Lomond	1	Humidity	1	English Town Road	1
Story Creek	2	Air-Temperature	2	Valley Road	2
Ben Ridge Road	3	Evaporation	3	Hogans Road	3
Avoca	4	Transpiration	4	Mathinna Plains	4
Tower Hill	5	Wind-Run	5	Tower Hill Road	5

From Table 1, we can calculate the time gap between the maximum value or minimum value of a rainfall event and another event within the same day by using Equation 3. Then, we can get two sets of time gaps which indicate the time differences between the rainfall event reaches the maximum value and another event reaches the maximum and the minimum values. The time gaps are described in a continuous data type. However, association rules can only take nominal or ordinary data types as inputs. To satisfy this requirement, the continuous values need to be transferred to a nominal style. Here, we use a simple clustering technique to achieve the conversion. Figure 3 shows the clustering method we used. The method transfers the continuous values into nominal items by generating different clusters. Each cluster

228   M. Zhang, B.H. Kang, and Q. Bai

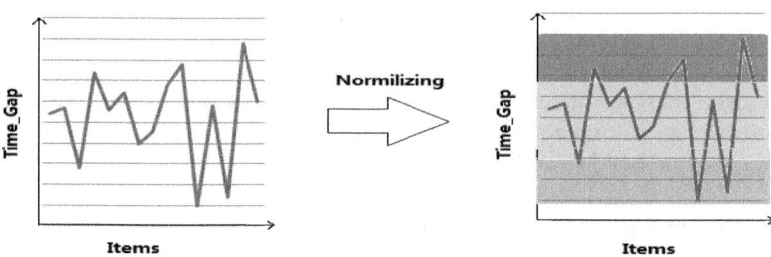

Fig. 4. Transfer data into nominal style

contains a range of continuous time gaps. For instance, the cluster (Max_Gap(0_4)) covers the time gaps between 0 to 4 hours.

$$Max\_Gap(Min\_Gap)_{JK} = Max(Min)_{JK} - Max_L \quad (3)$$

2.3 WEKA Workbench

We described the processes for data pre-processing in the previous subsections. Finally, we can operate association rule mining on a platform or workbench. There are a number of data mining tools which can conduct association rule mining. In this research, we select WEKA workbench to analyze hydrological data. WEKA, which was developed by the University of Waikato in New Zealand, provides a uniform interface to lots of algorithms for pre and post-processing, and evaluating the results of learning schemes on any datasets. The WEKA work bench not only includes a library that contains a number of data analysis algorithms, more importantly, it can also allow users to modify the algorithms in the library or add their plug-ins based on their needs [11].

WEKA requires a specific input file format named ARFF. Fig. 5 shows the data format of ARFF files. The attributes refer to the titles of items. The data in brackets

```
test_data_advanced.arff ×
         1,0        2,0        3,0        4,0        5,0        6,0        7,0
 1  %this dataset is to record the time gap between some items and rainfall.
 2  %all data is based on 24 hours series
 3  @relation 'water'
 4  @attribute location {BenLomond,StorysCreek,BenRidgeRoad,Avoca,TowerHill,Cox}
 5  @attribute item {Windspeed,Humidity,airtemperature,evaporation,transpiration
 6  @attribute compare_location {BenLomond,StorysCreek,BenRidgeRoad,Avoca,Tower}
 7  @attribute max_gap real
 8  @attribute min_gap real
 9  @attribute location1area {1,2,3,4}
10  @attribute location2area {1,2,3,4}
11  @data
12  BenLomond,Windspeed,RabbitMarsh,-6.5,-4.5,3,3
13  BenLomond,Humidity,RabbitMarsh,6.5,10.5,3,3
14  BenLomond,airtemperature,RabbitMarsh,2.5,1,3,3
15  BenLomond,Humidity,RabbitMarsh,11.5,-3,3,3
16  StorysCreek,airtemperature,RabbitMarsh,2.5,11.5,3,3
17  StorysCreek,evaporation,RabbitMarsh,0.5,0,3,3
18  StorysCreek,transpiration,RabbitMarsh,-3.5,4.5,3,3
19  BenRidgeRoad,Humidity,RabbitMarsh,4.5,0,1,3
20  BenRidgeRoad,airtemperature,RabbitMarsh,0,1,1,3
21  BenRidgeRoad,evaporation,RabbitMarsh,-0.5,0,1,3
22  BenRidgeRoad,transpiration,RabbitMarsh,4.5,-12.5,1,3
23  Avoca,Humidity,RabbitMarsh,-5.5,3,4,3
24  Avoca,airtemperature,RabbitMarsh,2,-11.5,4,3
```

Fig. 5. ARFF data file

(after each attribute) indicate the possible values of that attribute. The data after the label "@data" are values of items in transactions.

2.4 Generate Association Rules

We built up a dataset which concludes 443 instances to generate related rules. During the process, we input 400 instances to generate rules and set up 43 instances (10%) to evaluate rules. We set the support threshold as 10% to 100%, and the confidence threshold as 0.5. Due to the features of the hydrological data, the confidence threshold was not set to very high. Table 2 displays the result and evaluation of the association rules.

Table 2. The result of association rules

	Rules	Accuracy (40 instance evaluate)
Total number	10	Average 80%
With confidence > 80%	4	85%
With confidence (<80%)	6	75%

After the analysis, we get some rules for hydrological data and the following is an example:

$$Rule = \{(max\_gap:[3\text{-}7]) => (item: humidity)\}$$

This rule means that regardless the location, the humidity should get the maximum value 3 to 7 hours later than rainfall get the maximum value. For instance, if a rainfall event gets the maximum value at 9:00 am, the humidity will get the maximum value between 12:00pm and 16:00pm.

The rules are basically related with phenomenon types and time gaps. Based on identified rules, we can find the relationships between some specific phenomenons (e.g. rainfall and humidity), and furthermore, make some predictions on hydrological events.

In general, traditional hydrological model can generate more accurate results but with very high costs. For example, the hydrological model can give predictions about a specific location and phenomenon, e.g., water level in location A will increase by 10cms in the next 10 hours. However, these results are generated based on high quality input data. In addition, these models may require over 10 years data for calibration and training purposes. Such requirements will lead to very high cost on data preparation, and greatly limit the applications of the models. On the other hand, data mining methods have much lower requirements on data quality. Most data mining methods are purely data driven. Namely, the discovered information/ knowledge is based on the data availability. Hence, even without long period and high quality data, we still can find some useful patterns from the data. Meanwhile, these patterns are easier to understand for general users without too much domain knowledge.

3   Rule Presentation

In order to facilitate users to understand discovered knowledge, data presentation becomes to an important issue for the success of the approach. Data presentation is a

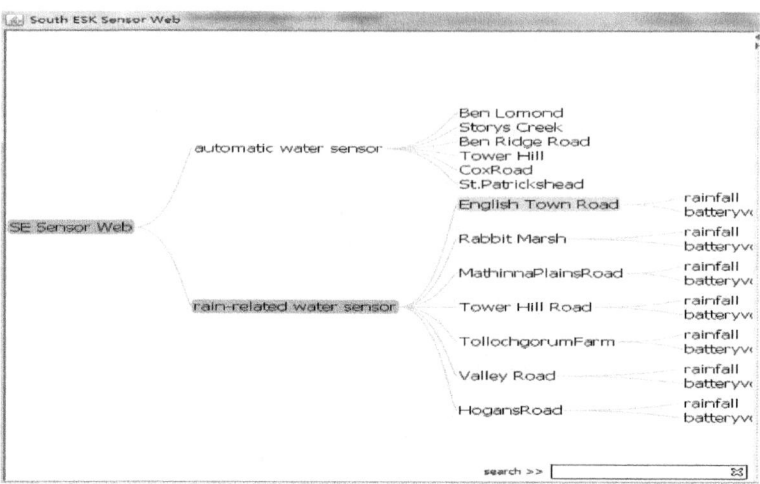

Fig. 6. Tree view structure of the sensor web

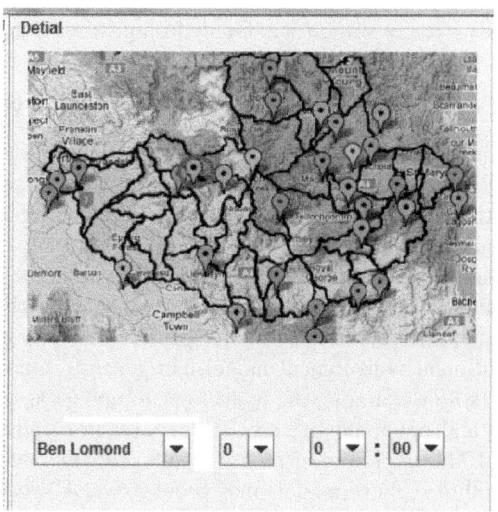

Fig. 7. Application of rules from data mining

suitable way to transfer the obscure data information into perceptible information [9] [13]. A good presentation can let data easy to understand and provide clear information from data to potential audience. Data presentation also can prune the redundant data and provide the friendly interface.

In this research, we focused on the presentation of discovered association rules and try to embed the presentation with the current interface of the South Esk Hydrological Sensor Web. In order to describe the rules clearly, we built up a tree view structure to describe the relationships between locations, sensors and phenomenon types (see Fig. 6). In this structure, locations, sensor types and phenomenon types are shown clearly. So it can also help the users to understand the relationships between observed phenomenon types and locations.

To present the rules, we provide a set of selection boxes to allow users to choose their preferred rules (see Fig.7). Based on the "maximum value time" of a rainfall event, there are four selection boxes to allow users to select locations, phenomenon types, value types and time gaps. When a user sets three attributes from any three boxes, the value of the other box can be generated based on the association rules in the rule base. For example, if the rainfall gets the maximum value at 10:00 am, and we select the location as BenLomond, phenomenon type as Humidity and the value type as Maximum Value, then the rules will be invoked and it can be found that the maximum value time will at 13:00 pm in same day. In addition, the application will give the support and confidence values of the association rule as well. This application of data presentation is the extension of the rules from data mining approaches which can visualize the rules and make rules easy to understand. In addition, it also provides a friendly interface to let user can manipulate rules and know how rules work in sensor data.

4 Conclusion and Future Works

Event prediction plays an important role in the water domain. In this research, we focused on using data mining approaches to achieve knowledge discovery. We select the association rules to analyze the relationships and patterns among different sensor observations on the Hydrological Sensor Web. Compare with traditional hydrological models, data mining methods have lower requirements on data quality and domain expertise. In this paper, we described how to collect and prepare data from the Sensor Web, and use a specific data mining workbench to achieve knowledge discovery by using association rules. In addition, we also introduced the presentation of discovered rules. The future work of this research will be the investigation of the applications other data mining in environment monitoring. In addition, we will work on the modeling of user preferences, so that to more user friendly interface for data/knowledge presentation.

Acknowledgement

This project is supported by the University of Tasmania and the Tasmanian ICT Center, CSIRO. The Tasmanian ICT Centre is jointly funded by the Australian Government through the Intelligent Island Program and CSIRO. The Intelligent Island Program is administered by the Tasmanian Department of Economic Development, Tourism and the Arts. This research was conducted as part of the CSIRO Water for a Healthy Country Flagship.

References

1. Agrawal, R., Imielinski, T., Swami, A.: Minig association rules between sets of items in large databases. In: Proceedings of the ACM SIGMOD Internatinal Conference on Management of Data, pp. 207–216 (1993)

2. Anthony, H., Vinny, C.: Route profiling: putting context to work. In: Proceedings of the 2004 ACM Symposium on Applied Computing (2004)
3. Arawal, R., Srikant, R.: Fast algorithms for mining association rues in large databases. In: Proceedings of the 20th International Conference on Very Large Data Bases, SanFrancisco, pp. 487–499 (1994)
4. Beven, K.: Rainfall-runoff modeling: The Primer. John Wiley & Sons, Chichester (2004)
5. Ian, H.: Data Mining Practical Machine Learning Tools and Techniques. Morgan Kaufmann, San Francisco (2005)
6. Ikuhisa, M., Michihiko, M., Tsuneo, A., Noboru, B.: Sensing web: to globally share sensory data avoiding privacy invasion. In: Proceedings of the 3rd International Universal Communication Symposium (2009)
7. Jeffery, W.S.: Data Mining: An Overview. Congress Research Service (2004)
8. Jiawei, H., Micheline, K.: Data Mining: Concepts and Techniques. Morgan Kaufmann Publisher, San Francisco (2006)
9. Klein, A., Lehner, W.: Representing data quality in sensor data streaming environments. Proceedings of the ACM J. Data Inform. (2009)
10. Liang, X., Liang, Y.: Applications of data mining in hydrology. In: Proceedings of the IEEE International Conference on Data Mining, pp. 617–620 (2001)
11. Mark, H., Eibe, F., Geoffrey, H., Bernhard, P., Peter, R., Ian, H.W.: The WEKA data mining software: an update. SIGKDD Explor. Newsl. 11(1), 10–18 (2009)
12. Mulligan, M.: Modeling catchment hydrology, pp. 108–121. John Wiley & Sons, Chichester (2004)
13. Pittelkow, Y.E., Wilson, S.R.: Visualization of Gene Expression Data. The Berkeley Electronic Press (2009)
14. Open Geospatial Consortium, OGC Sensor Web Enablement: Overview and High Level Architecture. Technical Report OGC 07-165 (2007)
15. Liu, Q., Bai, Q., Terhorst, A.: Provenance-Aware Hydrological Sensor Web. In: The Proceedings of Hydroinformatics Conference, Tianjin, China, pp. 1307–1315 (2010)

Author Index